Peace In The Midst
Of The Storm

Peace In The Midst Of The Storm

Denise Clayton Bryant

To order additional copies of this book, contact:
Xlibris Corporation
1-888-795-4274
www.Xlibris.com
Orders@Xlibris.com
86450

Dedication

First, this book is dedicated to He who gave me the wisdom, strength and ability to write the things that have been laid upon my heart every since my writing began. God has been an awesome, gracious God, One who Has preserved my life from its very beginning and despite the trials and tribulations I have had to endure, He has continued to enable me to do what He brought me into His world to do!

Secondly, this literary work is dedicated to my friend, my little sister and namesake, Angela Denise "Nesie" Cook, who encouraged me to move forward, in spite of the pain and anguish that had attempted to consume me at one of the most difficult times of my life, and proceed with the work that God had brought me to do!

"Come and hear, all ye that fear God, and I will declare what He has done for my soul. I cried unto him with my mouth, and He was extolled with my tongue. If I regard iniquity in my heart, the Lord will not hear me: But verily God hath heard me; He hath attended to the voice of prayer. Blessed be God, which hath not turned away my prayer, nor His mercy from me."

Psalm 66:16–20

ONE

KEEPING SECRETS IS a very dangerous practice. Eventually, the secrets we keep ultimately end up keeping us—from living in peace and from fulfilling the will of God in our lives. Unfortunately, everyone has them. As children, we are told that the things that go on within our own families are to be kept there, becoming almost sacred! We are warned of the dangers of *"airing our dirty laundry"* in public. Unfortunately, those family secrets, both collective and individual, often keep the family and its members in division and turmoil! There are many things that we try to hide; yet the Heavenly Father hides nothing! Through numerous stories, the Bible details the faults of some of the men and women that God used mightily. After all, we **all** have sinned and fallen short of the glory of God! From the very beginning of time, no one has been perfect—not Moses who, despite his negative self-concept, was willing to do the will of God; not even David, a man with an obvious weakness, who was a man after God's own heart; yet their lives were used to fulfill the will of God! I suppose that they would have preferred that their issues had been kept secret but alas, they have been written about for many generations to read about and ultimately learn from.

I should have known that exposing my infirmities and my own *"demons"* was just a springboard from which God would draw me to another level in my life. At the third printing of my first self-published book, I realized that He was in no way through with me yet! As I reached a new, more intensely spiritual plane, He showed me that there was something else . . . much, more for me to do. He revealed to me that my coming clean with my past and forgiving those who had deeply hurt me in my lifetime was the very tip of the iceberg! Of course, I realized that I had experienced a personal *"breakthrough."* I had come face-to-face with the demons of my past and reconciled some very tough issues. I had openly shared the experiences with my family, friends, and yes, strangers, too! The pages of my life had been in shared with readers who purchased copies of **Opening the Door** from bookstores across the country for about six months when I realized that God had brought me through the storms of life for an even greater purpose than to find my own sanity! Although He had chipped away the rock-solid edges of pain and misery that had been my interior for thirty years, He had something much more for me to do!

In the year following the publication of my first book, I encountered many people who could not only relate to my story, but had traveled some of the same road in their own lives! Hearing and reading about my testimony had somehow helped the damaging layers of their pasts begin to peel away. In the midst of rivers of salty tears, many confessed that the problems they had faced in their lives had not just begun. Things had not just happened to them after they became adults, or even after they had found themselves in unhappy marriages or empty, meaningless relationships! At the root of their problems were things that had happened to them during the most vulnerable time of their lives—their childhood! Many had grown up in families where certain *"unmentionable"* things had happened. After years of failing to mention those things, their families had continued and expanded, in crisis. What I heard about family crises all over the country had a profound impact on me. I began to think about that word—*family.*

After God had perfected all of His creation, He had created the family. *"Let us make man,"* He had suggested as the story began to unravel in the first book of the Old Testament. The Scriptures tell us that God had created man in His own image. He had made male and female, and then he blessed them and commanded them to be fruitful and multiply. The first man was given dominion over the fishes of the sea, the fowl of the air, the beasts of the field, and every creeping thing that moved upon the earth! The Creator saw that His creation was good, but He was not yet satisfied. He knew that it was not good for the man whom He had created to be alone, so He put that man to sleep and, sans scalpel, took a rib from his side. From the bone of Adam's bone and flesh of his flesh, woman was made for him. Theirs was the first marriage, and Adam and Eve became the *"first family."* God created them to govern his creation together. They had free reign of the Garden, and they knew what their responsibilities were. They were told what to do and what ***not*** to do. Adam did as God had commanded him and Eve, well, she helped him as she had been created to. Together, they lived and flourished in the Garden and all was perfect, **until** sin entered the picture!

We all know the story of mankind's fall from grace in the Garden of Eden. We've heard it preached about numerous times from the most sedate podium to the fiercest of pulpits on Sunday morning. It has long been disputed that it was Eve's fault for taking that first bite from the fruit of the **Tree of the Knowledge of Good and Evil.** Others argue that it was Adam's fault for even listening to her! Most male homosapiens would probably agree that Adam was **not** the responsible one! Their theory is just as shaky and almost as inadequate as the leaves behind which the banished couple tried to hide their nakedness, however. The Bible supports the fact that it was Adam who was ultimately responsible for the fall because God had given him authority over the woman. It was **he** who had received the commandment from God that they were **not** to eat of the tree. He was the *"head of household"* who sat silently by while the very foundation of his family was ripped asunder! Just imagine how many families have been lost, broken, and annihilated because someone saw it happening and said absolutely nothing! Hence, the beginning of dysfunction in the family!

After their eviction from Paradise, Adam and Eve had to find a means of survival outside of the Garden. Adam had to till the ground from which he had been made. As punishment for her part in their sin, Eve's sorrow would be multiplied in child bearing. How many women can attest to that? It has been said that the worst pain imaginable is that of giving birth to a child! Little did the mother of all creation know that the pain she endured in the birth of her sons, Cain and Abel, was just the beginning of her misery! She would suffer even greater anguish when one child of her womb violently slew the other. Thus, the family became even more broken, more torn, and more . . . dysfunctional!

Amazingly, many people don't understand how important it is to have positive family relationships. Far too many families are in a state of dysfunction, and many of the *"functioning"* families are doing so *"dysfunctionally."* I have often wondered if we could really take an honest look at our own families and see them as they actually are: some include brothers and sisters who literally hate each other behind strained smiles over annual Thanksgiving and Christmas dinners; some with mothers and daughters with thorny fields of resentment growing wildly between them; some which include husbands and wives who can hardly wait for the children to grow up so that they can finally get away from each other; and others which include fathers and sons who are at odds because some became *"daddies"* too soon and others that became *"fathers"* much too late! We see it all of the time. It's just as much a part of my family as anyone else's. No one is exempt from the bitterness. It is sad, but oh so true! I have, however, just recently realized something very significant about the family crises of our time. I have come to fully understand that the breakdown of the family is due in full part to the old wicked one himself! Satan must take full responsibility for the demise of love, respect and honor amongst kin because it is he who has continued to sow seeds of discord and resentment within God's first ordained entity—the *family.*

"Be sober, be vigilant; because your adversary the devil,
as a roaring lion walketh about, seeking whom he may devour:"

1 Peter 5:8

One afternoon, I came home from the school where I had been teaching for several years and turned on the *Jerry Springer Show.* I realized that things had gone much lower than I thought they could possibly go. In fact, they were even worse than I had suspected! The particular segment of the infamous show featured mothers and their daughters who were bitter and angry because they had recently discovered that they *both* had been seeing the *same* young man! My mouth widened in amazement! How on earth could a mother carry on an intimate relationship with the same *"boy"* with whom her daughter was romantically and, more likely than not, sexually involved? Talk about perversion! On the stage sat a very angry woman, seething because her daughter was **still** seeing the young man, even after finding out that her own mother had been sleeping with him, too! When the show went to commercial, as usual, Jerry smugly slithered *away* from the seated guests and the chanting crowd-*out* of the line of fire! The crowd went wild, cheering *"Jerry! Jerry!"* For a brief moment, I was reminded of the crowd of people who had showered Christ with shouts of *"Hosanna!"* and soon thereafter, just as passionately, cried *"Crucify Him!"* and spat at Him on His way to Calvary! In the cheers of the television audience, I could hear the jeers of the angry mob as they followed the innocent Savior of the world to the cross on *Golgotha's Hill.* What, I thought, must God have thought then and was possibly still thinking of us as we continue to nail His Son to the cross, day after day after day? Yet we continue to make mockery of the mercy shown to us by cultivating seeds of hatred between us and our own family members!

Obviously, families are in desperate need of healing! There are not enough psychoanalysts around to handle the steadily rising numbers of crises in every day society. What we need is a miracle, and I know of only one real *"miracle worker!"* To resolve the problems of the dysfunctional families in our time, the root of them must be sought out and dealt with. An old proverb says that the *"fruit doesn't fall far from the tree."* This is a very true saying, but it should possibly be taken a step further: *"When the fruit is bad, one must look at the roots of the tree!"* Where are the roots of the family trees today? I would venture to say that they are buried deep within the hearts of the individual family members.

The Bible tells us that the issues of life flow out of our hearts, so no individual healing can actually begin until people deal with their own individual **"issues."** Today, we seem to exist in a world full of broken people with broken pasts and continually breaking presents, which seems to make impossible any chance for completeness in our tomorrows! How can we resolve those issues? Where can we find much needed healing? We must go back to the root of the problems we have experienced in our lives and confront our issues—*face-to-face!* A close look will reveal that just as Satan was present and instrumental in the disarming of the first family and its members, he has continued to afflict our lives and the lives of our family members up to this very moment—but is time to break the cycle!

"The eyes of the Lord are in every place, beholding the evil and the good."

Proverbs 15:3

One evening, my adorable, then four year-old, Christopher, nearly tumbled out of the back seat of our Chevy Blazer, trying to get a better glimpse of the exquisite moonlit sky! We had just returned from a spur-of-the-moment trip to a local Wal-Mart store and he had conned his dad and I into taking him with us by sweetly declaring that *"if we loved him, we would,"* and so we had! It was a beautiful, clear night and through towering pine trees in our front yard, we could see portions of some of the constellations twinkling above us. As my husband unlocked the den door for us to go into the house, Christopher lingered near the lamppost in the front yard, staring up at the stars in their entire splendor. My eyes followed his gaze and I could not help but ask, *"What are you looking at?"*

In the most alarming innocence I had ever heard, he whispered, *"God's eyes."*

A chill ran down my spine in consideration of what my little angel had just said. *"God's eyes,"* I thought, watching all we do—even the things we think no one else sees us do! God still sees! He knows the secrets that we keep and think no one else knows. He is the invisible guest at every dinner table. Even in the privacy of a steam-filled bath, His presence permeates the vapors in the room! God is there! He knows, hears and sees *everything!*

As I followed Christopher's still reluctant steps into the house, I thought about all the things I had ever done, all the thoughts I had ever had, words I had spoken, well-intended or otherwise. Surely, if God had seen, He had also heard! I am aware that He knows the very content of our hearts, even when we say we don't really mind giving up our rights for another person's wrong or when we forgive the transgressions of others against us. My God! What about my transgressions against others? More importantly, what about *my* transgressions against *God?* I was instantly convicted by some of the things I had done in my past—some things I had done that had not even been revealed to those who thought they knew me best!

"My life is an open book," I once said to the students in a Multicultural Literature class that I had been teaching. *"I have no secrets,"* I told the attentive youngsters. Well, it was **almost** true! Certainly, I had voluntarily divulged my dismal, tragic past, the details vividly painted across the pages of my first literary work. Openly, I had shared with other people, some who were familiar and others, who were unknown to me, things I had never really shared with anyone before in great detail. Yet, there were many things that only God, Himself knew—things that had occurred in my troubled life. Seemingly, I thought that the veil had been lifted. I had bared my soul . . . well, just about, *anyway!*

On one of many occasions, my students sat attentively and listened intently as I shared with them my husband, Derrick's, *"semi-serious"* endorsement for me to run for *City Council.* Although I had never desired to seek public office, many times he had encouraged me to consider doing so. After all, he would say with regality, I had a *"clean slate,"* no dirty laundry that could be aired before the election results were in!

"No," I would reply, laughing, *"I don't want to be on the City Council."* Surely, I thought, God had something more meaningful in store for me to do! He had allowed me to reconcile my past and finally heal from a childhood of violence, and sexual and emotional abuse.

Right in my own classrooms, I had looked into faces of young people who were most likely living their lives caught up in painful indiscretions and destructive relationships of their own! I knew, with a degree of certainty, that on the faces of many of the young people I passed by, in the halls of the school on a daily basis, were eyes that had seen just as much horror as I, myself, had seen—possibly more! Some of them were living lives which epitomized the very torment of hell. I knew it! At times, I had seen my own life reflected in the sadness of many youngsters' countenance!

On occasion, hints had been provided to me in the letters I found slipped discreetly beneath my door some mornings upon entering my classroom. Why, I wondered, was Satan attacking so many young people? Oh, everyone knew that he really could care less whom he destroyed. That is still his main agenda, *"walking to and fro, seeking whom he may devour."* Narrowly, many times I, myself, had evaded his wicked grasp!

In the summer of 1998, Derrick, our boys, my friend, Terri, and I went on a cross-country tour to promote *Opening the Door.* It had been doing quite well since its publication in December 1997. We left Columbus, Georgia early one Friday morning, packed as tightly as we could stand it, in our black Chevy Blazer. We took as many copies of my book as we could carry with us and still allow us room to sit comfortably. In the months leading up to our trip, I had been in touch with numerous people across the country, so I had been successful at scheduling speaking engagements at several places as we made our way from hot and humid Georgia to dry and sunny California! I was very optimistic and quite eager about the opportunity to travel and share the book and the testimony it contained with as many people as I possibly could all over the country. I had been delivered, and I could hardly wait for the world to know just how I had received that deliverance! I was compelled to share my testimony with others because somehow, I believed that they, too, could be delivered, once they heard what God had done for someone like me—someone who had lived with so many issues for thirty plus years! I wanted to tell them my story and relate the rough road I had had to tread to obtain my own healing and deliverance so that they would understand that *without the test, there could never be any testimony!* Surely, I thought, people would hear what I had to say, look at the person I had become, despite the ugliness of my past, and be able to see God's handiwork. I felt like a miracle and figured that there must be somebody somewhere who needed to know that God was still in the business of performing them!

We set out on our way, heading for Shreveport, Louisiana. My first book signing on the tour was scheduled at a mall bookstore in nearby Bossier City at five o'clock that evening. As we traveled over the long highway, into and across the state of Alabama, my mind was filled with so many thoughts that I was somewhat oblivious to the noise that Christopher made as he busied himself with some action figures he had brought along for the trip. I looked out of the window and half-listened to the blues playing on the radio as we crossed the Mississippi State line. A huge, billowy magnolia was painted on the sign that welcomed us. Many, many times, we had traveled the road to Mississippi, Derrick's home state. He was born in Brookhaven, a small town which sits in the valley about fifty miles south of Jackson. Whenever we journeyed to visit, before we even got out of Alabama, he always frantically sought the airwaves for the sounds of **B.B. King, Johnny Taylor, Bobby Womack** or someone like the infamous **Lenny Williams,** whose *"oh-oh-oh"* song always drove me nuts! This time was no different. As soon as he found the right radio station, he began to croon along with the balladeer who was moaning his tale of woe and misfortune. *"My baby left me," dun, dun-a-dum, "cause I didn't have a dime!" Dun, dun-a-dum, "If I had-a known it, I wouldn't have let her drink all my wine! I got the blues . . ."* The singer didn't know it, I thought, but unless he wised up soon, he was going to keep on having the blues!

I gave some thought to that—the blues—the blues and the multitude of people who were experiencing them. Oh, not necessarily for the same reasons the blues singer was sang about, but the blues, nevertheless. I remembered having my own case of the blues on more than one occasion. My thoughts drifted back to a warm summer night when I was about fourteen years old. In my mind, I could still see myself sitting on the front porch, in front of our battered house up on Twenty-Second Street. The old frame house, with its faded green paint peeling away, sat down at the foot of a red dirt hill on a dead end red dirt road. It was well after midnight and there I was, sitting on the front porch alone, the anger inside of me forcing hot, salty tears from the wells of my eyes. I was angry and upset because my Aunt Meg, guardian to my three brothers and I, had just told me to get out of her house—*again!* She had said it many times before, and I had found myself sitting in that same spot, in an old green rocking chair on the front porch, staring out at the yard, dimly lit by the porch light. I suppose that every time she thought about what I had told her about her husband, my Uncle Ben, sneaking into my bedroom late at night to molest me, she would become furious all over again! She was probably angry with both of us, but it was *"me"* that she would tell to get out! When she looked at me, I could see in her eyes the contempt she must have felt for me, along with the frustration she felt that something within her had not been quite enough to satisfy her lustful husband. I am also sure that many mothers who have shared similar plights have felt this way. If their husbands or boyfriends felt it necessary to touch their daughters the way they should have been touching them, the poor women probably thought that the fault was their own, that something was missing, something somehow unfulfilled. I didn't understand that then, of course. It has taken me until this season in my lifetime to get to the truth of the matter. It actually took the hand of God, putting a series of events into motion to shake my very foundation, in order for me to discover that the fault was not in Aunt Meg. Even now, I wish she was alive so that I could tell her that. The fault was not in her. It was in Uncle Ben and the sin which he allowed to possess his life!

Men who molest children don't do it because the women in their lives are not able or willing to satisfy them. They are driven by the wiles of the wicked one himself! It is the sin of perversion that separates them from God. That is Satan's goal, after all, to separate us from God and His Love. Anyone who sexually abuses a child—a child, when the Bible specifically warns against those who would do them injury—puts the distance of the seven seas between themselves and the Lord! What a catastrophic thing to do! The sad thing is that, in most cases, the persons who have done this are not even aware of the jeopardy in which they have placed their very own souls!

Well, there I was, once again, sitting on that porch, surrounded by darkness, both inside and out of the old frame house. I could hear Aunt Meg inside, still fussing, ranting and raving about me coming home at midnight from the party that my older brother Wayne and I had gone to that Friday evening. He was sixteen and already had his driver's license. He had been granted permission to drive, and I had gone along with him to a friend's party in Aunt Meg's green Chevrolet Caprice station wagon. Although I had not been ready to leave the party, I had stopped dancing and gone over to remind my brother that I had to be back home before twelve o'clock. I wasn't really surprised when he waved me away. He was having way too much fun with his friends to give my personal problem much thought! By the time I persuaded Wayne to leave the party and drive me home, the bewitching hour had already crawled by, so we got home just after midnight. When we went inside, he went on to bed and I, on the other hand, was told to *"get out!"* So I did. I went outside and sat in one of the rocking chairs that had been sitting there, probably since the house was built. I had been sitting on the porch for about fifteen or twenty minutes, despising the very faded green and peeling paint as much as my own meager existence and straining my ears to hear an end of Aunt Meg's yelling. Finally, and much to my relief, the bellowing subsided. The house had become still, so I assumed that everyone had gone to bed. I had every intention of going inside and crawling into the top bunk where I slept in the room my brothers and I shared, but I didn't. Something deep within me had had enough! Instead of tiptoeing back into the house, I got up and walked right off of the front porch, up the concrete stairs and into the road in front of it!

There were no streetlights on that dark, dead end, red dirt road. Willow trees on both sides of the road communed with each other over my head so if there were stars above me, they could not be seen. Darkness draped itself around me as I began walking, with no particular destination in mind. My black leather loafers padded softly upon the moist earth beneath my feet. I went away from the house, past the dark crimson brick elementary school my brothers and I had attended, to the corner. At its end, the red dirt ended and the pavement began. For a moment, I stood and waited for a single vehicle to pass. It was way past midnight, and there was no traffic in view, so I jetted up the street! At the next corner, I sprinted across Hamilton Road and cut across a huge yard. An enormous red brick church building stood on the opposite corner. When I thought that I had gone far enough away so no one would be able to spot me, I slowed my pace.

It seemed I had been walking for at least an hour, but in retrospect, I think it had only been about twenty or thirty minutes. I had no idea where I was going. I only knew that anywhere else **must** be better than home! I felt like the Wizard of Oz's Dorothy, in search of a place somewhere over the rainbow. She loved her Auntie Em, and she believed that her aunt loved her, but she was unhappy with her life! I, too, was searching for my place—over the rainbow—but my situation was a little more ironic. Even though I felt that Aunt Meg could not possibly love me, I still loved her! I didn't even blame her for hating me! Heck! I hated myself and the slice of life that had been served to me! Perhaps if I could just make it to the Land of Oz . . .

By the time I got beyond what is now the Medical Center Hospital and some other medical offices, my footsteps quickened. Just as I turned onto Seventeenth Street, I heard the shrill voice of my middle brother, Michael, call out to me, *"Nesi!"*

I didn't even stop to look and see from whence the voice had come, but I heard a car turning onto Seventeenth, heading in my direction. My mind a blur, I took off running! Hastily, I crossed the street and ducked into the shadows between two frame houses. My heart was pounding!

"Nesi!" Michael called out to me again. *"**We can see you over there, girl!**"*

The Caprice pulled into the driveway, between two houses. The engine purred softly.

I held my breath, hoping that no one could see me. I waited, but the car didn't budge. When I realized that they obviously were not leaving until I came out, I sighed and stepped out of my hiding place. Slowly, I trudged towards the waiting station wagon where Uncle Ben sat patiently behind the wheel. Michael was in the front passenger seat, a mixture of joy and worry on his innocent baby face. He was wearing a pair of funny-looking pajamas with the words *"Zorro"* and tiny *Z's* all over them. I *almost* smiled as I climbed into the back seat. When I closed the door, Uncle Ben simply backed out of the driveway and started home. He never said a word to me then, but he usually had very little to say anyway.

"Where were you going anyway?" Michael asked me, smiling. For the first time, I noticed that his lips were a rosy pink.

I looked up at him, but said nothing. He, nor either of my other brothers, knew anything about the crimes that had been committed against me in the house while they slept peacefully in their beds at night. I didn't think about it then, but when I reminisce, I realize that they thought that everything was fine! After all, Uncle Ben and Aunt Meg had taken the four of us in after the sudden, tragic loss of our parents! For all they knew, Aunt Meg and Uncle Ben loved and cared for us as if they **were** our real parents! I guess they felt that we were pretty lucky to have someone to just step in when our father murdered our mother and took his own life. In many ways, I suppose we were!

I looked at my brother through the tears that were rapidly forming in my eyes. I could tell that he was glad to have found me. He was on his knees, turned around in his seat, watching me, all the way home. In fact, after we got there, he continued to watch me until I climbed up into the bunk bed, atop the one in which he slept. I laid down with Aunt Meg's yelling still ringing in my ears, and tried my best to figure out why she was so angry about my leaving. She had been the one who told me to get out! It made no sense to me at all. I slept in my clothes that night and cried myself into a deep, exhausted sleep.

". . . and God shall wipe away all tears from their eyes."

Revelation 7:17b

"What are you thinking about?" Derrick asked.

"What?" Startled, I turned to look at him.

"I said 'What are you thinking about?' You seem to be a million miles away," my husband said, with that smile that had first captured my heart several years earlier.

I smiled back. *"Nothing, really."*

"You excited?" he asked.

"Yeah, I am," I said. In fact, I was beyond excited! My insides were tingling!

After a long and somewhat cramped ride, we arrived in Shreveport, Louisiana and found our way to our hotel. As I mentioned earlier, in the weeks preceding the trip, I had made arrangements for our accommodations across the country and back, so we knew exactly where we would be spending each night during the tour. When we arrived at the hotel, we pulled into a circular driveway which ran directly in front of the lobby. Derrick stopped short of the shiny glass double doors to let me out of the car. I climbed out and went inside, while he went to park the Blazer in a space nearby. I entered the hotel lobby, which was elegantly decorated with green plants and beautiful pieces of warm, color-coordinated furniture. The floor in the lobby was a sparkling marble and squeaky clean. I was very pleased with what I had already seen.

Just ahead of me was a gentleman talking to the clerk, a young sharply dressed black woman. She completed his accommodations, and with a smile, handed gave him his room key. The man moved swiftly away from the counter, heading to his hotel room. I proceeded to the space he had vacated. When I stepped up to the counter, the clerk's smile abruptly faded and a dark, voluminous cloud rose behind her eyes.

"Yes?" she said, tartly.

I was a little taken back by her tone of voice, so I hesitated to speak right away. After a moment, I said, *"Hello, my name is Denise Bryant and I have reservations."* I smiled at her, hoping that whatever she had seen when she looked at me had dissipated. I knew that sometimes people could just not like you because you look a certain way. I didn't know what had brought to her face something that was beginning to look like a scowl, but perhaps a smile from me would turn things around.

To my surprise, the young lady sucked her teeth, as if she was annoyed at my very presence! Then, on top of that, she sighed an audible sigh!

My eyebrows raised of their own accord.

After typing something on the keyboard console in front of her, she looked up at me again. *"We don't have it!"* she quipped, dryly.

"Excuse me?" I said, amazed. I didn't think I had heard her correctly.

"I said we don't have it!" she snapped again, this time with finality.

I stood there, obviously at a loss for words. My husband walked into the lobby. Terri strolled into the lobby behind him.

"What's the matter?" Derrick asked, observing the look of confusion on my face.

The clerk was still standing in front of me, a look of disdain on her face, for some reason I *still* could not quite understand.

"She says that they don't have our reservation," I said, turning to look at him.

"What?" Derrick asked, incredulously. *"What do you mean 'they don't have our reservation?' They have to have it!"* A wrinkle crossed his forehead. *"Did you give her the confirmation number?"*

"No," I said, still looking at him. At his side, I could see Terri and the puzzled expression that had crossed her face.

"Well," he said, *"give it to her! They have to have it!"*

I turned back to the young lady, who seemed to have grown even more annoyed with me. *"Would you please check the confirmation number for us?"* I wasn't sure what was going on, so I spoke with a little more reservation than I was accustomed to speaking.

"You want me to check it now?" She asked, as if the request was highly unusual.

My husband intervened, his voice rising, *"Yes! We want you to check it right now!"* I could feel his irritation rising.

After another click of her teeth and another dramatic sigh, she began typing again. After a moment, she paused. Then she sighed again. *"We don't have it,"* she seemed pleased to announce, the queer smile returning to the corners of her mouth.

"I don't understand," I said, turning back to Derrick. I held up the trip booklet that I had been clinching in my hand. The slick cover had become even more slippery since my palm had begun to sweat.

He took the booklet from me and held it up where the clerk could see it. *"You see this?"* He asked. *"Every night, for the next fourteen nights, we have reservations at one of YOUR hotels in different cities across the country and back!"*

I don't think she was even listening to him, and I know she wasn't looking at him because she was *still* looking at me. I looked back at the young lady and I didn't know it then, but it wasn't her that I saw! There was something else there, but I couldn't quite put my finger on it.

"Would you please call the 1-800 number and ask them what happened to our reservation?" Derrick snapped at her.

To further astonish the three of us, she had the audacity to ask, *"You want me to call right now?"*

"Yes!" he said, struggling to contain his anger. *"We want you to call right now! My wife is an author and she is here for a book signing in . . ."* he glanced at his watch—*"thirty minutes! So yes, we need you to call right now!"*

The young lady sighed even deeper and strolled over to a phone on the wall at the end of the counter. She must have speed-dialed or something because I noticed that she only pressed a couple of buttons on the phone. Then she said a few words to someone on the other end, repeated the confirmation number that I had given to her, listened briefly and then hung up—without even saying *"thank you"* or *"goodbye"* to whomever she had been speaking to. Then she walked back down to the counter where we were standing. *"They don't have it, either,"* she said, matter-of-factly.

My mouth dropped! How on earth could they not have it when I had spent several days making those arrangements myself? For weeks, I had been on the phone, each and every day, talking to people at every one of my destinations about the my planned upcoming visits! I had talked to clerks at the *1-800* numbers personally! Together, they and I had plotted the stays for my entourage from Georgia to California and back again! They had my *Visa* number, for heaven's sake! How could they *not* have my reservation?

The entire time that the fiasco had gone on, I had noticed two other young women at the long, polished counter who had continued to wait on other people. Additionally, another Hispanic-looking woman had strolled in and out of an office behind the other young ladies. I knew that all three of them had all heard some, if not all, of what had transpired between us and the young lady who was going out of her way to be rude to us.

"May I speak to your manager?" Derrick said, obviously at the end of his own rope.

"You want to speak to her right now?" The young lady drawled, one hand on her hip.

I knew that was the final straw and the camel's back had been broken! As Derrick started to open his mouth to respond, I interceded, *"Please! We need to speak to her right now!"*

The young lady almost hissed!

"May I ask your name?" I said.

She told me, even spelled it for me!

I took a card from the counter top and scribbled her name on the back. On the other side was the manager's name.

"May I ask you a question?" I asked.

"Yes?" she replied.

I leaned towards the counter, in her direction. *"Have I done something to offend you?"* I asked . . .

"What?"

"I asked if I had done something to offend you," I said, again. *"I don't think I have ever been treated so rudely before, and I was wondering why you seem to be so angry with me."*

"Yeah," she said. *"Right."*

I tried to look no more surprised at her response than I had already been up to that moment.

Without another word, the young lady disappeared through the door in back of the lobby for a moment and then returned with a smug look on her face. *"She can't see you right now,"* she said, with obvious satisfaction. *"She's busy."*

Derrick exploded! *"Busy? She's TOO busy for a customer?"*

"Honey," I said, putting my hand on his arm, *"That's okay, it's okay. Let's go over here and use the phone."* I pulled him away from the counter. Terri followed. She, too, was seething.

We walked over to the elegantly decorated sitting area. I picked up one of the phones and dialed the *1-800* number which I realized that I knew by heart! A young man answered so cheerfully that it seemed ironic. I told him what had just happened at the clerk's counter. He was appalled! He asked for our confirmation number, and I gave it to him. Then, he told me something that I could hardly believe. He said, at that very moment, he could see our reservation on his computer, and if he could see it, surely the woman at the front desk could! And then, as he was speaking, a message popped up on his screen that our reservation had just been cancelled!

"Whoa!" he said, *"Someone just cancelled your reservation!"*

"What?!" I could hardly believe what my ears had heard.

"Yes, ma'am," he said. *"Your reservation was cancelled from that hotel location."*

I fell silent.

"What did he say?" Derrick asked.

I handed him the phone. *"He said that someone just cancelled our reservation from here."*

Derrick spoke to the man, but I could not hear a word that he said. Distress steadily crept upon me. The only thing I could think about was that if the reservation had been cancelled there, the rest of the hotel stays we had arranged must be cancelled, too! I don't know what kept me from bursting into tears at that very moment, but I tried my best to contain myself.

"I don't know," I heard Derrick say. *"Well, I don't think that would be acceptable at this point."* Then he turned to look at me, *"He said that they do have rooms available here. He said that he can arrange for us to get two rooms, if you still want to stay here."*

I shook my head 'no.' I knew that there must be a reason why our reservations had been cancelled. Something told me that we definitely were **not** supposed to stay there, so I wouldn't even entertain the idea of doing so.

"No," Derrick said into the mouthpiece, *"she doesn't want to stay here . . . . No, thank you . . . . Yes, we will call you back . . . . Goodbye."* He hung up the

phone and took me by the hand. *"You're gonna be late for your signing,"* he said, calmly.

"I know," I said, nodding.

In a hurry, we left that hotel and found two rooms on another side of the river, in Bossier City. The new hotel was a little more expensive than the previous one, but it didn't even matter to me. I was relieved that we had found other accommodations so quickly. We hurriedly checked in and went up to our rooms so that I could shower and change. Before stepping under a much-needed spray of hot water, I yelled to Derrick that he should call next door and have Terri to call the bookstore and let them know that we had been unfortunately delayed, but we would soon be on our way.

As the water soothed the tensions that had engulfed my entire body, I thought about the young lady, at the first hotel, who had been so rude to me. I could not understand what had provoked such negativity from her. I didn't know it then, but the answer to the question was on its way.

"Come on, Denise!" Derrick called from the other room.

"I'm coming!" I replied, and regretfully turned the soothing water off.

"We are troubled on every side, yet not distressed; we are perplexed, but not in despair; persecuted, but not forsaken; cast down, but not destroyed;"

2 Corinthians 4:8-9

The next day, we found our way around the city to a local pop music radio station. We had already called the DJ from our hotel and told him a little about my book. He was very interested and insisted that we should come right over and do a little on-the-air interview. Of course, we got ourselves together in record time in order to do just that!

The announcer was a really nice man who found the story of my having been attacked, in my ninth grade English classroom, appalling! Even more incredible, he thought was the tale of my sister, Debra, whom I had never known existed, having found me as a result of a photograph and the story about the attack in the local newspaper. He sat and listened in awe as I shared with him and his listening audience the story of my mother's and grandmother's brutal murders before my eyes when I was just eight years old. As I spoke, both on and off the air, Derrick circled the small space where I sat, with a camcorder aimed at us. He intended to capture the entire tour on tape. I smiled as I saw him take on the professional persona of a Hollywood cameraman, measuring the light for just the right amount of exposure! He really seemed to be enjoying himself!

After the interview, the DJ loaded the arms of my sons, fifteen year old Tjai and three year old Christopher, with cups and tee-shirts complete with the station logo, and pairs of big fuzzy dice which I knew would **NEVER** go around my rearview mirror! As we walked to the front entrance of the station, I suggested to Derrick that we try to contact the gospel radio station that we had seen, in the yellow pages, prior to coming to the R&B station. He said that he had seen a phone back in the rear of the station, near the sound booth, and he would go back and see if he could get a phone book and use the phone to call ahead and set up an interview. He said that we could stop by the other station while we were out. We still had some time before my second book signing. It had been scheduled for two o'clock that afternoon.

Terri, my boys and I waited in the front lobby, while Derrick went around to the back of the station. In a matter of moments, he returned with a look of amazement on his face.

"You won't believe this!" he said.

"What?" I asked.

"That other station? It's right back there!" He gestured over his shoulder.

"What?" I said, again.

"Yeah! And the announcer told me to bring you all on back!"

Terri looked at me.

"God is good!" I said, smiling.

"All the time!" she chimed back.

We followed Derrick to the back of the station. Frankie, the *"Faith Man"* Howell, a bold, exuberant man, was on the air. When he looked up and saw us coming into the sound booth, he raised a finger to let us know that he would be right with us. Since he knew that the announcer was on the air, Derrick whispered to Tjai to take Christopher around the corner to a lounge. He knew that if they stayed in the sound booth with us, it wouldn't be long before Christopher would make his own radio debut! I watched them leave, and then, I turned my attention back to the man who was busy preaching about the goodness of the Lord across the airwaves. As I stood there, I became distinctly aware of a presence in the booth, a presence I had not felt since we had been in Shreveport.

After a couple of minutes, Mr. Howell turned his audience on to a gospel medley and his attention to us. Large beads of perspiration rested on his wide, dark forehead. *"Who are you?"* he asked, pointing a finger in my direction.

It wasn't the question I had expected, but I answered nonetheless. *"My name is Denise Clayton Bryant,"* I said, feeling the warmth of Derrick's glare to the left of me where he stood. He preferred that I go by my married name only—**Denise Bryant**—that, he said, was just fine. In fact, he often teased me that I **COULD** simply be called '**Mrs. Derrick Bryant.**' He felt that by using my maiden name, I was somehow making some kind of liberation statement. On the contrary, each time the discussion came up, I told him that I had continued to use my maiden name so that those who had known me in my early years would know just who "**Mrs. Derrick Bryant**" is. That usually seemed to quiet the conversation for the moment.

Mr. Howell got up from the stool on which he had been sitting and walked over to where the three of us stood. He took my hand in his and shook it. "**It's a pleasure to meet you Mrs. Bryant.**"

"**This is my husband, Derrick, and my publicist, Terri Johnson,**" I said, gesturing to my companions.

He shook their hands as well, and then he turned his attention back to me. "**Now, tell me who you are.**"

"**Well, I'm an author from Columbus, Georgia and we are on a cross-country tour with my new book,**" I said. "**I had a signing at a local bookstore yesterday and I have another one today.**"

"**Ah, an author!**" Mr. Howell said, obviously impressed. "**What's the name of your book?**" he asked.

"**Opening the Door,**" I answered.

"**And what is it about?**"

I gave him a very quick and brief synopsis of the book and told him that I would love to talk about it on the air, if possible.

Mr. Howell became very enthusiastic about what I had told him. He wiped his brow, "**My God!**" He exclaimed. "**I KNEW there was something special about you! I saw it when you walked in the door!**"

I didn't know what he was talking about. I looked at Derrick and Terri to see if they had a clue. They didn't seem to know either.

"**Hold on a minute!**" he said, and turned back to his console. In a voice more animated than the one he had used to speak with us, he crooned, "**And that was Brother Hez-e-ki-ah Walker! Praise the Lord, Saints! Yes, yes! And now,**" he pressed a button to start another tape, "**If you haven't got your praise on yet, Sister Shirley Caesar will be glad to help you get on your way!**" The way in which only she can, the renowned gospel evangelist began ministering on the air through music.

The "**Faith Man**" returned to us. "**Now! My Lord! I am so glad you're here! You might not know it, Sister, but God sent you here! There is a demonic spirit in this part of the country! A spirit of incest and molestation! Right here in**

Shreveport!" he exclaimed, emphatically. *"You know, this is part of the Bible belt!"*

"Bible Belt" was a term I had heard many times before, but I had never given it much thought. After all, wasn't the Bible everywhere?

He went on, his voice rising like an exuberant gospel preacher to a hungry Sunday morning congregation, *"Yes, there are a lot of things like what your book is about going on in this part of the country! So much incest, so many young girls being molested, things like that!"* Then he laughed a deep, throaty laugh. *"Praise the Lord for bringing you here!"*

I breathed a sigh of relief, *"I'm glad SOMEBODY knows who the Lord is,"* I said. *"I was beginning to get worried about Shreveport!"*

At that, Derrick and Terri both laughed aloud.

"What do you mean?" Mr. Howell asked, wiping his brow with the back of his hand again.

I went on to relate the story about our experience at the first hotel we had attempted to check into. I told him how shocked I had been that this young woman, whom I had never even laid eyes on before, had shown me such blatant hostility. I exclaimed that I had done nothing to her to deserve the treatment she had rendered me.

Again, he was smiling.

I thought that was odd, so I stopped talking and looked at him.

"You don't understand do you?" he asked.

"No," I said. *"I had not done anything to her."*

"Yes," he said, *"you did."*

I could feel a quizzical expression crossing my face. *"What did I do?"* I asked.

He sat back on his stool and smiled broadly, *"You showed up, here in Shreveport,"* he said, *"and the Devil knew who you were!"*

Right then, a chill ran down my spine and suddenly, the tops of my feet felt unusually warm. That warmth began edging its way up my legs, my thighs, my entire body! I couldn't even speak.

"Sister, God has set you up!" He proclaimed, seemingly pleased with the revelation. *"Yes ma'am! God has something in store for you! He didn't deliver you for nothing! No sir! He knew exactly what He was doing!"* And then he pointed at Derrick, *"And you, brother, have been set up too, because you're married to her!"* Then he included Terri in his disclosure. *"You, too, Sister! So, get ready! You've been set up too, because you're with her!"* Then he turned back to me. *"Oh, God is going to do something awesome with you! Yes! Praise the Lord!"* He laughed again.

For some reason I could not understand, I began to cry. I felt tepid tears streaming down my cheeks. I turned to look at Terri and saw that she was crying, too. I tried to get a glimpse of my husband's face, but when I turned to him, he abruptly turned and left the sound room! I rotated back to Mr. Howell. He was still smiling.

"Denise, you didn't go through all of the things you've been through for nothing! God needed YOU to go through your storms because He wants to use YOU to help others to get through THEIR own storms!"

When he said that, I began to understand what he meant. While I was doing some serious writing, it had occurred to me that God had taken me where I needed to go in order to get to the place at which I had arrived. I had written something like that somewhere in my text

Now, here was this man, one whom I had never seen before, telling me the same thing!

'Don't let nothing stop you, Sister!" he said, expressively. *"God has started a work in you and the Word says that He is well able to complete it! You must NOT give up now!"*

At once, the words seemed to soak in, absorbed through my skin, in some supernatural way. I knew that what Mr. Howell had said was true. I realized that the war had begun, and Satan would soon know that I was prepared for the battle! I also knew that he would stop at nothing to discourage me! But more importantly, I knew that God had equipped me! I realized that I had witnessed my mother and grandmother's murders because I needed to be able to sympathize with those who would travel a similar road of grief. I had been sexually molested for a great part of my youth, because I would have to share my own humiliation with those who would be ashamed and devastated, as the result of the sin of others' perversion. God had *"allowed"* my painful experience with spousal abuse in order that I be able to see, through tear-streaked eyes, a heart as broken as my own marriage that had been filled with abuse! At that moment, I realized that God had indeed *"set me up,"* as the *"Faith Man"* had so aptly put it! Within my soul, I knew that I had come face-to-face with the wicked one, yet I was not afraid. Somehow, I was empowered by the experience and the implications it carried. God wanted to use **me**! It mattered not that Satan knew it. What was most important was that God had found use for me—someone who had been bereaved and berated, damned and deserted, cursed and criticized, and ultimately, sexually, physically, and emotionally abused! If He could *still* use someone like me, what about you?

On our way out of the radio station, I forgave the young clerk who had left such a sour taste in my mouth the day before. In fact, I began to feel sorry for her. She had been an instrument used by Satan to accomplish a task at which he had sorely failed! It was the very first stop on my two-week speaking and book signing tour, and he had tried to stop me before I could even get started! Little did he know, I had been emboldened as a result of his first attempt to dissuade me on the tour! I would go forth and tell anyone who dared listen about the goodness of the Lord! I would declare His mercy from Shreveport, Louisiana to Los Angeles, California and then, on the return trip, I was convinced that I would get a second wind to carry the word back across the country! In short, I was *"fired up!"* I made a vow to begin seeing with my heart instead of my physical eye. I realized that what I had observed with my own eyes had caused me to react carnally. What I should have been doing was seeing with the heart—the place where Christ had taken up residence. If I had, I would have seen Satan attempting to discourage me, instead of being hurt and offended by the young lady who had yielded herself for his use! She had not been my adversary. It had been Satan, himself, all along! One thing was certain—I would recognize him the next time he reared his ugly head in my presence! I was sure of that!

As we prepared to leave, a meek, diminutive man, Pastor Williamson, stopped in at the radio station and asked if I would come by and say a few words to a weekly assembly of ministers and lay people who met at his church, every week, in a tidy little Shreveport community. I apologized to him and explained that we would be leaving Louisiana the following morning, en route to Texas. Excited about what he had heard on the radio about my book, he asked me if there was any way possible for me to come back through the city and speak at his church. I looked over at Derrick, before answering. As we had been standing inside the sound booth talking to Mr. Howell, a few moments earlier, he had just commented that I had not yet learned how to say the word *'no.'* Before answering Pastor Williamson, I looked coyly over at him, hoping that he would say *'yes'* for me.

"Won't we be back in Shreveport on a Tuesday?" I asked, hopefully.

"Yeah," Derrick replied. *"What time is the program?"* He asked Pastor Williamson, opening the trip booklet he had been holding in his hand after he stopped recording. He studied our schedule for a moment.

"We have it every Tuesday at the noon hour," Pastor Williamson answered.

"Can we do it?" I said, eyeing my husband.

Derrick nodded and extended his hand to shake the older gentleman's hand. *"We'll be there,"* he said.

Two weeks later, we returned to Shreveport, making it to the quaint little church just minutes before my introduction was made. We eased into the service that had already begun. An usher escorted me to the front, to sit near the podium. Derrick, Terri, and the boys sat towards the rear of the church. I sat and listened as Pastor Williamson told the congregation about our seemingly *"chance"* meeting two weeks earlier. He said it *"seemed"* to have been by chance, but we both knew that chance had had nothing to do with it! He went on to say that he believed God had brought me to Shreveport for the purpose of being at that place, at that time, to speak to those who had come out to the weekly fellowship. After a very warm and complimentary welcome, he yielded the floor to me.

That day, I spoke about *"Overcoming Infirmities,"* something I had been speaking about before numerous audiences, during the rigorous fourteen-day trip. I referred to the woman who had had the spirit of infirmity for eighteen years. She had been so low that she could *"in no wise lift herself up."* Boy, could I relate to her! I, too, had been down in the depths of despair, having gone down a third, fourth, even fifth time! I could still see the little knobby-kneed girl with *"dirty brown"* hair, lying in the top bunk bed in a room I shared with my three brothers. I laid there, trying to figure out what just had happened, moments earlier, when my underdeveloped body had been fondled in the throes of perversion! The sound of the hardwood floor, creaking under my abuser's stealthy footsteps, retreating in the darkness, echoed in my ears. I had never known just what it was that had kept the woman in the Scriptures bent over for eighteen years, but I knew about the weight I had carried upon my own shoulders . . . the weight that had cast a ghastly shadow over my head for thirty.

The Scriptures tell us that the woman had a spirit of infirmity, and it had plagued her life for eighteen years. The infirmity was an evil spirit that had been so overwhelming that she had been bowed down by strong convulsions. She had had it for so long that it was, by social standards, incurable! She could not stand erect, which is something that places man above beasts. Her illness was a dehumanizing one! Not only was she deformed by it, but it was painful for her to even move! Yet, she went to the synagogue on the Sabbath day to worship! I shared with the congregation that some people wake up with a headache on Sunday morning and decide to stay home from church! It would seem to me though, that if you were sick, you would get to the *"doctor"* as swiftly as you can!

The woman went to church, despite her agonizing pain and, the Bible tells us, that she did not appeal to Jesus. In other words, she didn't go to Him, fall down, and ask Him to heal her. She had been suffering in her condition for so long, any hope she could have had that she would be cured had probably left her long ago. She came to church to worship I told the attentive listeners! Before she could even call upon the Master, He answered. She had come to be taught and to get some good food for her soul, and then, miraculously, Christ gave relief to her bodily infirmity. It occurred to me that this was what was meant in Matthew 6:33 which says that we are to *seek ye first the kingdom of God, and His righteousness; and all these things shall be added unto you.* Christ, in His gospel, calls and invites us to come to Him for healing of spiritual infirmities, and if we come to Him when He calls us, with our faith in tact, He will undoubtedly heal us!

That day, I shared with the worshippers that I had suffered with my own infirmity for a very long time. I had spent the last thirty years of my life, literally hating the person who had taken liberties with me to which he had not been entitled. Although I didn't go into a lot of detail, I disclosed that, at one point, I actually had threatened to kill him if he dared touch me again. I had meant it, too! I told the congregation of strangers, who were now so quiet that you could hear a pin drop, that I had hated my abuser, and I had carried that hatred around in my heart for so long that it had become a part of my being, flowing through my veins like the crimson substance which had sustained my life! I had heard it said that *"hate consumes,"* and I wondered how and why I had survived. Surely, the astronomical amount of contempt that had taken up residence within me had been sufficient enough to destroy me. Yet, God had let me go on—and I had chosen to continue to go on . . . hating.

As I spoke, something which I had not ever considered before occurred to me. I realized that God had fully intended for me to return to Georgia to reside. When I returned, I had not planned to stay indefinitely. I had merely come back to do what I felt was my duty, to care for my adoptive mother during her recuperation from a mild heart attack. After she passed away, I ending up staying because I had given her my word that I would. Obvious surprise showed on the faces of many as I shared with them that God had *"brought"* me back to Georgia so that I could face my abuser, in a direct manner, on a daily basis. It was the only way He could deliver me from the hatred that had threatened to destroy me! I saw the looks of shocks and disbelief on the faces of several people who were seated before me.

Yes, I continued, God had brought me back and placed me in a situation where I would have to physically look into my abuser's face, each and every day. It was the only way that He could actually *"draw"* that hatred that had taken up residence in my heart, to the surface. Each day, I had to talk to the man who had literally scarred me! I had to see him so that the hatred could be drawn up and out of me; much like salted pork draws a rising to its head.

Of course, those of you who have never experienced this or seen it done might not be able to understand what I'm saying. So I will say it like this: Consider putting an extremely hot towel on a blackhead. The heat will literally open the pores and draw the dirt out of the skin. It has the same effect the salted pork has on the rising. In either circumstance, the cause of the problem is drawn out and away!

I virtually believed that it did not bother me to see this man every day. I actually thought I had it all under control. Ha! **That** was a lie! I didn't have anything under control. I still hated him and try as I might, I could hardly contain it! It could have been Satan that caused the dirt to accumulate underneath my skin. But God, in His awesome goodness, had provided the heat necessary to draw the filth out—for good! *"That's what He was doing,"* I said, *"drawing it out of me!"* As the hatred rose to the surface, I had felt the weight that had resided on my shoulders become lighter.

Many people suffer from the spirit of infirmity in their lives today. It is the spirit of bondage that, through prevailing fear and grief, souls are actually cast down and disquieted within them. People are troubled! Individuals are bowed down with infirmities that threaten to destroy them! Some have already lost the battle! Many lives have been lost because of the evil spirit that has overtaken those in our society. Young people are dying by the thousands because so many are *"bowed down and can in no wise lift themselves up!"* Their lives are being snatched away by those who are *NOT* making their way to the church when its doors are open wide so that they can be healed of their infirmity! Many are coming to church each Sunday morning, taking part in the worship service, and then picking up their *baggage* and taking it back home with them!

The only way to overcome it, I surmise, is through the power of forgiveness! Although Satan has nearly convinced us that it is impossible to forgive others for their transgressions against us, we must realize that it is the only way that we can overcome our own infirmities! As long as you hate someone for something they have done to you, you will be bent over beneath the sin of unforgiveness. It **is** a sin! It goes against the Word of God! In the sixth chapter of the book of Matthew, Jesus said, *"If ye forgive men their trespasses, your heavenly Father will also forgive you: But if ye forgive NOT men their trespasses, neither will your Father forgive your trespasses."* I do not know anyone, including myself, who does not need forgiveness! So who are we *not* to forgive others for what they have done to us? Even if they have done that *something* to us more than once! In the eighteenth chapter, in that same book of Scripture, Jesus told Peter that we are to forgive those who hurt us *"until seventy times seven."* If you want to be delivered from your own infirmity, you have no choice other than to forgive the person or persons who have hurt or abused you—whether it was **verbally, emotionally, physically, or sexually as well!**

At the close of the service, I met and greeted several people who had sat through my hour-long dissertation. Many purchased copies of my book and I signed them, writing a personal message of encouragement in each one. I had just finished signing a copy of the book for an exuberant, elderly gentleman who chuckled as he told me that whether I knew it or not, God had indeed called me to preach. In a gruff voice, he had laughed, **"Yeah Lord! Just go on, Daughter! Preach the Word!"**

I had laughed, too, although a little uncomfortably.

When a brittle-looking woman approached me, her eyes bloodshot from crying, I knew that she was in need of much more than an autographed copy of my book.

"Can I talk to you?" The tall, slender, copper-skinned woman asked. Her voice was strangely fragile, almost as fragile as she herself looked! I looked up from my seat on the pew and wiped a bead of sweat from my brow. Almost stoically, she stood before me, her arms folded across her chest, tightly, as if she was trying to keep herself from falling.

"Sure," I said, in response to the woman's request to talk.

"Sister Denise, my name is Shirley" she said, a weary sigh escaping from her lips. She stood rigid in front of me, her arms still folded across her chest. **"Something you said really touched me today,"** she said, holding onto herself.

I smiled, trying to put her a little at ease.

"When you were talking about the way God brought you back to Georgia so that you could face the person who abused you every day . . ." her gentle voice trailed off.

"Yes . . ." I said, encouraging her to continue.

After a moment, she went on. The tears that had begun to form in the corners of her dark brown eyes were becoming much too immense to stay there. **"I had been trying to figure out why, after fifteen years, my father had suddenly come back into my life. "After fifteen years . . ."** she said the words again.

I stood up to face her, behind the one pew that separated us. Then I stepped out into the middle aisle and walked around to stand directly in front of her. I reached out and touched her arms, which were still folded.

"After not seeing him for fifteen years," she said, **"for the last three months, I have been seeing him every single day."** Her tears began to flow freely.

Impulsively, I put my arms around her. Almost immediately, I felt a strange sensation, one I had never experienced before! It was as if the energy was being drawn out of me! At once, I was weak, and I felt my knees quiver beneath me. I pulled away from her and looked into her eyes. *"Your father molested you?"* I asked, trying to ignore the sudden weakness I felt.

She nodded, her shoulders shaking.

"Did your mother know?" I asked.

"No," she answered, quietly.

I studied her face. *"Did she live in the same house with you?"*

"Yes." she replied.

"She knew," I said, for some reason unknown to me.

Silently, she lowered her eyes.

I was too tired to keep standing, so I sat down on the closest pew, and then I took her hand and gently pulled her down on the cushioned seat next to me. She was an attractive woman who appeared to be somewhere in her mid-thirties. Her pretty black hair had been smartly styled into a thick French roll on the back of her head. She looked as if she had it all together, but somehow seemed very uncomfortable with herself. I had seen it myself, many times before, in the eyes that looked back at me from the mirror.

"How long did you say it had it been since you last saw him?" I asked.

"Fifteen years," she replied. *"I hadn't seen him in fifteen years, and then three months ago, he just showed up. Now, I see him every day."* She paused, as if she thought she had to. *"When he came back into my life, I asked God 'why?' I thought I was rid of him! I didn't understand . . . until I heard you say what you said today."*

"Believe it or not," I told her, *"I have been speaking at several places across the country for the past two weeks, and today was the first time I said something like that."*

"Well, I'm glad you said it today," Shirley said, wiping her eyes with a damp, crumpled tissue.

"So what now?" I asked, noticing, for the first time that the other people in the small church had moved away from us, out of earshot. We were alone in the rear of the church, near the door.

She shrugged, *"I don't know."*

I took a deep breath, and then I told what I thought she should do. I told her that she needed to go and talk to her father **and** her mother. She needed to tell her father that he had hurt her deeply by abusing her. He needed to hear that from her, and she needed to say it to him. She desperately needed to say it so that the dirt and filth could rise to its surface. He, in turn, needed to hear her say it so that he could acknowledge, to his daughter and to himself, that the hurt, which he had inflicted, was real . . . that it had not been a scene from a forbidden flick upon a silent screen. He had sinned, and it had not gone unnoticed. He truly needed to know that! Then, I explained to her that her mother had had her part in the sin committed against her by her father by disregarding the issue, whether intentionally or subliminally. *"Sometimes we sin by omission, as well as by commission,"* I said.

As I spoke these words to this woman who had been bent over by her own infirmities, Aunt Meg's voice rang in my ears, *"You slut! What makes you think somebody wants you?"* At once, I realized that her retaliation wasn't really against me. What she was really saying was *"Why does he want you? What's wrong with me?"* No doubt, Shirley and I had much in common—not just with each other, but with millions of other women all over the world!

There are women and men, too, who have been sexually, emotionally or even physically abused all over the world! Little girls have been given a false concept of what *"love"* really is by fathers, stepfathers, brothers, uncles, and other relatives who sought to satisfy some *perversion* of their own minds by abusing others who were weaker than them. The abuse itself was and *is* perverse!

It took me a long time to make some sense of my own experience with sexual abuse. It took thirty years for me to see through the dense clouds in my mind and recognize that it was not just a matter of my caregiver taking advantage of me and making my life a living hell. It was a real live attack of Satan and his attempt to make it my eventual residence for all eternity! He had set out to get me, just as he had targeted other individuals like Shirley, other men and women, both young and old, throughout the world. The abusers had simply been *"middle men,"* fulfilling the enemy's perverted will. Through them, he had sought to deceive and devour. Oh, he is so proficient at that! But he is a liar, a deceiver, and the truth never has been, nor will it ever be, in him!

After Shirley and I prayed together for her deliverance, I assured her that God had set her free! That day, I vowed, was her day of deliverance! As we embraced, she shed tears of joy! I also told her that Satan was not going to be very happy about her being set free. I am sure that he is still ticked off about my deliverance! He doesn't want us to be delivered because he knows that we can't keep anything to ourselves. We will tell *everybody*! And when we begin to share our testimony, others begin to overcome! Since he is not very happy about it, he urgently sets out to *undo* what God has done! His goal is to put you back where you were. He begins to constantly remind you of what others have done to you so that you can renew your hatred of them! But, we must *not* allow him to succeed! We *must* hold onto the Word of God and the freedom that it gives to us! Every time Satan reminds you of the sin committed against you, just tell him, in no uncertain terms, *"Get away from me, Satan! I've already forgiven him or her for that! I've already overcome that! I've got the victory and I am not giving it back!"*

*"Stand fast therefore in the liberty wherewith Christ hath made us free,
and be not entangled again with the yoke of bondage."*

Galatians 5:1

One Friday, I was home from school due to a recurrent bout of strep throat, and I happened to turn the television on to an episode of *"Forgive & Forget."* The show's host, *"Mother Love,"* had tears in her eyes. She had been interviewing a young lady who was sitting alone on a sofa, crying, as she related her experience of abuse by her own father. The young lady, a guest from a previous show, was still grieving over the fact that her mother had not appeared behind the door to give her a long overdue apology. The mother had refused to accept the young woman's confession about her husband's sexually molesting her as a youth. Instead of acknowledging the story as true, the mother denied that it had ever happened, and she was so angry with her daughter that she would have nothing else to do with her! In fact, the young lady tearfully reported, her mother had poisoned the minds of her other family members against her, and her own brother had not spoken to her in over four years! Four years! For four years, the bloodline between this woman and her brother had been severed because she had come forward with the truth of her victimization! *She* had been the victim, *not* her mother!

My husband called me from work while I was looking at the show. I spoke to him, somewhat detached, while I was still trying to hear what was being said by both the woman and Mother Love. Briefly, I told him what had just transpired and he said something about it being a shame. The shame, I thought, belonged to the mother and father! Here this young lady was, feeling shame—not for something that she had done, but for something that had been done to her! Her story was not a new one though. Shame was what had kept Shirley stiff and fragile for most of her life! That same shame had kept me insecure and untrusting of anyone—particularly males—for most of my life! Countless relationships have been ruined because of it! Many have struggled with weight problems as a result of it! Drug addicts have been created in denial of it! Marriages have failed from the repercussions of it! Success in life has been crippled in the waves of it! Shame has wreaked havoc in so many lives that its track record is virtually impossible to keep up with!

Like almost every other woman I know, I, too, have been in constant combat with my weight. I can remember a time when weight was not a problem for me, but I also know that it was during my childhood that sexual abuse began. In retrospect, I realize that I had found some security in food that I could find nowhere else in my life! I know everyone has heard that business about finding comfort in overeating. I have heard it, too! And I don't know if comfort was what I actually found. At least, I don't recall feeling comfortable before, during or after stuffing myself with food. I am not making any excuses for my hips and thighs either! I am simply convinced that gaining weight was the only answer I could find in my attempt to hide the shame that had become the essence of my being! There are many, many people who have tried to cover the shame of their abuse with bulges and unwanted weight. In their minds, if they don't look very enticing, perhaps others won't be tempted to take advantage of them. Even at the risk of physical discomfort, we have settled for fat, rather than the attention of abuse. It might not sound rational to some, but it makes perfect sense to me—one who has subconsciously done the very same thing! The one thing that had never occurred to me before is that God could still see who I was—inside, as well as out. Remember? He knows the very contents of our hearts!

"Keep thy heart with all diligence; for out of it are the issues of life."
Proverbs 4:23

TWO

WHEN I THINK about God's frustration and disappointment with the sin and corruption in Sodom and Gomorrah, I wonder in amazement that He has not taken even greater and more drastic measures with mankind today! The Old Testament details the stench of perversion that spiraled towards Heaven, pierced the very nostrils of the Father and struck a nerve so powerful that He had to say *"Enough!"* Men were sleeping with men in that day, just as they are today! In some places, there is an ongoing movement to make homosexuality socially and legally acceptable. Recently, homosexual marriages have even been detailed in magazines and on television shows. It seems that many have forgotten that God didn't accept perversion in the days written about in the Scriptures, and since He has said in His Word that He *"changes not,"* it is safe to assume that He does not accept it in 2010! It is equally as perverse as the notion of men sleeping with their own daughters! Sons! The fruit of their very own loins!

In our modern society, there are women who have been hurt so much by men that they are convinced that the only person who can fully understand them and meet their emotional, physical, and sexual needs is another woman. On the other side of that pendulum are men who sincerely believe that there is a female actually trapped within their masculine bodies. Unknowingly, they suffer from a *"division of the body"* initiated by the fallen angel himself, whose objective has always been to divide and conquer! The mind, or the psyche, in disagreement with the body, represents complete division or *"schism"* within the body, whether it is the body of Christ or the physical body of a human being. If Satan can cause **gender-identity** confusion within the individual, he can certainly gain control over him or her! The result is a broken individual. Broken people constitute broken families . . . families, very much in need of healing.

> *"That there should be no schism in the body; but that the members should have the same care one for another."*

> *1 Corinthians 12:25*

Homosexuality has always been a touchy subject with people, particularly if a member of their family is admittedly *"gay."* To say that the majority of families have one or more members with homosexual tendencies might sound a bit *cliché-ish,* but it is a pretty accurate statement. Nowadays, it is becoming less and less a family *"secret."* Not only are same-sex couples openly frequenting public beaches and restaurants, they are making their private affairs very public in the professional and business world, in the sports world, and even within the student bodies of public schools! Although society has seemingly decided to accept these unnatural relationships, the Word of God has not changed one jot or tittle on the subject!

I have often heard it said that the root of the problem is desire—whether unfulfilled or met, however the real problem is and always has been **sin**! Because of the sins of the fathers, sons are following suit! Somewhere, however, the chain can and must be broken! Where do we begin? It starts within the family. Although the family makeup has drastically changed in our society, God's intention for the family has not. Remember? He changes not!

> *"For I am the LORD, I change not; therefore ye sons of Jacob are not consumed."*

> *Malachi 3:6*

We have strayed far away from the original plans God initially had for the family. One of my former pastors once began a series on the family. When he announced the beginning of the series, I almost exploded! For a while, I had been working on a book about family secrets and here he was about to begin a teaching series that directly related to what I had been writing about! I was so excited! I went to his office after service one Sunday and told him that I was elated that he had begun to talk about the family—the way God intended for it to be. With great enthusiasm, I shared with him my initial inspiration to write a book about healing within families. He seemed to be just as excited as I was! In that morning's worship service alone, I had gleaned many thoughts that I wanted to expound upon. Today, families are definitely in need of healing. They truly need restoration! We must have restoration, but it won't happen until healing takes place. The kind of healing I'm talking about is not possible unless we confront the *"issues"* in our lives, and God knows, we all have them!

When Christopher, reminded me that God *"sees"* all that we do, it was a wake-up call for me! God **does** see all that we do! If we had a thought, He knew exactly what that thought was. That is a scary thing, isn't it? I realize that it makes us seem very vulnerable, but that is how we should feel! We are, after all, nothing but, as I once heard someone say, *"just dust!"* We need to take closer looks at the images that greet us in the mirror every day. We must look deeper, with the eyes of the heart!

I had met Pastor Brooks and his lovely wife, Aria, some months after my first book was published. About a week earlier, I had taken a copy of the book over to the bookstore to see about the possibility of putting some copies there for sale. The clerk was ecstatic about the book and thought that her pastor and I should meet, so she arranged a meeting.

When I walked into the church, I was impressed, not only by the loveliness of the sanctuary and the elegantly decorated offices, but I was delighted to be met with such warmth and genuine kindness! Immediately, I felt at ease there. Pastor Brooks greeted me with a hearty handshake and spoke words of welcome in a tempered accent. I asked where he was from and he told me that he hailed originally from Trinidad, and then, from up north in Massachussetts. Mrs. Aria spoke softly to me with an accent that was much more noticeable.

We sat in Pastor Brooks' office and talked for about an hour and a half. He was very curious to know about the book, although the bookstore's clerk, Liza, had already given him a brief summary. He later told me that he was in awe about the experiences that I had so openly shared within its covers. To look at me, he said, one would never know that I had been through as much as I had. He also told me that this *"incest and abuse thing"* was very new to him because he had grown up in an environment where something like that was virtually unheard of—at least, to the best of his knowledge! When he said that, I smiled, knowing that just because he had not **heard** of it did not in any way mean that it had not happened to some of the same people he had grown up with, gone to school with, played in the yard with, or laughed or cried with! In fact, it could not be counted out that some of those who had been abused sat in the congregation to which he spoke every Sunday morning and each Wednesday night! He had, no doubt, shaken hands which some who had wiped away tears of anger and resentment. It was possible that numerous others, who had been violated in their pasts, were part of his fellowship. Some of those who had asked for prayer in troubled marriages had been the same people who were actually having trouble *"getting over"* the pain of childhood sexual molestation, abuse and neglect. He just had not heard about it . . . yet.

By the end of our meeting, Pastor Brooks had a revelation. He said something that I had not considered before, but it was something that I would never, ever be able to forget. He told me that, as a pastor, he could preach and teach others about the power of God to deliver people from the pain of sexual, mental, physical, and emotional abuse. He knew that he could tell them about Job and his experiences, his pain, his desolation, his frustrations and his struggle to overcome the attacks of the enemy. Pastor Brooks said that, yes, he could tell people that despite their pasts and the pains which accompanied them, God could help them to become overcomers! But, he told me, I could *show* them! He said that I was a living testimony of deliverance! His words struck a chord deep within me! If I had been committed before to sharing my testimony with others, now I was even more resolved to do so! I left his office with a new and greater determination to witness! I never told him that, but I think he knew.

Over the next couple of weeks, I was scheduled to come to his church to minister during a Sunday morning worship service. The date had been set for June fourteenth. I was very eager to go and share with the members there the wonderful things that God had done in my life. I felt compelled to tell them about the abuse I had suffered in the past, so that they could see just what God could do—to show them that He could truly deliver! He had, in fact, delivered me! In the days preceding the fourteenth, the words echoed in my mind . . . *I can tell them, but you can show them!"* I purposed in my heart to do just that!

On the Sunday that I was scheduled to speak, Derrick got off from work at his station, but he had to accompany some other members of the Fire Department's Honor Guard to perform in a special ceremony. He said that he would meet me at the church as soon as he was finished with his duties there. I went on ahead alone. Terri met me in the parking lot. When we got to the church and walked into the sanctuary, I was in awe of the sight before me! Everyone was on his or her feet, praising God! The praise and worship team was on the platform and the congregation had joined them in singing collective high praises to God with everything within them! It was an awesome sight! By the time I got to the front row, where seats had been reserved for us, a warmth engulfed me that I had never before experienced in my life! I felt as if a blanket of comfort had been wrapped around me, and that blanket was one of praise! I put my purse down in my seat and raised my arms up towards Heaven, as others around me were doing. I closed my eyes and felt, for the first time in all my years of going to church, singing, praying and praising God, the glory of the Lord upon me! That is the only way I can adequately describe it!

When the time came for me to speak, Pastor Brooks introduced me to the congregation. As I got up from my seat and walked up to the platform, I could feel the air of expectancy around me. I knew that the church family had already been made aware that I would be coming to speak to them in the worship service that morning. I looked into faces that were anxious to hear, see, know, and share in the experiences and the witness I had to share. I began by telling them a little about myself and about how I happened to come to their church. Then I got straight to the point of my being there that day.

I shared with them my decision to return to college and pursue a degree. I talked about my endeavor to become a teacher, after having dropped out of college thirteen years earlier. I described my enthusiasm and determination to obtain a Bachelors of Science Degree so that I could pursue the career that seemed to have *"found me"* in education. I told them that I really believed that I was supposed to become a high school teacher. I thought I had found my niche in life! Then I switched gears and talked about the traumatic incident that occurred during my second year of teaching in a rural South Georgia high school. In **Opening the Door,** I had written about that experience, describing, in great detail, the day I was attacked by a seventeen-year-old freshman student. Throughout the sanctuary, eyes widened as I spoke of the fear I felt that my life might have ended in that classroom, that day! I went on to tell them how my story was published in the local newspaper and as a result, I met my sister, Debra, whom I had never known to exist!

The congregation was very attentive, and I knew that although the story sounded like an unbelievable one, every word of it was true! As I have been known to do, I told amusing anecdotes throughout my message—of course, I didn't want people thinking that the story had a tragic ending, because it really did not! In fact, God had still reigned in my story! He had given me the victory and ultimately, received the glory! But something very profound happened to me that day at that church. After I had finished speaking, Pastor Brooks extended an altar call to the congregation. He gave the invitation for everyone who had ever been abused—sexually, physically, emotionally, or mentally—to come to the altar so that we could pray for his or her deliverance. Then something happened that totally blew his mind! Nearly every member of the congregation began moving into the aisles and coming towards the altar! I looked across the platform at him, and I could see glowing amazement in his face! He obviously had no idea that so many of his members had experienced abuse in their pasts! Later, he admitted that what had happened that day had actually overwhelmed him! He really had had no idea! On the contrary, I had not been that surprised. I already knew that my story was only one of countless others like it. I had simply done something which most people were reluctant to do—I went *"public"* with my story.

> *"The thing that hath been, it is that which shall be; and that which is done is that which shall be done: and there is no new thing under the sun."*

> *Ecclesiastes 1:9*

Pastor Brooks prayed for the people as they came to the altar. He stepped down from the platform and prayed, touching men and women, even anointing boys and girls, and believing with them deliverance from the pain they had sustained in their lives. I prayed along with him and watched the people as they continued to move closer and still closer to the altar. While I was praying, I thought I heard a voice say *"Go."* The voice was like a deep whisper. I turned to the right to see if anyone was standing beside me and to my surprise, there was no one there! Then, discounting it as my imagination, I turned back to the scene in front of me. Tears streamed down many faces in the congregation.

Someone on the platform was pouring oil into Pastor Brooks' hand. I turned to watch him as he rubbed his palms together and then went back down the steps to continue praying for the people who had assembled there. Then I heard the voice again! *"Go!"* it said. That time, I was sure that it was not my imagination. I had really heard a voice speaking to me! The voice had told me to *"Go!"* I wasn't sure where I was supposed to go, but I knew I had heard it. Just then, Pastor Brooks turned and motioned to me to come down the steps to where he was. Quickly, I obeyed. He touched my hands and whispered to me to touch and agree with some of the people at the altar. *"Pray for them,"* he whispered. *"The anointing is in your hands!"*

The warm blanket wound itself around me once again. I began to touch the people nearest me and pray aloud for their deliverance. A woman in front of me was crying uncontrollably. I touched her on her forehead and, to my surprise, she fell slowly backwards into the arms of two gentlemen who had been standing directly behind her! Gently, they laid her down on the floor, and another woman spread a blue lap cloth over the prostrate woman's legs. For a moment, I stopped and looked down at her. *"Go on,"* I heard Pastor Brooks' say. He could sense my astonishment at what had just happened. I felt my entire body tingling! I nodded at him and moved down to the next person on my right. I realized that the Holy Spirit was having His way, and I had become an instrument being used to fulfill God's will at that moment! That was the first time anything like that had ever happened to me in my life. Little did I know, it was just the beginning!

I have since realized that the seemingly audible voice I heard that day was the voice of God! I heard the command to *"go,"* and I stepped out on the Word that He had allowed to be sown deep within me. When I made the decision to open the door to the past which had kept me bent over for thirty years, the Word of God had kept me from self-destruction—that was what Satan had been working on since the beginning of my life! I had held onto the faith that had been planted deep within me and had continued to grow, despite the pain and abuse I had to suffer. When God delivered me from that pain and abuse, He had not done it so that I could keep it to myself! No, God doesn't bless us so that we can keep those blessings to ourselves. In fact, He wants us to witness to others about all the wonderful things He has done in our lives as our testimony!

People need to know that God is *still* in the miracle-working business! I always tell the groups and congregations to which I have been privileged to speak that if they want to see a miracle, like a song I've heard before says, just look at me! I know that God has done something phenomenal in my life, and I am always eager to share that something with whomever I meet! I truly believe that the afflicted can become overcomers upon hearing the testimonies of those who have overcome.

*"And they overcame him by the blood of the
Lamb, and by the word of their testimony."*

Revelation 12:11

While I was writing **Opening the Door,** something pretty unbelievable happened to me. I had already printed a hard copy of the first seven chapters, but since then, I had written chapter eight in its entirety. Somehow, I lost the manuscript from the computer, so all I had were the seven chapters that I had printed out. The day I discovered it, I was overwhelmed! I left my seat at the computer and went to the bedroom to tell Derrick the terrible news.

"You will never believe what happened!" I exclaimed to my husband as I flopped down on the bed and let out an exasperated sigh.

"What?" Derrick asked, not even taking his eyes from the television screen. He was propped up against the pillows on our bed, deeply engrossed in the day's episode of the **Ricki Lake Show.**

"I lost my whole manuscript!" I declared, disbelief filling my voice.

"What!" He said, raising up from his pillow to look at me. *"How?"*

"I don't know how," I said. *"I tried to get back into it this morning and it was GONE!"* I couldn't believe it myself! I had been working on it for three months and had just finished typing what would have been Chapter Eight in the book. I was devastated to know that I had somehow simply wiped it out of my computer.

"Didn't you save it?" he asked, with a raise of his brow.

"Yes," I replied. *"I had saved it—before I wrote Chapter Eight! I even have a hard copy of the whole manuscript, but I printed it BEFORE I wrote that last chapter."* For all intents and purposes, Chapter Eight was history and I, alone, knew it!

"Well, what are you going to do?" he asked, falling back against the cushiony pillows.

I shrugged. *"I don't know,"* I answered. *"Probably nothing."* I stared off into space, my thoughts drifting. It had already occurred to me that the contents of Chapter Eight probably shouldn't even be in **Opening the Door** in the first place. It contained details about something I had shared with absolutely no one—not even my husband! The lost chapter described the shame that I had carried deep within me for what seemed like my entire life! I had finally *"come clean"* with the story and after getting the courage to do so, it had simply vanished! After a while, I knew that it had not been the right time to share the story. The book was in print without the devastating details of my teenage pregnancy and consequent abortion.

The day that the memory replayed itself in my mind, I had just rushed in from work. Frantically, I tossed my purse on the bed and charged into the adjoining bathroom. I had waited until I got home to go and had barely made it! *"Whew!"* I said, aloud. As I plopped down on the toilet seat, a scene that I had long ago stored deeply into a hidden place in my mind flashed before my eyes. I recognized my then fifteen-year-old self, sitting on a toilet in an all-too-familiar bathroom. In a haze, I saw myself wince from the pain of induced labor as the fetus, I had believed was less than twelve weeks—when in actuality, it turned out to be a bit later, was forced from my womb and splashed into the aquamarine-colored water of the toilet bowl! In a state of shock, I had raised myself up on unsteady feet and peered down into the bowl. What I saw shattered me forever—tiny, translucent arms, at the end of which were miniature hands, little, puny and equally translucent fingers. My knees shook violently as the air throughout the room began to dissipate! I gasped and then everything in the small bathroom eclipsed into a cloak of utter darkness. It was not until later that day that I realized I had passed out on the cold hardwood of the bathroom floor!

The actual memory of that experience caused me to tremble. When Derrick walked into our bedroom, he startled me back into the present. *"Hey!"* he said.

"Derrick!" I almost shouted. *"I need to tell you something!"*

"What, Baby?" he asked, pulling off his work boots. He had been installing cable all day long, as he usually does on his days off from the Fire Department.

"You know, I just had a flashback," I said. *"I saw myself sitting on a toilet seat about twenty years ago—"*

"Wait a minute," he said, dramatically holding up a palm to stop me. *"Is this another one of those terrible experiences you've been telling me about?"*

"Yeah," I said.

"Well, that's okay," my husband said. *"You don't have to tell me."*

"But—"

"No," he interrupted me, shaking his head. *"I already told you. I don't need to know everything about you in order to love you."*

Weakly, I smiled. He had told me that just when I started baring my soul in **Opening the Door.** I often joked about his reluctance to *"handle"* the tragic details of my past. Even though I usually made light-hearted fun of the whole thing, I had often told others that women were not necessarily the weaker sex because they seemed to be able to handle much more than men could, on the average. Since he felt that he *"didn't need"* to know, I decided not to tell him. I decided to write about it instead.

As a teenager, I had been an absolute novice about the *"boyfriend-thing."* I didn't really see what all of the *hoopla* was about, with regard to dating, but since all of my girlfriends were doing it, I didn't want to seem like an oddball or anything. So, I had jumped into the dating game with both feet as a sophomore in high school! I knew virtually nothing about dating and even less than that about sex. Like many, many young girls, I surrendered my virtue way before I should have. Like many of those same young girls, I wanted, and felt that I needed, someone to love me or, at least, make me feel as if they did. At home, I had been accused of being sexually active long before I had ever considered doing anything like that. After I exposed my Uncle Ben's recurrent episodes of *"touching"* me in my tiny bedroom, during the late night hours, I was cursed, denounced, insulted, humiliated and outcast! I was told that *if* it had actually happened at all, it had been *my* fault! Even though I was obviously the victim, Aunt Meg had seen to it that I was the guilty one. She almost convinced me that I had obviously wanted and asked for it, and Uncle Ben had simply given me what I had so desperately craved! At the time, I did not know that it had been the only way she could realistically deal with it—the only way she could avoid feeling rejected by her own husband! If she really believed that I had initiated it, I guess she thought she could make herself feel better. She tried desperately to convince herself that the person with the problem was *me,* not her! After I had gone to her and told her of my misery, Aunt Meg did absolutely nothing about it! For what seemed an eternity, it went on and on and on, stopping only when I got sick and tired of being sick and tired about it myself! When I had taken all of the abuse I could endure, I decided to take drastic actions to stop it myself. I told Uncle Ben that I would *kill him dead* if he ever touched me again . . . and I think he believed that I meant it! He never touched me again.

It is so inexpressibly painful to be the victim of abuse. Only those who were or who have been victims of it can understand the real agony of the situation. I speak to those women, men, boys and girls right now. You must know that you are not alone in your misery. Many people you know have walked the same desolate path on which you have found yourself. A lot of them have concealed their pain beneath frozen smiles and layers of denial and rejection only to find their self-esteem buried deep within. Like you, they have low self-esteem and like you, they don't know how in the world to rise above it! There is an answer though. If I had not undergone the transformation from *"victim"* to *"victor"* myself, I would not be able to share this with anyone. I have seen the eyes of victims of abuse and heard tremors of it in the voices of young women many, many times. With tears in my own eyes, I have read notes written to me by teenagers who have suffered, in their very own homes, abuse from those who are supposed to love and protect them!

I went to speak to two groups of youngsters at a youth detention center in Killeen, Texas once. I was a little stunned to see so many teenage girls in the room—almost as many girls as there were boys being housed at the facility for various crimes and misdemeanors they had committed. In the first group of youngsters I spoke to, there were about thirty girls and a small group of boys—about ten or so. As I stood before them, I looked into the eyes of youngsters who looked like my own children. Some of them could have been twelve years old, while others were as much as eighteen or nineteen. They were just children, misguided, misdirected and missing the mark in their own lives! As I spoke to them, I thought about what the fifth verse of Psalms, one twenty-seven said about children: *"Happy is the man that hath his quiver full of them."* They were a room full of fallen arrows that had either not been properly aimed or had fallen off course somewhere. Instead of enjoying the carefree days of summer, they were here, seated before me, uniformed in bright orange khaki shirts and pants with colorless cheeks.

"God's grace," I said, *"kept me out of places like this!"* I knew with certainty that those kids were not very different from me. Some of the glossy eyes that looked back at me had seen things children ought not have to see. Victims of sexual abuse sat in that room. Fatherless children sat in that room. Children who had been neglected were there. Some studied the checkerboard print of the linoleum floor in front of them as if they were expecting some sudden change in the pattern as I spoke about my own experience with abuse. *"I know how it feels,"* I said. *"You feel as if you are dirty! You think that everyone who looks at you knows your terrible secret. And you feel as if it's your entire fault, too. In fact, you've probably even heard that from someone."*

When I said that, a young, black girl jumped up and ran out of the room. A tall, slender woman in a khaki uniform went out after her. I could not help but to look after them both. I tried to continue, but it took a moment for me to get back to what I had been saying. I went on to tell the young people that although I had grown up in a bad situation, I had been able to rise above it and overcome my circumstances. I knew that they wanted to know how, so I told them. It was with God's help, I said! In spite of losing my mother at the age of eight and then being sexually abused until the age of fifteen, I continued to pray and trust God to help me. For a long time, I confessed, I felt very bad about who I was. I told them that I had successfully concealed my misery from most of the people who **thought** they knew me. Throughout my life, I said, I had maintained a determination to defy the odds, and even when told that I would never amount to anything, I had been bent on proving to everyone that I would! In school, I always did my best because I wanted the satisfaction of knowing that I had. It wasn't for my mother. Although I felt that she was in heaven, watching over me, she was gone, and I knew that I would never be able to see or talk to her again. It certainly wasn't for my father because I had literally hated him for thirty years! I didn't try to excel for my adoptive parents, because, for one thing, I was a victim of their abuse and secondly, I knew that nothing I did would ever be quite enough to redeem myself in their eyes! I excelled academically for me! I did it for myself! I told those young people that the best reason for them to change their lives for the better was for them! They owed to themselves! I don't know if anyone had ever told them that before, but if not, I wanted to make sure they got that message before I left them that day.

I told the kids at that youth detention center that, quite often, I received notes from students at the school where I taught. Most of these notes are unsigned. *"I don't want you to know who I am. I just want you to pray for me . . . I need help, but I can't tell you anymore right now . . . I don't know what to do . . . Help me . . . Please pray for me . . ."* And so, I do. I knew that God knew who they were. I encouraged them to pray for themselves and to ask God to help them to turn their lives around. I told them that just because they had made some mistakes in their lives, it did not mean that their lives were over! They simply needed to do things differently from the way they had done them before.

At the end of the first session, I asked the matron to bring the young girl that had run out back into the room. She left for a moment and returned with the distraught girl at her side. When she reentered the room, the young girl was crying. *"Are you okay?"* I asked, putting my arms around her shoulders.

She almost fell into my arms and laid her head on my shoulder, sobbing.

We just stood there for a moment like that. Then I pulled back so that I could see her face. *"What's wrong?"* I asked.

"I don't know," she said, shaking her head. *"I'm going to be getting out next month."*

"Well, that's good . . . isn't it?" I asked.

She shook her head again. *"No, not really."*

"Why not? You'll be going home, won't you?"

"Yes ma'am," she replied. *"But I don't want to."*

My heart quickened. In an instant, I realized that this frail-looking teenage girl had come from an environment probably much like mine. Home was a place she dreaded returning to. I could feel her pain. I understood her agony. I grieved for her. Again, I put my arms around her. *"I will be praying for you,"* I whispered in her ear.

"Thank you," she whispered back, softly.

I wished there had been something more I could have said or done to help her. I felt such empathy for that young lady that day, but since then, I have discovered that things are going to be much worse for the person who abused her. In fact, all of those who have physically, sexually or emotionally abused children will have a day of reckoning that I don't even think they know about! To the fathers or mothers, stepfathers or stepmothers, boyfriends or girlfriends, uncles, cousins and anyone else who has abused the children entrusted to their care, the Bible warns of the terrible danger of mistreating those children. When a child is abused, instead of being nurtured the way Christ taught that he or she should be, they will, instead become another mis-directed arrow and, in all probability, not be guided towards righteousness. Chances are that the child will have a twisted picture of *"right and wrong,"* and we all know, more often than not, those children usually choose the wrong path in life. These are the children about whom Christ spoke when He said *"Suffer the little children to come unto me, and forbid them not: for of such is the kingdom of God."* Those who abuse children make it difficult for those children to find the Lord. In most cases, they don't know what the righteous know—that God is love!

Job 6:27 tells us that those who take advantage of children who are left fatherless are cursed: *"Yea, ye overwhelm the fatherless, and ye dig a pit for your friend."* Another scripture found in Deuteronomy 27:19 says *"Cursed be he that perverteth the judgment of the stranger, fatherless, and widow."* It is important for you to know, if you have ever abused a child, that you must make amends for the life you have affected. If you don't confess your sin and repent, promising God that you will never again abuse anyone, your life will be forever cursed! This is a life or death matter! God saw what you did and he knew the perversion that filled your heart and mind. Repent before it is too late! It will take a great leap of faith on your part, but if you want God to forgive you, you must seek the forgiveness of the victim of your abuse, as well. If they don't accept your heartfelt apology for the pain you caused them, that is between God and them. Don't let another day pass without coming to terms with the sin that has threatened your entire eternity!

"Repent therefore of this thy wickedness, and pray God, if perhaps the thought of thine heart may be forgiven thee."

Acts 8:22

Healing must take place on **both** sides of abuse. The abuser needs healing just as much as the person who has been abused. The main issue is that of forgiveness. People must realize that without forgiveness, healing is impossible! I talked about this in **Opening the Door**, but it is crucial enough to revisit here. When I realized that in order for me to be able to get completely free of my past, I needed to come face-to-face with my abuser, get things out in the open and tell him of the pain I had endured my whole life! That is exactly what I did.

Thirty-one years after the first time he had violated me, I had sat down and confessed my anguish to Uncle Ben. I told him that I had often grieved over the destroyed relationship between me and Aunt Meg as a result of what he had done to me. I had never been able to have a solid relationship with any other males in my life, because as a child, I had been provided a demented picture of *"love"* that kept me from knowing its true meaning. The pain surfaced once again as I poured out the brokenness I had suffered, and I asked him if he had ever even thought about what he had done. I was a little surprised when he told me that he hadn't. I didn't really believe him, but that didn't even matter. He never said the words I thought would mean so much to me to hear. He never said *"I'm sorry."* It didn't stop me from forgiving him for his trespasses against me. I told him that I forgave him right then and there. I forgave him for the destruction he had brought into my life. I forgave him for abusing my adolescent body and scarring me for life. I forgave him because I had no choice not to. I knew I had to do it if I ever intended to be complete. I wanted to finally be whole. I needed to be free!

Later on that night, when I spoke to Derrick at the Fire Station, I told him what I had done. He was shocked!

"What did he say?" he asked, breathlessly.

"Nothing," I replied.

"He didn't even apologize?" he asked. I could tell he was a bit bothered by that.

"No," I said.

"Well," my husband said, *"are you okay with that?"*

"Yes," I answered. *"I did what God wanted me to do. I'm finally free."*

> *"If the Son therefore shall make you free, ye shall be free indeed."*
> *John 8:36*

I have been told by some victims of abuse that they don't think they will ever get to the point that they can forgive the person who has hurt them. Some have even testified that because they have had to live with the pain in their lives for so long, they have found it not only difficult, but in some cases, impossible to forgive. I have to tell you that it does not matter how long you have had to live with the pain of abuse in your life. You can **still** be free of that pain! I suffered with my own infirmity for thirty years. I began hating my biological father when he murdered my mother. I was only eight years old! Shortly thereafter, the sexual abuse began, which continued until my sophomore year in high school. I know what it's like to be angry and filled with negative emotions. Thirty years is a **very** long time!

I am reminded of the man in the Gospel of John who had an infirmity for thirty-eight years. At each designated season, he was carried down to the pool at Bethesda to wait for the angel to come down and trouble the water. The first person who stepped in after the troubling of the water would be made whole of whatever was wrong with them. This man was impotent, something in his life had gone very wrong. He didn't even have the strength or courage to get up on his own and walk to the water. Each and every time, someone else would always get there first! Well, the Bible says that one day, Jesus came down to the pool and noticed the man lying there. Seeing him in his despondent state, Jesus asked him if he wanted to be made whole. Like many usually do, the man gave a *"lame"* excuse, citing his inability to get to the water because someone else always beat him to it. But I love what Jesus did! He ignored the man's excuse! Instead of asking the man why he didn't move closer to the water or perhaps get someone to help him, He simply told the man to *"**Rise, take up thy bed and walk.**"*

That is exactly what He wants you and I to do. We need to stop making excuses for ourselves! Of course, God knows that we are hurting, and He knows the depth and extent of our pain! It is not that it doesn't matter to Him. It is just that He knows it doesn't have to destroy us forever! Like the Apostle Paul, we are *"troubled on every side, yet not distressed; we are perplexed, but not in despair; persecuted, but not forsaken; cast down, but not destroyed."* We must rise; take up our beds of affliction, pain and abuse and walk! No matter what has happened in our lives, we have to rise above it! We cannot afford to wait for anyone else to move us! We cannot afford to wait another minute! Whether you are the abuser or the abused, Jesus is saying those same words to you, *"**Rise, take up thy bed, and walk.**"*

"I can do all things through Christ which strengtheneth me."
Philippians 4:13

THREE

I AM ALWAYS AMAZED that school teachers are actually expected to daily pour prolific knowledge into minds that are virtually cluttered with painful memories of abuse—past and present! They are being held accountable to penetrate layers of hurt in order to make learning the main thing, when just peeling away the layers requires radical measures! Every day, in the public school setting, I saw adolescent girls, going to their classes, trying to ease their protruding bellies behind student desks, as inconspicuously as they could. I looked into many sets of eyes and knew that things had not gone according to their parents' plans. For the majority of the young girls, it had not been their intention to become pregnant. Their mission had been to obtain love and acceptance. Instead, what they got was added responsibility—responsibility that they were not yet ready to undertake. As a result of their search, their already complicated lives became even more complicated!

Psychologists have readily diagnosed teenage pregnancy as a possible result of increased sexual activity among our youths. I keep waiting for them to get to the real root of the problem though. It goes much deeper than just sex. In fact, the hunger and thirst is not even satisfied by the sexual act! I honestly believe that it is not actually about sex. It is about unfulfillment. We are a people of unfulfillment, and we keep trying to fill the voids in our lives however we can, as much as we can, whenever we can and from whomever we can. Unfortunately, we keep looking out when we really should be looking in!

*"Even unto this present hour we both hunger, and thirst, and
are naked, and are buffeted, and have no certain dwelling place;"*

1 Corinthians 4:11

One summer, I remember being extremely excited about my job with the city youth opportunity program. It was my first time being hired because prior summers had found me too young. This time, I was included in the large group of young people who eagerly went to work in the early summer morning hours. We were anxious about becoming adults, as youngsters are today . . . earning our own money, cashing our own paychecks, and becoming our own persons! I had been assigned, along with a moderate group of young people to walk the streets of a community called Beallwood, seeking out refuse in the residents' yards that could be removed by the city: old, broken down automobiles, abandoned washers, dryers, and other large appliances, stacks of lumber that had **not** been used for added-on rooms, things like that. When we would locate the refuse, we had the responsibility of talking to the residents and making the arrangements necessary to remove the rubbish out of their yards. I particularly liked talking to the people in the community. I felt as if I was doing something really important—helping to clean up the community, which was very near in proximity to my own.

One morning, I woke up feeling really rotten. My stomach churned in a way I had never experienced. When I brushed my teeth, I had gagged uncontrollably! What in the world, I wondered, was wrong with me? I skipped Aunt Meg's oatmeal, toast and bacon breakfast that day, claiming that I wasn't hungry. The truth was that I knew that if I ate, I would most likely throw up! So I just didn't eat. Even the ride over to our worksite made me feel worse, the churning increasing in my stomach! All day long, I was sick and I couldn't understand what was causing me to feel that way. Instead of talking to the residents myself, I stood *"light-headed"* at the curb and waited for my co-workers to do all the talking. By the end of the day, I could hardly **wait** for Aunt Meg to pick me up.

At home, that evening, I sat down at the dinner table with my brothers, Aunt Meg and Uncle Ben. I didn't want to eat, but I knew I would never be able to leave the table if I didn't. I opted to sip slowly from my glass of iced tea. Two sips sent me rushing from the table, making it just in time to the bathroom! When I had nothing left in my stomach to expel, I heaved vehemently! Afterwards, I didn't even attempt to go back to the table. I went to my room and laid across the bed. For a while, I looked out of the window at the slowly setting sun. I heard someone come into the room. I assumed it was Aunt Meg, even though she never said anything. I couldn't even turn my head to look. After a moment, she went away, without a word. I soon fell asleep.

Over the next couple of days, my appetite disappeared but the churning in my stomach remained. I didn't know what was wrong with me, but Aunt Meg did. In the kitchen, one morning, I was fixing myself a cup of coffee, (She had let us drink coffee when we became teens, although I still don't allow my fifteen-year-old to drink it.) and she was at the stove preparing breakfast. She didn't say anything to me and I didn't say anything to her. I had begun to feel very uncomfortable around her lately and tried as quickly as I could to fix my coffee so that I could hurry and get out of the kitchen! I escaped into the dining room and sat down at the table. As I sipped the hot drink, the thought I had been fighting over the last week or so pervaded my entire being. **What if I was pregnant?** I had just become sexually active at the very end of my sophomore school year and now, towards the end of the summer, here I was, devastated by the fear that the unthinkable had happened to me! I didn't know what to do or how to find out whether it was true or not!

That night, after everyone had gone to bed, I sneaked into the kitchen and called my Aunt Margie in Atlanta. I had always been able to talk to her about everything. She was my mother's youngest sister, and although she was grown and married, I could relate much more to her than my other aunts. Since I had no sisters to connect with, I found a connection with Aunt Margie. In a low voice, I told her about the symptoms I had been experiencing over the last couple of weeks. At once, she knew that I was pregnant and like a responsible adult, she told me that I simply *must* tell Aunt Meg!

"*No!*" I said, a little louder than I knew I should have. "*I can't tell her! She'll . . . she'll kill me!*"

Aunt Margie laughed and calmness echoed in her voice. "*No, she won't. She'll be upset, but she won't kill you. She'll know what to do. She'll help you.*"

Something inside me wouldn't let me believe her. I had already seen Aunt Meg's wrath in full effect. I knew that to tell her this news would make matters which had seemed to be incapable of getting any worse do just that!

"*You have to tell her,*" my aunt said. "*She'll know what to do.*"

She made me promise that I would tell my awful secret as soon as daylight came before I hung up the phone. I didn't sleep a wink that night. My head was filled with imaginings of the worst kind! I didn't know what Aunt Meg would do when she found out, but I knew my life would change for the worse! I peered through the darkness out of the window. Through the tall, billowy trees on the side of our house, I could see the moon, shining, betraying the dark night sky. Inside, I was filled with impending gloom.

The next morning, I walked into the kitchen to fix my usual cup of coffee. Aunt Meg was there, hovering over the stove, intently stirring a pot of steaming hot grits. I froze near the doorway. *"Aunt Meg,"* I said, *"I have to tell you something."*

She kept stirring the shiny pot full of hot, sweltering grains.

I took a deep breath and felt a tingling sensation in the top of my head. *"I'm pregnant."* There! I had said the words. I waited for the pot to come flying off of the flaming eye of the stove and into my direction. It didn't. Aunt Meg didn't turn around. She didn't say anything. My knees began to quiver.

"Aunt Meg?" I said, timidly.

"I know," she said, finally, standing still at the stove.

A puzzled expression rested upon my face.

"I've known for a while," she said, simply.

I was silent.

She turned away from the stove to face me. *"What are you going to do?"* she asked. Her voice, calm and not accusing, was not what I had expected it to be.

"Huh?" I replied.

"What do you want to do?" she asked. *"Are you ready for a baby?"*

I shook my head *'no.'* I felt certain that I was in no way ready for anything remotely like that kind of responsibility. God! I was only sixteen!

"Alright," she said, wiping some flour from her hands onto her apron. *"Don't tell anybody else,"* she warned, as if I had not already done that.

"Okay," I said, my eyes lowering to the faded linoleum floor. *"I won't,"* I said.

"Go on and get dressed," she said, quietly. *"I'll take care of everything."*

I didn't know exactly what she meant by that, and somehow, I didn't think I needed to. I just knew that I needed help and Aunt Margie had said that Aunt Meg would provide it. I supposed that adults knew what to do in situations like that, and I had no choice but to accept my fate—whatever it was going to be. I began to wonder what I would do with a baby of my own. I shuddered! I knew that I wasn't ready for the experience! The very idea horrified me!

That Friday evening, I found out what Aunt Meg had decided to do about my problem. She ordered me into the car that night and drove to a woman's house way on the other side of town. She never told me who the woman was or why we were going to her house. She turned off the car, got out on her side and told me to do the same. Aunt Meg pushed the doorbell on the screen door, but I didn't hear it ring. In a moment, a quiet, reserved woman opened the door and quietly ushered us into the house. It was very dark both inside and out of the woman's green and white framed house. She led me to a dimly lit room and told me to get undressed from the waist down, and then she disappeared. I did as I had been told, slipping out of my oxfords and socks and then I carefully laid my denim jeans and panties on a chair near the bed. After a couple of minutes, she opened the door, came back inside and closed the door behind her.

In bits and pieces of my recollection, I remember that the only instruction the woman gave to me was to *"lie down"* on a bed that had been covered with crisp white linen. In the faint light of a strange room, my pregnancy was terminated. I didn't know what she was doing to me, but it felt as if I was being poked and prodded with some kind of long, narrow, and very sharp instrument. It hurt like nothing else I had ever felt before! As the lining of my uterus was being ripped away, I felt myself slowly plummeting from God's grace! My stomach began to cramp after a moment, and I was told to *"get up and get dressed."* The woman left the room, closing the door behind her. As if in a trance, I did as I had been told. I could hear the muffled tones of Aunt Meg and the woman talking in the next room. When I appeared in the doorway, they both fell silent. The woman handed Aunt Meg a small brown bag and told her to see to it that I took its contents as she had directed when we got home.

The drive home was somber. Aunt Meg said nothing to me. In the strained silence, I could feel the deep pains that had already begun making their way to the surface. The pain was not physical. It was a mental and emotional pain that I would experience again and again throughout the rest of my life! I had no idea of the depth and magnitude of the scar that had been made within me that night. I only knew that somewhere inside me, a life had been ended. Repeatedly, I have since regretted the terrible sin I committed that night. I have punished myself a thousand times for lying down and making the mistake that had taken me to that place in my life! It was not until years later that I sincerely asked God to forgive me for my sins. Broken, I confessed that although I was young at the time, I was still responsible for the choices I had made—not necessarily the choice to terminate that pregnancy, but the choice to surrender my virginity to someone in a desperate attempt to feel loved! Time and time again, I have grievously remembered looking down into that commode and seeing the child that I had helped both to create and to destroy! Because He is merciful, I believe that God has forgiven me. It took much longer for me to forgive myself, but in time, I did.

Most Christians don't want to talk about, much less remember, the trauma of abortion. Of course, the *"self-righteous"* frown upon any young woman who has made that choice in her life, but I am convinced that it is no more or less a sin than that of lying, cheating, stealing, or that of committing adultery. Moreover, all of us have sinned and fallen short God's glory, haven't we? We are still seeking reconciliation with Him—and we all should be! I have had to look honestly at my own sins and wickedness, those that I committed both knowingly and unknowingly, by commission or omission, and I realize that Satan has tried, in many ways, to destroy me. Like others, I found myself separated, alienated from God, by my own actions. True, at times, I wondered why He had left me, but my own self-inventory revealed to me that He had not been the one who moved. It was me! I moved away from Him in order to move closer to the comfort zone created by my own sin! I thank God that despite my mistakes, despite my shortcomings, despite my bad choices, I eventually made my way back to Him!

Those of you who have lived with the pain and guilt of having terminated a pregnancy in your past need to know that it is past time for you to obtain reconciliation in your life! This is not to *"excuse"* the sin we have so perilously committed, but it is to stress the importance of confessing our wrongdoings, seeking forgiveness, and then going on to seek repentance for them. Only then can we be reconciled to God and reenter His presence! It is not His will that we be estranged from Him. He already knows about the act—He was there when we performed it! He knew the condition of our hearts before, during and long after our sins were committed! He was a silent witness to the wickedness of our deeds. What a powerful thought! Imagine the things we would have not done had we actually realized that God was there—watching! Unfortunately, we gave very little thought to his presence and as a result, we did some things that can never be undone! And He has always been there—lovingly waiting for us to come to ourselves, like the father in the parable of the prodigal son. We have continued to do *"our own thing"* and go *"our own way,"* but each and every day, He has looked down the road, hoping to see us coming back home to Him! You must decide right now to ask God to forgive you for the things you have done in the past! You must confess your sins and repent, vow never to repeat them again, and then ask Him, with the sincerity of your heart, to let you come back to Him! In the name of Jesus, you can be forgiven! You can be reconciled to God! Listen to that still, small voice within you and you will find your way back to the Father.

"If we confess our sins, he is faithful and just to forgive
us of our sins, and to cleanse us from all unrighteousness."

1 John 1:19

When I became a mature Christian, I realized that the mistakes I had made as a young girl were all part of the snare Satan had devised to destroy any chance I could ever have for a real relationship with God in my life. My scenario was similar to those of other young people I have met in the past and those I have yet to meet in the future. Like them, I craved love and affection and, as a result, sought out an intimacy that should have been reserved for marriage. In a false sense of security that I thought I found in the arms of adolescent males who were neither ready nor able to love me like I really needed to be loved, physically, emotionally, or spiritually, I lost my innocence. Many young ladies and young men have done the same, exact thing! In the absence of loving, nurturing mothers and fathers, many have rushed into the arms of someone who was just as young and inexperienced as they were. They, too, sought to fill the void in their own lives. Together, they formed an abstraction, each half of the pair trying unsuccessfully to meet the needs of the other. The end result—the loss of innocence and the beginning of dysfunction! The only satisfaction gained was that which Satan acquired from knowing that once again, he thwarted the divine plan of God.

I have many regrets. My greatest one is the ignorance of my youth, but I thank God that He is full of grace and mercy! He has graciously looked beyond my many faults and ultimately saw my needs. When we have sinned, we must seek full repentance so that we can avoid repeating the sin. It is important to first confess, or reveal our sin by verbal declaration of our intention to turn completely away from it—and not repeat it again! True confession is a cry for help from the person who is broken and contrite at heart. But that is just the beginning of getting free from sin. In order to please God, we have to absolutely and completely change our mind, abandon our schemes to sin and change our entire lifestyle to one of true holiness! That is when we truly repent! We can purge our lives of the sins we have committed, never to repeat them again. If you want to find your way back into the Lord's presence, that is what you will have to do.

"And you, that were sometime alienated and enemies in
your mind by wicked works, yet now hath he reconciled."

Colossians 1:21

The number of people who have kept secret the details of their past transgressions is astronomical! It is evident by those who go through life with bowed-down heads or those who hesitate to meet the eyes of others in general conversation. When tears seem to flow so freely, yet no explanation for those tears can be verbalized, it is apparent that the scars are much deeper than the surface! They are so deeply rooted and so self-convicting that many cannot stand to even think about the battles that caused them. How many times have you seen someone with tears in their eyes and out of genuine concerned asked them *"What's wrong?"* only to have them burst completely into uncontrollable tears? It has happened to me, too! In fact, I think I could have held myself together better if someone had *not* asked me what was wrong! Many times, I could seldom find words to express what was really wrong with me. At others, I didn't really know myself! Oh, something could have happened to trigger the emotional outburst, but there was most likely a deeper problem that had been festering, like a sore, within the recesses of my heart—some issue or another.

One thing that I have discovered is that we **ALL** have **ISSUES!** For a very long time, I was a lot like that woman who had been bent over for eighteen years. I could truly relate to her because I had had some issues of my own—for thirty years! Before my deliverance, it was a wonder I could stand up at all! A still, small voice within prompted me to face my issues—head-on—so that I could finally straighten up! I would admonish anyone in a similar situation to get away from everything and everybody and get to a place where you can just be still and listen for that voice inside of you. It is probably way past time for you to deal with your issues so that you can straighten yourself up.

Recently, a woman confessed to me that she had been sexually molested by her grandfather when she was six years old. Six years old! Who, in their right mind, could find a six-year-old child remotely sexually provocative? Tears spilled from her dark brown eyes as she confessed to having kept the terrible secret and having been bowed down and bent over her entire life! She had been insecure and had never felt quite adequate in her entire life. She had seldom been able to make eye-to-eye contact with other people because she always felt that they could see through her to the awful shame she was carrying around with her! Incredibly, she was ashamed! She was ashamed at having been victimized and violated! Isn't that ironic? This lovely woman had done absolutely nothing to be ashamed of, yet she was ashamed of wearing the stain of the sin that had been committed against her! If anything, the person who had betrayed her trust, her grandfather, should have been the one ashamed! He was the one who had wronged her! She had simply been the victim!

For a few days, I had been ministering to the congregation at a small North Carolina community church that she attended. At the culmination of the services, the humble, petite woman testified that she had been delivered!

She told the church full of other people that she had been set free from a lifetime of infirmity! With just a word from the Lord, she was delivered! As we embraced each other, I rejoiced with her and thanked God for what He had done in her life!

I had a similar experience when I met the pastor of Antioch Missionary Baptist Church, in San Antonio, Texas, Dr. E. Thurmond Walker, during my first Summer cross-country tour. I had been speaking to the youth at a revival at Simmonville Missionary Baptist Church in Killeen, Texas. Dr. Walker was the revival preacher at the time. After I had finished speaking to the large group of youngsters assembled in the sanctuary, I had gone out to the foyer to sign some copies of **Opening the Door**. At that time, Derrick had joined Terri and I, along with the lines of people who wanted to purchase copies of it. As I was speaking with a young lady at one of the tables, a strong, powerful voice floated out of the sanctuary into the foyer. The voice was so resonant that I had to stop talking. I leaned over the table in an attempt to look through the glass doors so that I could see where it was coming from. Up in the pulpit, I saw a diminutive, dark-complexioned man, but from a distance, I couldn't see him very clearly. One thing was for certain though; he was preaching the Word of God with a voice that thundered like the mountains of Zion! With strong, muscular arms, he gestured before the captivated congregation and seemed to emerge from behind the sacred desk.

"Who is that?" Derrick asked, coming to my side. The lines of other people had all but emptied.

"I don't know," I replied, still straining for a glimpse of the minister. *"Do you know, Terri?"* I asked, turning to face her.

"Uh-uh," she said, and turned back to restacking the remaining books on the table in front of her.

"Well, I don't know who he is either," I said, *"but I'm going back inside so that I can hear him!"*

"Me, too!" Derrick said, leading the way, through the glass doors and back into the sanctuary.

We found seats on a left rear pew and sat down. Two of our boys, Tjai and Christopher, were sitting on the pew in front of us. As I sat and listed to Pastor Walker, I was captivated. I could not help but be reminded of my pastor, Rev. Tony Thompson, who had recently passed away. Dr. Walker spoke as if he himself had just been with Almighty God! Rev. Thompson had always delivered his Sunday morning messages as if he had gotten the words straight from the Lord! Derrick and I sat, spellbound, until the end of Dr. Walker's message.

After church, Rev. Dubose, Simmonville's enthusiastic, warm-hearted pastor, invited my family and I to go to dinner with him and several his church members. It was late, but we had not eaten, so we graciously accepted the invitation. We went to a restaurant in the heart of Killeen and it seemed that the establishment was a popular late-night eatery. It was packed, nearly to capacity! I was standing next to Derrick. He was talking with another young man we had just met about the wonderful message we had just heard. While we waited for our waitresses to find seating for our large dinner party, another young man, wearing a black baseball cap, approached me.

"Ah, Sister Denise?" he said, his voice sounding a little hoarse.

"Yes?" I said, turning to him with a smile. I thought he might be someone from the church I had not yet had the pleasure of meeting. There had been so many people there that night.

"How are you?" he asked, taking my hand in his.

"I'm just fine," I said. *"And you?"*

"Oh, blessed! Blessed in the Lord!"

I knew that I had never met him before, but there was something strangely familiar about his voice. Then, it hit me! *"Was that you?!"* I asked.

In the meekest manner I had ever before observed, he lowered his head and he chuckled, *"Yes, that was me."*

The *"Voice of Thunder"* was standing right in front of me! *"Oh, I didn't know it was you! I was sitting all the way in the back and . . . well, I thought you were an older man!"*

Dr. Walker laughed, *"Is that right?"*

"I did, too," Derrick said. *"You sounded like one of those good old Mississippi preachers!"* Of course, he thought that *everything* of any substance came from there!

Again, Dr. Walker laughed. *"Well, you know Sister Denise, I wanted to speak with you to invite you about coming to our church?"*

"Okay," I said, quickly, then I remembered what Derrick had said about saying *'yes'* before knowing when and where. *"When?"* I asked.

"Well, I'm not sure of the exact date yet, but we're getting ready for a women's retreat and you would be the perfect speaker for it," he told me.

"Okay, Pastor, and where is your church?"

"In San Antonio," he answered. *"Just up the way a bit."*

"Well, just let me know, and I would love to come!" I said, shaking his hand.

"Here, Pastor Walker, is one of her cards," Derrick said, handing one of my business cards to him.

"Alright," he replied, taking the card from Derrick. *"We'll be in touch!"*

When Sister Doris Newton, the Women's Retreat Coordinator, called me a couple of months later, I was elated and eagerly began to look forward to going to San Antonio! In the days, weeks, and months that followed, she and I became friends over numerous phone conversations and email messages. We kept constant contact, excitedly discussing the upcoming retreat and the miracles we expected God to perform there! Almost immediately, a bond of sisterhood was formed between Doris and I! Over the telephone, our spirits intermingled and seemed to become one.

In October of 1998, I found myself en route to San Antonio, Texas, to be the guest speaker for the Women's Retreat, hosted the Antioch Missionary Baptist Church. As usual, I waited until the night before my flight to pack. *(I don't know why, but if I pack too early for a trip, I usually forget three or more items.)* Derrick stayed home with the boys, while Terri accompanied me on the trip. We left Columbus on Friday morning, eagerly anticipating getting to San Antonio. When I checked my baggage in at the airport, I felt satisfied that I had remembered to bring everything with me, with the exception of a bath sponge! We had a brief stopover in Memphis, Tennessee. We almost had to run through the huge Memphis terminal to get to our connecting flight! I could have sworn I had seen radio *"fly-jock"* Tom Joyner rushing past us in the airport! If both he and we had not been in such a hurry, I would have stopped to validate his identify, but we only had five minutes to board our plane! We hurried to our designated gate and breathlessly checked in.

The flight from Memphis to San Antonio was much better than the one from Columbus to Memphis had been. For one thing, the plane was larger! On the small plane from Columbus, I had felt every bump in the clouds! My stomach and I were thankful for the smoother ride from Memphis to San Antonio. Before long, the pilot announced that we would be landing on the San Antonio airstrip, momentarily.

As Terri and I got off of the plane and walked inside of the terminal, Terri asked me if I knew what Doris looked like.

"No," I said. *"I don't."* I peered around the busy terminal, hoping for a sign or something. I didn't have to look very long.

In a few minutes, a pretty, petite lady with twinkling eyes and a bright, sunny smile approached us. *"Denise?"* she said, walking towards us.

"Yes!" I said, moving in her direction. *"Doris?"*

"Yes!" she replied. *"I'm so glad you're here!"* We embraced each other and the miles between Columbus and San Antonio dissipated. Immediately, I felt a spiritual sisterhood with this meek woman with whom I had established a telephone connection over the past few months.

"This is Terri," I told her.

"Hi, Terri," Doris said, turning to embrace my companion.

"Hi," Terri said, returning Doris' embrace. *"How did you know it was us?"*

"When I walked in the door, I could the see the light around you!" she turned to look at me.

The three of us laughed.

"My car is right out here," Doris said, leading the way.

Since we had some time before we were scheduled to arrive at the conference center in New Braunfels, she had decided to show us around the city a little bit. I fell in love with the huge metropolitan city of San Antonio! Everywhere we went, we were greeted by some of the friendliest people I had ever met! Doris took us to a wonderful restaurant for lunch and as we waited for a vacant table, the three of us browsed through an elegant boutique that was right inside of the restaurant! After a much-too-short wait, we were seated at a quaint glass—topped table and a courteous young lady placed a hot, steamy, buttery, cinnamon roll on a saucer before each of us.

"Oh my goodness!" I exclaimed, noting the creamy butter melting over the sides of the hot, succulent roll.

Doris smiled, as she sipped a dainty cup of hot beef bouillon the woman had placed in front of her.

"This looks so good!" Terri said, sliding her saucer toward her for easy access. The woman put an even more delicious-looking roll on the saucer.

"I'll be back with more!" she said, in a lively, animated voice.

"Oh, no!" I said.

"I'm not dieting this weekend!" Terri exclaimed, taking a delicious bite.

"I guess I'm not either!" I said. I eyed the roll and decided I would try to wait until I had eaten my lunch to indulge. After a couple of minutes of watching Terri indulge, I determined that I simply couldn't!

We thoroughly enjoyed our lunch that afternoon. The exotic eatery was called *"Michael's."* I vowed that should I ever return to San Antonio, I simply *had to* return to *Michael's,* too! After lunch, we had a forty-minute ride to the conference center in New Braunfels. Several ladies had already arrived ahead of us. We checked into our villa, and I decided to rest for a few minutes and then freshen up for the evening's meeting. While I was in the shower, someone stopped by to deliver a very large, beautiful gift basket for me. When I came out of the shower, Terri told me about it. The Women of Antioch had sent it over to me.

"They didn't have to do that!" I said. Doris had already made me feel more than welcome! After taking a closer look at the basket, I was glad that they

had sent it. Among the many lovely, aromatic gifts inside was the one thing I had forgotten to bring with me—a bath sponge! I carefully opened the peach cellophane wrapping to take it out. *"**Look Terri!**"* I exclaimed, holding it up.

During the first meeting of the Women's Retreat, that evening, I got a chance to meet some of the women who had gotten together to prepare the lovely basket for me. I felt surrounded by love and true sisterhood in the lavishly decorated conference room. We got to know each other over a delicious dinner. Coprah Ann Rector, the wife of the late former pastor of Antioch was seated next to me. She and I talked, and we found that we had much in common, sharing our passion for travel and meeting new people! She was a lively, very beautiful and gracious lady whom I felt like I had known all my life! She immediately took to *"mothering"* me and with a broad smile, she told me to let her know if I needed absolutely anything!

When the time arrived for me to address the waiting congregation of bubbling, spirited women, I eagerly stepped up on the platform. As I stood behind the podium, I thought about Doris' having asked me a few weeks earlier if I could talk for two hours. I smiled. I had responded that I could literally talk for hours—and that was *"for"* and not *"f-o-u-r"* hours! I ended up proving it that evening! During that first session, I shared with the ladies my overcoming some of the infirmities I had faced in my own life. In the first two hours, I gave funny anecdotes about my life with Derrick and the boys, intermingled with the tragedy I had experienced in my childhood. The women laughed about my comical tale of Derrick's and my first meeting at one of the city's Shoney's Restaurant, and they wept at my account of sexual abuse at the defenseless age of eight. The evening was a rollercoaster ride of emotions. Up and down, we rolled together! Deep into corners of intimacy, we delved and then, as the details of my story unfolded, and normal color returned to the tear-streaked faces, I told them just how I had gotten over!

Jesus had been my deliverer, I told them! It was He alone that had lifted me up from the despair that had satiated my existence. I admitted that I had been sexually abused. I confessed that I had been the victim in a physically abusive first marriage. I also confessed that I had, at times, considered suicide as the only possible answer to my problem-infested existence. But in the midst of it all, I told the ladies, Jesus had rescued me from the despair that had engulfed my entire life! I looked into eyes that had cried tears like the ones I, myself, had cried. I felt a powerful, spiritual connection with these women, some of whom I was sure had been abused in their own lives, either physically, emotionally or sexually. I didn't doubt that some of them were still involved in abusive relationships. The message I had come to San Antonio to deliver was that there was hope, even in the most hopeless situations—hope in Jesus Christ!

At the end of the first meeting, I was approached by a very pretty, yet fragile-looking, young woman. The woman, whose name was Vanessa, could not stop crying as she told me about the pain and misery she had been living with for most of her life! I was deeply moved by her story that her father had chased her mother through the house they lived in and fatally shot her in the back. When she fell, she toppled over and covered her five-year-old daughter, Vanessa, on the floor. She had been raised by her grandmother, and from what I gathered, her life had been an unhappy one. She was now married to a wonderful young man, but still seemed unable to get beyond the trauma of losing her mother in such a violent manner.

"You just don't know what I've been through," she cried. *"No one knows!"*

I reached out to touch her arm. *"You are not alone,"* I told her.

"I know, but it's so hard . . ." she sobbed, nearly uncontrollably. *"I just can't stop thinking about it! My mother fell on top of me! She covered me!"*

When Vanessa said that, I began to understand what she was so grieved about. She felt that she had lost her *"covering!"* *"You know what?"* I said.

She looked at me. She really was very pretty, I thought. She had long, dark hair and her skin was smooth and almond tan.

"You don't have to cry about not having your mother to cover you anymore," I told her. *"God has been covering you every since you were born!"*

The look on her face convinced me that it was something she had not considered before. *"Oh, my God!"* she said. Again, the tears began to flow.

I hugged her. *"Sister girl, you're going to be alright!"*

> *"And God shall wipe away all tears from their eyes; and there shall be no more death, neither sorrow, nor crying, neither shall there be any more pain: for the former things are passed away."*
> **Revelations 21:4**

The next morning, I witnessed Vanessa's miraculous deliverance from the grief that had possessed her since she was five years old! During the early morning's worship service, I had played the piano while the large group of women stood on their feet, swaying to the music and singing high praises unto the Lord! Vanessa was sitting with a group of her friends at a front, center table. After I had finished playing, I got up from the piano and walked to the podium. At the front of the stage, I embraced a woman who had been conducting the worship service. As we hugged each other and praised God together, a light caught my eye from just over her shoulder. I looked in the direction of the round table that Vanessa shared with about seven other women. In the center of their table burned a brilliant light! At first, I glanced around at the other large tables in the room to see if they had candles on them as well. The other tables had candles on them, but none of them were lit. I presumed that someone had lit the candle on Vanessa's table. Before I could give it another thought, I saw something happen that I can only identify as *"supernatural!"* As I looked in the direction of Vanessa's table, I saw something that looked like wisps of smoke rise up into the air above her head. She cried out something inaudible. Tears ran down her face as she rocked back and forth. In the light above her, I could see something that resembled large dust particles, swirling out of her and rising up above her head! The wisps of smoke rose up high above the table and the other women at the table began to cry out loudly. I looked around to see if anyone else could see what I saw. Everyone seemed to be caught up in the Spirit that had seemed to have inundated the whole room! Then, to further amaze me, the illumination on Vanessa's table moved to a nearby table! My mouth dropped as I watched the light move from one table to the next, virtually stirring up the emotions of each group of ladies who were seated around it! It was an awesome sight to behold! I knew that I was witnessing the power of Almighty God! The beam of light moved around the entire conference room, touching every table and igniting every woman seated around it! I was in awe, just to have been allowed to experience the vision. I found myself saying *"Thank You, Lord! Thank You, Oh God!"* I realized that the Holy Spirit had entered into our midst and just to have been in His presence was awesome and overwhelming!

I knew that Vanessa had been, as had been numerous others in the conference room that morning, set free of the infirmity that had monopolized her existence! She had surrendered her anguish to God and wholly submitted herself to the Holy Spirit! As a result, her physical body had been purged of the guilt and shame she had carried around inside for many years! For the first time in her life, she was truly free!

I know that many others were emancipated at the retreat because the next day, in the following Sunday morning's worship service, many, many women came forward to give their testimony of deliverance to the large congregation! As a matter of fact, the testimonies of the women who had attended the retreat had such an impact on the congregation, people who had not even been at the conference center were profoundly affected! One after another, women came forward and confessed their guilt and shame about things that had happened to them in their lives. One by one, they tearfully surrendered those infirmities to the Lord before a congregation of almost a thousand people! What an awesome, powerful, and magnificent display of God's awesome power!

Later that day, Pastor Walker told me that he had been overwhelmed by the outpouring of the Holy Spirit that had taken place at the conference center in New Braunfels. He said that he had driven up that Saturday morning, just to check on the women and see that everything was running smoothly. When he walked into the conference room and realized that the Holy Spirit was *"having His way"* with the women, he had quietly closed the door and eased back downstairs. It had been an awesome experience for me, too, I told him. In fact, since the San Antonio experience, I have never been quite the same!

The same spirit that had pervaded every crevice of the conference center that weekend flooded over into the worship service on Sunday morning. Pastor Walker spoke with the same boldness I had first heard him speak in Killeen, Texas. The enormous congregation swelled in the spirit with every round he climbed in his explosive sermon entitled *"The Power, The Pain, The Paradox and the Promise."* I was still on a spiritual *"high"* from the women's retreat and to sit under the powerful anointing so soon thereafter kept me perched on the edge of my seat throughout the service!

At the culmination of the seven forty-five service, Pastor Walker asked if I would address the church body during the Sunday School hour, the time leading up to the ten forty-five service. From the pulpit, he light-heartedly teased that the women had returned to their homes from the retreat in such a heightened spiritual state that the men wanted to know just what I had said to them. I laughed! I couldn't remember everything I had said to the women. It had, after all, been like a group of close friends, sprawled out in someone's living room, a bunch of the girls, talking about the goodness of God. What did I say? My goodness! God had given me a lot to say!

Instead of dismissing the church members to go to Sunday School, Pastor Walker graciously introduced me to the congregation. He encouraged me to take *"all the time I needed"* to share with the anxious church members just how I had overcome a past full of violence, pain and abuse. I gladly gave my testimony to them and when I had finished, I sang *"I Believe I Can Fly,"* the song that had been the spark which ignited my deliverance. I told them how my two-year old son had brought God's message of healing in my life by singing words from the song in an answer to my audible prayer to *"rise above"* my past. By the time I finished the song, the church was engulfed in the spirit of worship! It was an overwhelmingly refreshing experience!

At the close of the second service, people began to come forward to give their testimony of healing and deliverance. Many who came forth were some of the same women who had been at the retreat. They openly shed tears of joy at having received God's answer to their long-awaited prayers for release. Like me, they had also buried horrible experiences deep within the recesses of their hearts. Like me, they too, had all but given up their hope of joy and peace in their lives. Like me, they had felt the spirit of God, setting them free—once and for all—from despair! Others came to the front who had not attended the retreat, but had been touched by the prevailing Spirit within the sanctuary that morning. At the close of service, there was hardly a dry eye in the entire sanctuary!

It was obvious that many more people than I have ever known have suffered from brokenness. So many women have been carrying around seeds of bitterness that were planted deep within them when they were fragile, little girls. Many have been too broken to positively contribute to relationships and marriages. As a result, they have been unable to relate to the men in their lives. They have found it difficult, and at times, impossible to relate to men in their present, because the pain caused by the men in their pasts has been too great . . . too lasting. I once heard a minister say that when two broken people come together in marriage, they seldom become one. Instead, what you really end up with are two broken people. I honestly believe that is the main reason that so many marriages end in divorce! It is difficult to *"trust"* someone when those to whom you've been *"entrusted"* have proven themselves *"untrustworthy."* There is only one way to rectify the problem . . . through healing, which begins within the family.

The San Antonio experience turned out to be an amazing, supernatural one! That is the only way I can describe it! My life was changed forever as a result of the weekend I spent with the Doris, Pastor Walker's lovely wife, JoAnn, the other gracious *"Women of Antioch"* and their church family! A bond of love was established between us, a spiritual connection that miles will never be able to diminish!

> *"The Spirit of the Lord is upon me, because He has anointed me to preach the Gospel to the poor; He has sent me to heal the brokenhearted, to preach deliverance to the captives, and recovering of sight to the blind, to set at liberty them that are bruised."*
>
> *Luke 4:18*

FOUR

ONE MARTIN LUTHER King, Jr. holiday, Derrick and I packed the boys into our black Blazer and headed to Birmingham, Alabama. It was our intention to go over to the Books-A-Million Bookstore to get things set up for a book signing that had been scheduled for the following weekend. Since it was a holiday, and the boys and I were out of school, we decided that it would be a good day to ride over and get things set up. It would also give us an opportunity to see David and Eula Johnson, Tjai's godparents, who reside there. So early that morning, we loaded up the car with books and our youngsters.

When we arrived in Birmingham, we decided to go downtown to see if we could possibly get something put in the paper so that residents would know about the book and be interested enough to come out to the signing. When we arrived at the stately newspaper building, we went inside and approached a young woman who was seated at the information desk.

When we reached her desk, Derrick held out a flyer that contained some information about *Opening the Door.*"

Hi," he said.

"Good morning!" she said.

"My wife is an author and we were wondering if we could talk to someone in your entertainment department," he said. *"Maybe we could get an announcement about her book signing next week in the paper."*

"Oh, okay," she said, flashing a smile in my direction. She pointed across the lobby at a man in uniform who sat behind a desk, reading his copy of the day's paper. *"Go over there and ask that gentleman to call up to the entertainment desk for you."*

"Thank you," Derrick said.

"Thank you," I said, echoing him.

"Tjai," Derrick called to our oldest son. *"You and Little Derrick sit over there and wait for us. We'll take Christopher with us."* He held onto our two-year old's hand.

"Yessir," Tjai answered. *"C'mon Derrick."* He led his younger brother over to a plush green sofa in the lobby.

Derrick, Christopher and I walked over to the man in uniform. He was on the telephone talking to someone. We waiting patiently until he had finished talking and hung up the phone.

"Excuse me," I said.

He looked up from his seat. *"Yes ma'am?"* he said with a smile.

"I was wondering if you would call the entertainment desk for me, please."

"Yes ma'am," he said. The gentleman put his newspaper down and spent a couple of seconds locating the right extension from on a list on the desk in front of him. Then he picked up the receiver and dialed the number. While he waited for someone to pick up on the other end, he asked, *"What is your name, ma'am?"*

"Denise Clayton Bryant," I answered.

He nodded. *"Sir,"* he said, speaking into the mouthpiece, *"I have a 'Ms. Denise Clayton Bryant' down here and she would like to speak to you."* He nodded and then handed the receiver to me.

I explained to the man at the other end who I was and why I had come to the city of Birmingham. I told him that, if he had time, I would like to come up and talk to him about the book and, I asked if he thought I could get something in the newspaper to let people know that I would be back in the city the following weekend. In a hasty, impatient tone, the man told me that, first of all, he was extremely busy and didn't really have time to talk to me at the moment, and secondly, he said that if I wanted to leave some information for him, he would *"try"* to take a look at it when he had time.

My heart sank. *"Oh,"* I said. *"Thank you."* Dejectedly, I hung up the phone.

"What did he say?" Derrick asked, noting the look of disappointment on my face.

"He said he doesn't have time to talk to me," I replied.

Derrick sighed.

Silently, we stood there for a moment.

"Mrs. Bryant?" The voice of the woman seated at the receptionist's desk pierced the silence.

Derrick and I both turned and looked at her.

"Come over here for a minute," she said, beckoning us.

I followed my husband over to the desk, dragging Christopher behind us.

She held up the flyer Derrick had given her earlier. *"Is this a true story?"* she asked.

"Yes," Derrick replied. *"My wife was attacked in a school around this time last year."*

She looked at me, her eyebrows raised. *"And you met your real sister after that?"*

"Yes," I answered. *"She saw my picture in the local newspaper."*

"Hum . . ." she said, thoughtfully. *"I don't think you need to talk to the entertainment editor,"* she said. *"You need to talk to Mitch Nelson. He's the religious editor."*

"Oh," I said, a glimmer of optimism returning to my voice. *"Do you think we could talk to him?"*

"I don't see why not!" she said, smiling. *"Go back over there and ask the security officer to call him up and let you talk to him."*

I didn't want to get my hopes up too high, but I didn't see where I had anything to lose, so I said, *"Okay, thank you so much!"* We went back over to the security officer's desk and did as we had been instructed.

The officer called Mitch Nelson's desk and told him that I needed to speak with him for a moment. Then he handed the receiver to me.

Briefly, I told Mr. Nelson my reason for coming to the newspaper that day. He seemed genuinely interested in my story and asked me if we could come up to see him on the sixth floor. I smiled and nodded at Derrick, as I told him that we would be right up!

We spent the next hour and a half talking to Mr. Nelson, the newspaper's religious editor. He was a warm and very kind gentleman who kept telling me that the story I that I shared with him was *"incredible!"* He told me that he would be sure to get the story in the paper in time for people in the Birmingham area to know about the book signing. He even called the staff photographer down to take pictures of me outside of the building! After a very eventful interview, Derrick, Christopher and I got on the elevator to go back down to the lobby where Tjai and Little Derrick had been patiently waiting. As the car made its way down to the ground floor, Derrick turned to me and commented that, as usual, the devil had tried to discourage us.

"*Yes,*" I said, "*but when God is in the building* . . ."

Derrick laughed and nodded his head.

After leaving the newspaper building, we stopped by David and Eula's house for a short visit. Although they lived two hours away from us, we still maintained a very close relationship with their family. David and Eula were our oldest son Tjai's godparents. In fact, at that time, they had witnessed his entrance into the world fifteen years ago. I was Minister of Music at a Baptist church we all attended. When I literally ran away from a horrible first marriage to Tjai's biological father, they had been there for me, giving me some much-needed support. Even after I left Atlanta to live in Los Angeles, they continued to treat me both like a daughter and a sister. When they met Derrick, they immediately fell in love with him, treating him like a brother!

Although our visit with the Johnson's was much too short, we still needed to get to the bookstore to get things set up. As the sun began to set over the city of Birmingham, we bid reluctant good-byes to the Johnsons and piled the kids back into the car so that we could run over to the bookstore before its closing. When we got there, Tjai took Christopher and Little Derrick to the children's section while Derrick and I went to the customer service desk. We asked to see the manager, and, in a matter of minutes, an enthusiastic little lady who had already read the book literally bounced out of her office to talk with us. Her name was Mary, and she told me that she could hardly wait to meet me in person, and then she told everyone in the store who would listen what a wonderful work it was! She was like a cheerleader, telling nearby members of the bookstore's staff that they simply **must** read the book as soon as they could and encouraged them to invite their friends and family members out to the signing the following weekend. The delightful woman held my hand and walked me up to a front register. The clerk was waiting on a tall distinguished-looking gentleman, wearing a black and white tweed hat at the time.

"*This is Denise Clayton Bryant, the author of that book I was telling you about!*" she chimed, clasping my forearm.

"*Hello,*" I said to the woman.

"*Hi,*" she replied. "*Mary's been telling everybody about your book!*"

I blushed and smiled.

"*You know what?*" Mary said, to no one in particular, "*She needs to go on that show they have here! What's the name of it?* "*Good Morning, Alabama,*" *or* "*Good Day*" *or something like that* . . ."

"Good Day, Alabama, I think," the cashier chirped.

"Yes!" Mary said. *"That's it! Now, what's that woman's name that's on there?"*

"I don't know," the cashier said. *"Linda, Lynette, or something like that."*

"Her name is Lydia Lawson," the customer said.

Mary, the cashier, Derrick, and I turned to look at him.

To me, he said, *"Mrs. Bryant, what is the name of your book?"*

"Opening the Door," I replied.

He took his bagged purchase from the cashier and walked over to where Derrick, Mary and I were standing. He reached into his pocket, took out a business card and handed it to me.

"Give Ms. Lawson a call and tell her that I told you to contact her," he said.

I looked at the card that he had given to me and then back at him.

"I'm associate producer of the show," he told me. *"But, I'm on vacation. Just call Lydia and she will make arrangements to get you on the show."*

"Thank you," I said.

"No problem," he said, adjusting his hat on his head. *"Good luck with your book, Ms. Bryant."* With that, he walked out of the store.

"Now, ain't that something!" Mary exclaimed.

"Yes, that's definitely something," I replied with a grin. I looked over at Derrick. He was shaking his head in disbelief.

Shortly thereafter, we left the bookstore. We still had a two-hour drive ahead of us, and it was already dark. The kids wanted some ice cream, so we went through the drive-through at Chick-fil-A. Derrick bought four dishes of creamy vanilla ice cream and headed for the highway. Tjai was riding *"shotgun"* with his dad in the front seat while I sat in the back with Little Derrick and Christopher, who was seated between us. In a hurry, we got started on the long stretch of road out of Birmingham.

After the kids had eaten their ice cream, they each drifted off to sleep. I noticed that it had begun to rain. We had been riding for about an hour when the strange scent of vomit reached my nose. In the darkness, I touched the front of Christopher's shirt. It was wet. *"I think Chris threw up,"* I said to Derrick in the front seat. *"Honey, roll the window down for me so I can wet this napkin."*

Derrick rolled the window down for me, using the controls on the armrest of his door. Quickly, I stuck the napkin out of the window and was alarmed to find that what had begun as rain was now nickel-sized pieces of hail! *"Derrick! It's not rain,"* I shouted. *"It's hail!"*

Responding quickly, Derrick rolled the window back up. It was a little too quickly though! I had not yet gotten my hand back inside of the car and found it caught in the window! *"Ouch!"* I shrieked. *"I think you broke my hand!"* I yanked my hand back inside the car.

"What!?"

"My hand!" I said, as it begin to throb. *"I think you broke my hand! Turn on the light!"*

Derrick flipped the interior light on so that I could take a look at my hand. When he did, from the corner of my eye, I saw Christopher's left arm convulsing. Instantly, I forgot about my hand and looked at my baby. *"Chris!"* I yelled. *"Chris! What are you doing? Christopher! Stop doing that!"* With my hand, I tried to still his jerking arm.

"What is it?" Derrick asked. He reached up and repositioned the rearview mirror so that he could look back at us.

"Derrick! Something's wrong with the baby!" His left arm was jerking violently in strange, mechanical thrusts! Without any hesitation, I snatched Christopher's small, convulsing body up into my arms. His eyes had rolled to one side. I screamed, *"Derrick! His eyes!"* I tried to turn him around in my arms and make him look at me. He wouldn't. His eyes were glazed and focused on something else in the darkness! I couldn't see what it was. Instead, I saw my own life flashing before me!

Derrick slowed the car down and pulled over to the side of the road. He brought the car to screeching halt and turned around in the front seat. *"Denise, give him to me!"* he yelled, reaching for Christopher. His voice sounded strangely hollow in my ears. I handed our son over the seat to his daddy.

"Mom, what is it?" Tjai asked, waking up in the fog of excitement that had begun to escalate within the car.

Unintentionally, I ignored him. *"Derrick, what's wrong with him?"* I screamed, my eyes wide and horror-filled.

A thick line of saliva ran out of my two-year old baby's innocent mouth.

"He's having a seizure!" Derrick exclaimed. *"Here, Denise, take him!"* With unusual swiftness, he passed Christopher across the seat, back to me, and whirled around quickly to the wheel. *"We have to find a hospital!"*

"What's wrong?!" Tjai screamed. I could hear panic filling his voice.

"Huh?" Little Derrick said, waking up from a sound sleep on the other side of the car.

I looked around wildly. My heart began to race! Where would we find a hospital? I didn't even know where we were! All I knew was that something was happening to my baby and panic had engulfed me!

"Where?" I yelled. *"Oh, Derrick! What is happening? Why is this happening?"* I ranted, asking questions which I knew neither of us could answer.

Derrick slammed his foot on the gas and we took off! *"Don't let him close his eyes,"* he instructed me.

Of course, that was exactly what Christopher did—close his eyes! *"Oh my God!"* I cried. *"Derrick, he closed his eyes!"*

For the next couple of minutes, the car was filled with complete havoc! Tjai had begun to scream loudly, asking questions that neither Derrick nor I could answer. We desperately wanted to know what on earth was going on! I glanced at Little Derrick. Panic had seized him and his face appeared taut and strained. A little ways down the road, we spotted a service station on the left. Derrick sped the car up and hastily pulled off the road, in front of what looked like a Texaco gas station and convenience store. He parked the car and jumped out. In one fluid movement, I thrust open my door, leapt out, and followed him into the store, with Christopher, limp in my arms. Tjai and Little Derrick hopped out and trailed us into the store.

Derrick spoke to the station attendant in desperate elevated tones, asking him to call for an ambulance for us. I laid Christopher down on the counter between us and the attendant. In one breath, I was pleading the blood of Jesus, begging God to have mercy and not let Christopher die and, in the next, I was audibly calling Satan a liar and telling him that, no matter what, he could not have my baby! By this time, Tjai had become hysterical! I could hear Derrick telling him to *"calm down"* and that everything was going to be all right. Little Derrick seemed frozen, his face pale and ashen. Another little boy, probably the attendant's son, who had been standing nearby, took little, nervous steps backwards trying to get away from my shouting. I was yelling at the top of my lungs, praying to Father God and cursing Satan, all at once!

In what seemed like about five minutes, an ambulance pulled into the service station parking lot and two paramedics hopped out. They rushed into the service station and ran to the counter. Derrick and I moved aside so that the men could get to Christopher. Derrick told them what had just happened in the car. They quickly picked Christopher up into both of their arms and loaded him onto a raised stretcher. One of them quickly strapped my baby's frail arms beneath rugged black straps while the other busied himself, taking Christopher's vital signs. I watched in horror and felt the world around me begin a curious dance in slow motion. Meanwhile, I kept praying, hoping God was not too busy to give attention to our desperate situation.

After the paramedics loaded the stretcher into the back of the ambulance, the driver directed me to get into the front seat. Tjai and Little Derrick hurried to get back into our car with their dad. The three of them followed the ambulance to a nearby hospital.

"Ma'am?" the driver said, calling me out of a dense haze.

I looked at him, attempting to see through the tears that had filled my eyes. I was clutching Christopher's tennis shoes to my chest.

"Don't worry ma'am," he said, comfortingly. *"It looks like your son has had a seizure."*

I glared at him. My mind raced. A seizure? What on earth was he talking about? Christopher didn't have seizures!

"Has your son ever had a seizure before?"

"A seizure? No!" I said, incredulously. *"He's never had a seizure before!"*

"How old is he?" He asked.

"He's two," I replied, and I realized that he must have been trying to distract me from the siren that blared atop the vehicle speeding along the interstate.

"He's going to be all right, ma'am," he said, reassuringly.

A huge lump had found its way into my throat, and I could no longer speak. I lowered my head and began to talk to the Lord, in my heart.

After a brief ride, we pulled into the Emergency entrance at a hospital. When we went inside, we were met by one of the warmest and kindest groups of people I had ever met in my life—from the attending physician to the competent staff in the emergency room! The moment we walked through the heavy double-doors into the emergency room, the staff gave Christopher their utmost attention. I was comforted by the pains everyone took to assure us that everything was under control. During the first hour after we arrived at the hospital, Christopher had three seizures, which the doctor told us were medically termed *"grand mal"* seizures. Because of the number and severity of the seizures, we were told that he would have to be kept overnight. Chris was admitted as an in-patient and assigned to a room on the third floor. No matter what they did to prepare him for admission—including starting an IV—he never even knew what was going on. After the third grand mal seizure occurred, he fell into a deep, peaceful sleep. The doctor told us that it was normal for people who had seizures to go to sleep afterwards. Although I was still very worried about this *"new thing"* that was happening in our lives, I felt a little relieved.

"Where were you folks going on a night like this?" the emergency room physician asked.

"We were on our way home," Derrick answered. *"We live in Columbus, Georgia."* Although I couldn't take my eyes off of our toddler, stretched out in the hospital bed, I could hear a little tension in my husband's voice.

"I see," he said, lifting one of Christopher's eyelids and shining a light into his eyes.

"My wife is an author," Derrick continued. *"We had driven over to Birmingham to get things set up for her book signing next weekend."*

"Oh, an author? What's the name of your book?" He turned to ask me.

"Opening the Door," I replied, still watching Christopher.

"We have some flyers with some information about the book out in the car," Derrick said, sensing my reluctance to get into anything that might take my attention away from our son at the moment. *"I'll go out and get one."*

"Okay, thanks," the doctor said, *"if you don't mind."*

For a few minutes, Derrick left us to go out to the car. He soon returned with a handful of flyers and a couple of books. He handed a flyer and a book to the physician.

After a moment, the doctor asked, *"How much is the book? I'd like to get one."*

Derrick told him and he left the room to get his checkbook. When the doctor returned, he asked me if I would mind signing the book for him. I signed it and he left to see about his other patients. A few minutes later, two nurses came to talk to us—about the book.

Derrick and I were in the treatment room, waiting for another nurse to come and take us upstairs. About twenty minutes after he had fallen asleep, Christopher did something that made me feel a whole lot better. In his semi-conscious state, he said something that my ears had longed to hear him say. Eyes still closed, he simply whispered, *"Mommy."*

I looked at Derrick and he looked back at me.

"Did you hear that?" He asked. *"I'll bet he's going to do that when he makes it to the pro's, too,"* he said, smiling.

Relieved, I smiled back at him.

A tall, slender nurse came to take us up to a room that had been assigned to Christopher for the night. *"Mrs. Bryant, I don't want to impose,"* she said, as she pushed Christopher's stretcher down the hall, *"but, I read a couple of pages in your book, and I was wondering if you have anymore, because I'd like to buy one from you. I mean, I hope you don't mind. I know this is a difficult time for you all and—"*

"It's all right," I said. *"I don't mind at all."*

After we got Christopher settled in his hospital bed, Derrick left to take Tjai and Little Derrick to a place where they could spend the night. There just happened to be a hotel conveniently located next door to the hospital. They had been sitting in the Emergency Room's waiting area every since we had arrived. When he came back to the hospital room, he found me sitting in a chair next to the bed where Christopher was still sleeping soundly. Derrick told me that he had told the on-duty manager what had happened to bring us to the small community of Alexander City. This woman, whom I never had the opportunity to meet, told my husband that she would watch over our sons for us while we kept vigil at the hospital with Christopher! I could not believe the outpouring of kindness that had been our good fortune to receive from the people in Alexander City! In my heart, I continuously thanked God that He had set his *"angels"* around us in the midst our traumatic ordeal!

By the time we checked out of the hospital the next morning, about fifteen more people had purchased copies of **Opening the Door** from us. That really had no prolific impact on me until the following weekend when, with Christopher's doctor's permission, we returned to Birmingham for the scheduled book signing. He had suggested that we take Chris with us so that we could keep a close eye on him, so our toddler accompanied his dad and I on the trip. We had prepared some decorative jars of candy to take with us. We planned to stop at the hospital in Alexander City and give them to the wonderful people who had shown us so much hospitality during the previous weekend. Earlier that week, I had scanned a picture of Christopher, dressed in western-gear and sitting on a pony, printed several copies of it, and taped one to each of the jars and which were filled with candy. I had planned to take a jar of candy to the hotel where Tjai and Little Derrick had stayed and several to the Alexander City Emergency Room staff who had cared for him the previous Monday night. It was a small gesture of thanks for the overabundance of kindness we had received while we were there.

We stopped at the hotel, only to find that the manager who had watched over Tjai and Little Derrick for us the previous Monday night was not on duty that day. Again, I did not have the pleasure of meeting this angel that God had put there for us. We intended that the jar of candy be given to her upon her return to work and continue on to the hospital. When we walked into the hotel lobby, the woman that had taken care of Tjai and Little Derrick the previous week was not there. In fact, the male attendant told us that *no* female had worked at that hotel for several years! My lips dropped! Derrick handed the jar of candy to the attendant, and he told him that we appreciated *"their"* having taken care of our sons the previous week. As we walked out of the lobby, I realized that God had obviously put one of *His* angels in that hotel to watch over our boys while we had stayed overnight in Alexander City!

When we walked into the emergency room entrance, we were met by one of the nurses who had been working the night that we came in. She had also purchased a copy of **Opening the Door** from us. When she saw us, she was elated!

"Well, hello!" she said, greeting us with a big smile. She warmly embraced me. *"I am so glad to see you, Mrs. Bryant!"*

"Well, thank you," I said, returning her embrace. *"We just stopped by to say 'thank you' for the kindness you all showed us last Monday night."*

"And there's that little angel!" she said, smiling at Christopher.

"We brought you some candy!" he said, grinning an irresistible pink-lipped smile.

"We wanted to do something to show you all our appreciation for the kindness you showed us last week," Derrick said. *"We brought these for you all."*

She beamed. *"That's so sweet of y'all! Come on back!"* She escorted us back to the Emergency Room treatment area.

When we got back to the place where I remembered having been so distraught the previous week, several familiar faces greeted us. *"Mr. and Mrs. Bryant!"* someone called out in passing.

Derrick and I waved. *"Hi! Good to see you!"* Derrick called out to a nurse in crisp teal scrubs.

"Hey!" someone called out from behind me.

I turned around to see a young, blonde woman. *"Hello!"* She was the nurse who had returned to Christopher's room the morning after she had gotten off duty to buy a copy of my book. She had read the first chapter in someone else's copy that night and, at the end of her shift, she had rushed home to get some money to buy her own.

"Mrs. Bryant," she said, holding both of my hands in hers, *"You just don't know how much your book has helped me! It is . . . it is . . . I just don't know how to tell you,"* she said, searching for the words she wanted to say. *"I've been there, and well, your book really helped me!"*

I hugged her. *"I'm glad,"* I said.

As Derrick, Christopher and I left the hospital that day, I felt a sense of revelation in my heart. As I waited for Derrick to open his door and unlock mine from his side, I started laughing.

"What's so funny?" he asked.

I lifted my two-year old into the car and, as he was usually prone to do, he jumped over into the back seat. *"Christopher is not going to have any more seizures,"* I said. *"You know that, don't you?"*

Derrick smiled and nodded his head in agreement. He knew exactly what I meant. We both knew that God had ordained our being at that hospital, in that city, on that night, at that time! Had it not been for Christopher's seizures, we would never have stopped there. God had had it all under His divine control! We knew that there would be no reason for Christopher to have another seizure. It has been thirteen years now, and he has not had a single, solitary one! That experience served to further convince me that, in the midst of our most traumatic experiences, **_God is ever-present, ever-loving, ever-giving and forgiving._** Even when Satan tries to wreak havoc in our lives, God is our anchor of stability, keeping us upright, steady and optimistic! He takes that which Satan means to destroy us with and uses it for our good—**_EVERY_** time! I realized that Christopher's seizures provided someone an opportunity to hear from God. Our small inconvenience in exchange for another's blessing! Our wilderness experience in exchange for another's crossover into God's promise to heal and deliver! Knowing that God had orchestrated the events of that night in Alexander City has brought me a tremendous sense of peace and confidence in Him to keep everything that happens in my life under His divine control!

> _"For our light affliction, which is but for a moment, worketh for us a far more exceeding and eternal weight of glory."_
>
> _2 Corinthians 4:17_

Personal healing is long overdue. As the clock rolled forward into the new millennium, people were already tired and weary, having carried around the weight of their issues for their entire lives! How can we go forward when so much threatens to hold us back? Stifle us? Stunt our growth? How can we form meaningful and lasting relationships when we are so incomplete in forming our own? It is time for mending in our personal lives. It is the only recourse! Many people need a word from God, a signal that they can put down the baggage they have carried from pillar to post in their lives. They need to hear that their past mistakes are forgiven, that they too, can forgive those who have brought pain into their lives. Families need healing. But there can be no healing within the family until its members fill their own prescriptions!

As I said earlier, I had the privilege of hearing a series about the family. I had become very excited about it because I had just begun to work on this book and I knew that I could glean much from the ministry that I would be able to share with those who would read it, once in print. There would be a lot to add to the thousands of ideas floating around in my mind since God had begun to speak to me on that wise. Eagerly, I had sat in service after service, jotting down some of the pearls of wisdom He had so willingly shared with me. There were many ideas, some of which came as news even to me, which I made mental notes to include within the pages of my next literary effort!

Sometime in March, the pastor had begun to teach on the downward trend of the concept of family in our society. That Sunday morning, I sat up straight in my seat! The Family? Wow! I was anxious to hear him address a topic which had been working its way to the forefront of my writing. The eloquent speaker told the congregation that there had been a loss of distinction between men and women in our society. Although God had made a distinction in His creation, he said, society had begun to move towards the acceptance of a *"unisex"* society. God! I thought. It was so true! We had begun to make God's Word fit our culture instead of the other way around—the way it should be!

God had first formed Adam, gave him a place to live, a job to do, and a commandment to keep or the responsibility of leadership—before giving him his wife, Eve! God had created man with the idea in mind that man would **lead** his family. He would be the head! He would be the protector! He would cover his wife and children! He would **not** go on extended trips to the grocery store and never be seen again! He would **not** abuse his wife or children. He would **not** stay home and let his wife go out and win the bread she would later come in too exhausted to bake. Most importantly, he would **not** forget the responsibilities he had been given by his Creator!

Listening to the pastor raised a new consciousness in me. What happened to the original plans? In the weeks and even months that followed, the answer was revealed. Satan had thwarted God's original plan for mankind. Man had fallen from grace and things had continued to go downhill from that point on. It was no wonder that the family had continued to be dysfunctional! We have continued to fall farther and farther away from God's original plan. Sin and perversion saturated our parents' and our grandparents' lives and continues to seep through all we say, think and do!

There is only one solution to the problems in our families. **Family secrets must no longer be kept secret!** I am not suggesting that you go out and put your **"business in the streets,"** as it were. What I am saying is that those age-old unmentionable things that you have kept deep within, in hopes that absolutely **no one** would ever uncover, must be rooted out, confronted with and disposed of—once and for all! In other words, it is time to come out of darkness so that we can walk in the light of God's wonderful love! When we are bowed down beneath the burden of infirmity in our lives, we are indeed living in darkness! The darkness has kept us from seeing ourselves and other people in our lives very clearly. We have been unable to see *who* we are and, as a result, we are not completely sure *whose* we are! I'm talking about you **and** me because I have been exactly where you may be right now!

This darkness issue is very real! In the Old Testament, Daniel spoke of the secrets that are kept in the dark. The Scriptures say *"He revealeth the deep and secret things: he knoweth what is in the darkness, and the light dwelleth with him."* God knows those things that we have tried to keep hidden deep down inside of us! We have been unable to find healing because of the darkness. We have suffered failures because of it. We have not been able to find peace in the midst of it. It is time to come out of the dark! There is peace in the light of God's love! Jesus said *"I am the light of the world: he that followeth me shall not walk in darkness, but shall have the light of life."* There is only one way to get that light of life—through faith in Jesus Christ!

There are so many people, young and old, male and female, who have not been able to find happiness and contentment in their lives because of the darkness that hovers about them. I know because I have, as they say, *'been there and done that!'* Most families have deep, dark secrets that threaten to unravel their very threads. We are all guilty of holding on to some things much longer than we need to and letting go of others much too easily. So just how do we let go? Or do we even have to do that?

I once had the extreme pleasure of speaking to a singles' group at a large Baptist church on the west side of Dallas, Texas. That day, my topic was *"Beginning at the Source,"* and I talked about my experience in the *"dating world"* and how I had come to the realization that no one really needed to *"look"* for *"Mr. or Miss Right."* On the contrary, I told the rather large group of single men and women, we simply needed to follow the Savior's guidelines in Matthew 6:33 where He told us to *"seek ye first the kingdom of God and his righteousness; and all these things shall be added unto you."* What *things* was Jesus talking about? I posed that question to the group and gave them a moment to think about it. There are things like jobs, cars, homes, hefty savings accounts, good friends, honorable reputations, right decisions and **yes, healthy, solid, and meaningful relationships!**

Derrick accompanied me and sat, as he usually does, away from me and the group, simply observing the facial expressions of the people in the audience. He later told me that several times throughout my message, he saw faces change, the darkness, and at times, despair, being exchanged for much-needed light! Yes! Christ, Himself, left the truth of the matter in plain, leather-bound view! Seek God *first* and all of the things you truly desire will be *added* to your life! So what about all the bad relationships we have all fallen victim to? How did we even get ourselves into them? I talked to the singles about my own *foolish* choices, because that's exactly what they were, and about how I had tried to do things *my* way. I thought I knew what was best for me so I did *my thing* only to discover that my knowledge was limited and my wisdom even more minuscule! How can we, I asked, possibly know what that man or woman is going to do five, ten or fifteen years from now? Six months from now? Heck! Tomorrow? We cannot see into the future, but there is one who can! And besides Him, there is **no other!**

"Yes!" I heard a young woman say. She had obviously gotten her revelation!

"Look for a man who is willing to fulfill the call of God upon his life," I told them. This man would certainly love God with all of his heart and the woman in his life would reap the wonderful benefits of his knowing how to truly love her! Men, likewise, should pray for a wife who knows how to love and serve the Master because then, and only then, will she know how to love, respect, honor and submit herself to her husband. The ways of the world **OR** the Ricki Lake Show won't be able to influence her to demand her independence from the man God has given to her.

"Delight thyself also in the Lord; and he shall
give thee the desires of thine heart."
Psalm 37:4

In high school, I guess you could say, I had a lot of *"friends."* We were average teenagers, experiencing some problems much like those young people experience today. When we graduated from high school, we were starry-eyed and anxious to leave our parents' homes and get to our respective institutions of higher learning so that we could be on our own and go virtually *"buck-wild!"* Upon *"Day One"* in college, we began our desperate search to find the answers to the questions that had burned so deeply within us throughout the *first* most stressful four years of our lives in high school! Surely, somewhere amidst those hungry eyes that met us and looked over the newest batch of *"fresh meat,"* we would be able to find what we were looking for!

In college, I became acquainted with and fell in love with the idea of being on my own. I also fell in love with Stevie Wonder, having spent endless nights listening to his *"Songs in the Key of Life"* albums as the black vinyl spun around and around on the turntable in the room I shared with my best friend, Trena. *"Love's in need,"* Stevie crooned over and over again on the little turntable in our dorm room, *"of love today."* I listened and found that I absolutely understood the blind poet's prolific message. Love was **definitely** in need of love today! What was that supposed to mean anyway? I realized that not only had I never been truly loved before, but I wasn't even sure what *real* love was. And I was not alone. Amidst the new friends and acquaintances I made at Mercer University in Macon, Georgia, very few of them knew either!

I bonded with a group of intellectual and charismatic young ladies on campus. Although we had much in common, I found myself in awe of their individual, unique talents and academic abilities. I discovered, almost immediately, that they had much to offer. Simultaneously, I noticed that they had not yet realized it. Unceremoniously, we became a *"clique"* and called ourselves *"Brown Sugar, Incorporated."* It was not very long before the whole campus knew about us and recognized the colorful tee-shirts we wore daily, with the letters *"B.S.I"* sprawled across our chests. Around the campus, we were nearly famous! The party was not a party unless **we** were on the guest list!

One very cold night, we braved a snow storm and ignored a severe weather advisory to walk to a party that was being hosted off-campus by the Sigma fraternity! One of their hungry-eyed brothers had trudged through the ice and snow just to bring us back to the party! Naively, we thought they wanted us there because, as I said, a party just wasn't a party without *"B.S.I."* in the house! Retrospectively, it was not our excellent company that they wanted, but it was actually the *"brown sugar"* that they were really after!

During my brief stay at Mercer, I underwent a curious transformation. I'm not sure whether or not it was because I was away home and my family or my new independence as a college freshman, but I began to ask the question *"why?"* You know, like why was I there? Why was I alive . . . still? I began to question God about my existence. What was His purpose for my life? What exactly did He want from me? I had already been convinced that He had some higher purpose in mind for me—after all, He had spared my life the terrible night of my father's murderous rampage. I was sure that my life had been preserved for some reason! In the tiny cramped dormitory room that Trena and I shared, I began to wonder just what that reason was.

I am confident that Satan heard me when I spoke to God aloud. I had not yet been introduced to the power and presence of the Holy Spirit and, as yet, did not know that through Him, I had a prayer language. So, I prayed out loud, and undoubtedly, Satan had heard every word! While I was waiting for an answer to my prayers, the wicked one sent a few diversions my way, hoping that I would become consumed in other *"things,"* and forget about God's call upon my life. That's exactly how he operates. While God begins to move you in the direction you need to go in order to fulfill your destiny, Satan begins to move people into your path to distract you and get you off target. If you just looked back over your life, up to this time, I am sure that you would be able to recall some of the people who entered your life, seemingly for no apparent reason. It was probably not until after they had long left the picture that you realized how much pain and anguish you suffered as a result of the relationship that was established between you and them! You should know that they were only a diversionary mechanism, a decoy sent to trip you up!

In the months that I spent at Mercer, Satan sent some diversions my way, some, in the persons of several young men—at least four—all named *"Greg."* For a while, I began to wonder if my destiny was to end up with someone by that name. That was very strange to me! Another diversion came in the person of a young lady I'll simply call *"Simone."* Simone had been deeply hurt in her youth. When I met this song bird at the audition for the annual Freshman Talent Show, I had no idea just how hurt she had been. She was a fair-skinned girl who wore a short, cropped afro. Her eyes were almost as bright as her smile, and she smiled a lot! I soon discovered that she was very talented and after hearing the rich, strong vibrato in her voice, I knew that she had grown up like me—singing in a church choir somewhere.

One Saturday evening, I had changed my mind about going to a campus party and elected to spend my evening with my thoughts, prayers ... and Stevie Wonder. The sun had gone down and I had not even bothered to turn on the lamp on my desk, so the room was dark, except for a tiny red light glowing on the stereo. I was lying across my bed, lost in the music, when there came a knock at the door. At first, I was going to pretend that I wasn't there, but I realized that the music was a dead giveaway. The Resident Advisor had asked us not to leave music on in our rooms when we were out of the dorm. If she was knocking on the door, I had no choice but to answer, so I got up and padded to the door in my socks.

It wasn't the R.A. Instead, it was Simone. *"Hey, girl!"* she chimed with a wide smile on her pretty, round face.

"What's happening?" I asked, holding the door slightly ajar. I didn't feel much like company, so I didn't invite her in. I thought that she might realize that since I had not fully opened the door to her, I obviously wanted to be alone. To my dismay, she didn't take my subtle hint.

A slight breeze followed her as she whirled past me and bounced into the room, *"dapping,"* the way I had seen many of the guys on campus do. *"Ooo! Stevie!"* she cried in an animated voice. *"I just loooove this album, girl!"*

I simply looked at her for a minute.

Simone was immediately lost in the music that blared from the small, black speakers on either side of the turntable atop my dresser.

I could tell that she planned on staying for a while, so I sighed and closed the door. I walked over to the desk, turned on the lamp and then I went back to my bed and curled up against the headboard, clutching my knees to my chest.

"*What you doin'?*" Simone asked, turning her attention away from Stevie and on to me. "*Just coolin' out?*" She was still swaying.

"*Yeah,*" I said, putting my head back against the wall and closing my eyes.

"*I thought you girls went to the Kappa thing,*" she said.

I opened my eyes at looked across the room at her. Before I could respond, the next song began to play

"*Oooo!*" she squealed, snapping her fingers and closing her eyes. "*That's my jam!*"

"*I was going to,*" I said, "*but I changed my mind.*"

"*Oh,*" she said. "*I was doing the switchboard thing. Just got through.*"

I nodded. I had seen her behind the desk in the lobby when I had come into the building earlier that evening. She was busy chattering with someone on the phone and had not even noticed me.

"*So,*" she said, "*you like Stevie, too?*"

"*Yeah,*" I answered. "*My favorite.*" *Songs in the Key of Life* was a two-record set of some of the most profound songs Stevie Wonder had written before or even since then, as far as I was concerned.

"*Me, too!*" Simone chirped.

"*Oh,*" I murmured, trying to keep my responses monosyllabic. I didn't want to encourage her to visit for very long.

I leaned my head back against my headboard. For a moment, I closed my eyes. I was suddenly aware of a sharp silence in the room. I opened my eyes and saw Simone looking at me.

She had laid down on Trena's bed.

My roommate and I had put the feet of our beds together so that we could sit up late at night and talk to each other and study together. The space on that side of the room was just large enough for our twin beds to fit so that our headboards rested on opposite walls. We had spent hours upon numerous hours leaning up against the heads of our beds, in deep conversation. Now, Simone lay stretched out on Trena's bed, her head at the foot of the bed, propped up on both elbows! To be honest, the way she was laying at eye-level with my lap made me feel very uncomfortable.

"*So,*" she began, "*you don't have a boyfriend.*"

It didn't sound like a question, so I didn't feel compelled to answer.

When I didn't respond, she went on. "**Do you?**"

"**Nope,**" I replied. That wasn't entirely true, since, technically, I **did** have a boyfriend back in Columbus. *"I mean, I don't have a boyfriend here at school,"* I said, correcting myself.

"So, where's your boyfriend," she asked.

I went on to explain that my boyfriend, Richard, was a senior, still in high school. *"Oh,"* she said, matter-of-factly.

Another silence.

"Do you?" I felt obligated to ask.

"Nah," she drawled, *"Men are just too trifling!"*

I smiled.

"I don't do too well in those kinds of relationships," Simone said, voluntarily. *"You know what I mean?"*

I didn't.

"What about you?" she asked.

"What?"

"Do you have a strong relationship with that guy in Columbus?" She seemed genuinely interested enough.

"Yeah, it's pretty serious, I guess," I replied.

"So . . . you like—love the guy or something like that?"

I wasn't quite sure where my uninvited guest was trying to go with her line of questioning. *"What are you getting at?"* I asked.

"Nothin,' I was just asking. That's all." She fell silent.

I gazed out of the tiny window above the dresser at the night sky.

"Don't you ever get lonely?" Simone asked.

Lonely? When did I have time to get lonely? Since coming to college, I had become a sort of off-the-record-of-course counselor, giving advice when asked, acting as mediator beyond disgruntled friends, helping to mend broken relationships, and at times, just being a good listener for many of the friends I had made on campus. *"No, I can't say that I have much time to get lonely,"* I said, resolutely.

"Oh, I know you always seem to be with somebody," she said. *"Everybody likes to talk to you and tell you their problems. They act like you don't have any problems of your own."*

"Yeah, sometimes," I said, letting my head rest against the headboard and closing my eyes again.

"Don't you need somebody sometimes?"

I wasn't quite sure what she was getting at, and I wasn't sure that I wanted to know. A little hesitantly, I asked, *"What do you mean?"*

She took a deep breath. *"I mean, don't you wish you had somebody here with you sometimes?"*

"To do what?" I asked, opening my eyes and looking at her in the dim light.

"You know, somebody to comfort you . . . hold you . . . make you feel good."

Unsure of what I should say, I didn't say anything. Shrugging seemed like my only recourse, so . . . I shrugged.

Then Simone said something that totally threw me. *"You know, you and Trena are always walking around in tee-shirts and stuff! Y'all got big breasts, big, pretty legs and all!"* Then she laughed a strange, deep, throaty laugh.

Right then and there, the atmosphere in the tiny dorm room changed dramatically! The air became still, like the calm before a storm. Suddenly, instinctively, I wanted Simone to leave, to go to her own room, to go somewhere other than to reside in my room with me! Like I had seen so many people do in the movies, I feigned a yawn, dramatically stretching my arms above my head. *"Simone, girl, I'm tired! I think I'll just go on and go to sleep!"* I said.

To my surprise, she said, *"Go on and stretch out, girl! You can go on to sleep!, If you don't mind, I'm gonna just keep on listening to Stevie for a while and then I'll turn it off and I'll go when I get finished."*

My heart skipped a beat! What in the world was happening? I swung my feet around and sat up straight on the side of my bed. *"No, girl! I don't want to be rude! Why don't you just take the albums to your room and listen to them? I'll get them back tomorrow!"* In an instant, I had hopped to my feet.

"I don't wanna take your stuff, girl!" she said.

"Oh no, it's alright! You can take it with you! I insist!" I walked over to the turntable and abruptly halted the blind performer's performance. I slid the album into its cover, picked up the other one and turned around to hand both of them to her.

Slowly and somewhat regretfully, Simone got up off of Trena's bed. *"Well . . . if you really want me to."*

Of course I really wanted her to! I wanted her to go because I had a feeling that she was into something I had absolutely **NO** interest in getting into myself! I held the album set out to Simone and waited for her to take it from me. Reluctantly, she did. Then, I walked to the door and opened it. Looking somewhat defeated, she left the room.

When I closed—and locked—the door to my room that night, I felt that I had barely escaped entry into strange and unfamiliar territory! In the weeks that followed, I learned that Simone had confessed to being bisexual. This musically talented daughter of a Baptist minister had been sexually abused. At the age of thirteen, she had been raped by a customer in a back storage room of her grandfather's grocery store in a rural town in south Florida. Her emotional scars ran deep and I was sure that she had been to places in which I had no desire to go!

Simone was one of many young women I have met that were beautiful and gifted, yet had been tripped up by Satan! As a result of things that had happened to her, things over which she had absolutely no control, she had decidedly gone *against* the Word of God. She had chosen the wide path, the one that most surely led to destruction! God had blessed her with a beautiful gift of song, and her voice was one of the most melodious that I have ever heard, but Satan had tricked her in an attempt to get her off course! She has crossed my mind a time or two, and I have wondered whatever became of her. I pray that she has gotten her life together and is following the will of God today. I say this for those of you who have found yourself at a similar crossroad in life. Don't let Satan fool you! Just because you have been abused by someone, that doesn't mean that you need to swear off of members the opposite sex altogether! The man or woman that God has in mind for you is somewhere, waiting, just for you! In the meantime, don't be foolish enough to believe that God has changed his mind on the subject of human sexuality.

Although Satan may have successfully convinced many young women that there are other women out there who can and will love them better than a man possibly could, or whether he has persuaded some young man that the only person who can truly love him is another man, we must *never* forget that Sodom and Gomorrah were destroyed as a lasting memorial of God's dissatisfaction with that lifestyle! Any way you look at it, homosexuality is *perverse!* Perverseness is *sin* and the wages of sin is *death!* Remember that Satan's main objective is man's destruction and spiritual death. He wants to see you and me *dead!* I have no desire to play into his wicked hands nor will I conscientiously be a part of his evil plans! I want to live the life that Jesus promised to those who love and diligently seek him!

> *"The thief cometh not, but for to steal, and to kill, and to destroy:*
> *I am come that they might have life, and that they might*
> *have it more abundantly."*

> *John 10:10*

FIVE

THERE IS A very truthful poem which describes the affects of environment on a child's behavior. The poem is entitled *"Children Live What They Learn."* I used to have a framed version in my eldest son's room when he was about five years old. According to the poem, if a child lives with criticism, he learns to criticize others. While teaching high school, I came into contact with young people who were overly critical of others. I discovered that they lived in homes where most of the words that were spoken to them were those of criticism. Do parents actually realize just how profound is the affect they have on their children's lives, based upon the way they live their lives in front of those children? What a questions for the ages! We are producing replicas of ourselves, whether we know it or not! I would venture to say that little boys who never see their fathers showing love towards their mothers grow up to be men who don't know how to show love to the women in their lives. Little girls who never have the opportunity to grow up with strong, responsible, loving and committed fathers in their lives grow up not knowing what a real husband or father is supposed to be! As a result, they make the wrong choices, based upon erroneous ideals. They almost inevitably end up with someone who is very much like their father, and more often than not, it is **not** to their advantage.

If a child lives with anger, he learns to hate. I remember making myself a promise that I would not let my son, Tjai, grow up in a home where the only example he had to follow was that of a cursing, abusive, drug-using father! I swore that I would prefer that he has **no** example at all rather than a poor one! I was determined that I would never let him see his biological father physically abuse me, as I had watched my father physically abuse my mother. Early in our ill-fated union, I realized that the man I had married was my father—reincarnated! What was really crazy was the fact that I had never even loved him! Over the years, I found myself wondering just why I married him. We were such opposites—in every way! Each time, however, when I looked at my kind-hearted, handsome, hazel-eyed, curly-haired son, I knew that I had had to endure the hardship of my tumultuous marriage in order that he exist! For that, I thank God!

One day, one of my students, whom I will call *"Eric,"* told me that his father hated him. At first, I was surprised to hear such an open admission, since we were in a full class at the time. After I had time to observe this young man and the obvious pain he felt in the knowledge of his confession, I realized that he honestly believed that his father did, indeed, hate him. My heart grieved for him because it was quite obvious that he wanted, as all children do, his father's love. The rest of the class laughed and teased Eric for a few minutes about what he had said. However, a few students seemed to know the father in question and agreed that Eric's father surely had no real love for his son. That made me even more sad. The man, of whom I had yet to make an acquaintance, obviously had not visited the book of Proverbs, nor had he seen what had been written about fathers in any of the Scriptures.

Later that evening, I was at home, still feeling the pangs of Eric's sad confession, I opened my Bible and read passage after passage about the love and duties of a father. In Proverbs 4, I read about the responsibilities of fathers and God's requirement that they give good instruction and wisdom to their children. I wondered what kind of instruction Eric's father had given him. Had he taught him the things he needed to know in order to grow into a good man? Or had he perhaps crossed the boundaries described in Ephesians 6:4, which say *"And, ye fathers, provoke not your children to wrath: but bring them up in the nurture and admonition of the Lord?"* Well, we all know that children are expected to obey their parents and honor them so that they may live long lives. We do, however, have to be realistic and admit that it is very difficult to do that when that fourth verse is completely ignored!

In Eric's attention-craving behavior, I saw the negligence of his father. In his sometimes overzealous way of expressing his dissatisfaction and discontentment with the world around him, I heard the voice of criticism, and I could even sense the lack of affection in his life. Sometimes, when I got close enough to touch him, I could feel him gravitate towards me, hungry for motherly—or even fatherly love! I have heard some of my colleagues speak of their experiences with Eric. He had been a difficult student to deal with—at times threatening their safety, both in and outside of the classroom. He had been more challenging than they have felt compelled to tolerate. He has rightly earned his negative reputation. I do, however, realize that Eric's behavior was a cry out for help. *"Please, somebody! Anybody! Please fill this gigantic void in my life!"* Funny, he never even heard himself, but I did. In my brief drama of life, as a teacher, I have encountered many Erics.

Daily, I gave journal assignments to my students. It was a way for them to do some on-the-surface thinking about some deeply seeded issues they never had the opportunity to express. It was a means for them to write about what they had been thinking about. It was an avenue of self-expression where they could say what they desperately wanted or needed to say—words they were afraid to allow to escape from their lips. I wrote journal topics on my daily class transparencies and projected them on the screen in the front of the classroom. Usually, I gave the students time to write their thoughts down, and then, I asked for volunteers to read what they had taken pains to write. This *"sharing"* activity helped students to understand the classmates they sat next to and across from each day. It has also helped me to understand my students in a way that I never could have imagined!

On one transparency, I wrote *"If I had the opportunity, I would tell my father..."* The ellipses indicated that the students were to complete the sentence and then write a one-paragraph response to the topic. The students had a lot they wanted to write and needed more time to respond than usual. As a result, we didn't have time to read their responses in class. I took them home and later that evening, I sat down in my office and began to read what my students had written. The responses were interesting, to say the least, but most of all, they were sad indictments against many of their fathers.

One student wrote: *"If I had the opportunity, I would tell my father thank you for putting me down with those non-confidence lectures, instead of building me up with words of wisdom. I would also tell him that through all the insults he imposed upon my character, it gave me even more ambition to make something of myself. And when I do plant my own seed, I will be more of a father to my children than he ever was to me. And, I will set an example for them to be unlike him, to know that money can't hold a family together, but love, and faith in God."* Reading what the young man had to say brought tears to my eyes! Here was a teenager, about to graduate from high school, go into the world and make his mark upon it. What he was taking with him was bitterness, deeply rooted as a result of the seeds of rejection and criticism that had been sown into his life by his own father!

A young lady wrote: *"If I had the opportunity, I would tell my father thanks for nothing! You have never been there for me throughout my whole life! The only memory I have of you is the rotten way you treated my mother, cursing her and abusing her. You have never shown love to her or to me and, because of you, I don't even know what real love is! They say that little girls grow up to marry men who are like their fathers. I don't know what kind of man I will end up with, but I do know the kind of man I do not want to end up with is one like you!"*

I was grieved and confident that God **must** be, too! The sentiment of those two students was echoed by one student after another, as I read page after page. The pain that poured from the scrawled words and phrases stung my eyes! Those young people were living lives visibly scarred by the absence, abuse, or neglect of their biological fathers. Those children, who literally represented our future, were bitter and angry about the hands of fate that had been dealt to them by the person who helped to bring them into the world. The bitterness and anger was packed up in the luggage they were dragging into the future with them! I could not help but wonder, considering the root of the trees, what kind of fruits they would yield.

On Father's Day, I sat and listened to a sermon that I would never be able to forget. The message was entitled *"Fatherhood: A God Given Assignment."* I sat on the front row and listened intently as the pastor dealt effectively with the very contents of my heart! I was in the midst of doing some earnest writing of this book, and I had just written about the journal assignment I had given to my students. That morning, the pastor addressed some of the same issues that I sincerely believed had undermined God's divine plan for the family. I was so enthused that immediately, after the eight o'clock service, I rushed to his office and exclaimed to him that he absolutely **must** let me transcribe his message so that it could be put in book form as soon as possible! I saw his eyes light up as I insisted that he seemed to be walking along beside me as the pages of my own writing came together. I told him that I had been thinking about how devastated the lives of young people had become as a result of the breakdown of the family structure in our society. He agreed. In his message, he had said that the problems in our society stemmed from the failure of fathers to assume their God-given responsibilities to father their children. I told him that I was currently writing about that same thing and, although I would probably quote him on some of the things he had said, I would be careful not to include his entire message in my book! I believed that God had already given him the contents to be included in his own book.

I am sincere about the fact that, when it comes to fathers or father figures, I had the worst examples on both accounts. My biological father abused my mother, abused me and my brothers. He did not love his wife like Christ loved the church. I am convinced that he did not even know how to do so, having had a very poor example to follow himself! He simply did the same things he had learned to do while watching his own father. In order to control people, he misused and abused them. When he lost control, he resorted to murder and suicide. My adoptive father abused me, too. First, he sexually molested me. Then he called me a liar when I confronted him with the truth! I was sure that he never loved me because he never showed it. Instead, he pretended that he had had no part in violating me—that I, in fact, was making the whole thing up! *Hadn't the doctors said that I was unstable? Wasn't I mentally unbalanced after having witnessed my mother's brutal murder? Did I even know what I was saying?* I actually believe that he convinced himself that he had done nothing wrong to me. When I began writing this book, it had been twenty-seven years since he last touched me. Although I forgave him, he never said *"I'm sorry."* Unfortunately, he passed away a few years ago, so he'll never have the opportunity to say it now.

Even though I have never been able to boast of a positive earthly *"father-daughter"* relationship, I can still say that I have been blessed! I have always had the benefit of a heavenly Father who loved me when I thought no one else did. In fact, He has loved me even when I felt that I was unlovable! What I mean by this is that when I retaliated against the absence of fatherly love in my life, I made some bad choices, some big mistakes! In search of love, I began to *look* for it, as the song says, *"in all the wrong places."* Even while I wallowed in the depths of sin, God was merciful enough to look beyond my faults and see my real need to be loved. And He loved me! Even when I gave the greatest part of me to someone undeserving, God loved me. Even when I lied to my adoptive parents about where I had been all night long and sneaked into the house as the sun came up, God allowed new mercies to be mine every morning! Time after time, I have confessed and repented for the sins of my adolescence, my teenage and young adult years! Time after time, I have thanked God for having had mercy upon me long enough to save me! And what an awesome testimony He has given me!

I understand how the need to be held can fool a young girl into thinking that the arms into which she lands belong to someone who truly *"loves"* her! I can see how a teenage girl, who has never been exposed to the loving caress and *"right"* touch of her father, could misinterpret premarital sex for real love. At a young man's suggestion of *"making love,"* she believes that this is the way to obtain it—as if love is something that can actually be manufactured! In her enthusiasm to be desired, she doesn't know the difference between *love* and *lust.* She doesn't know the difference because she has never had real love before. Her daddy never gave it to her. Wasn't he the one who was supposed to hug her? Let her sit in his lap at the end of a hard day's work? Let her step up with bare feet on top of his work boots? Hold her in his strong arms and waltz her around the living room? Wasn't he supposed to show her how a *real* man was supposed to treat a woman in the way he embraced her mother? In the loving words he spoke to the woman in his life? In the passionate way he looked at her mother? Shouldn't he have been the kind of man that she, herself, would hope to find in a husband some day? A man just like her dad? Without the proper example, not only would she be lost, but she would have a very difficult time recognizing real, genuine, Christ-inspired love! Without that love, her life would never be complete!

> *"And to know the love of Christ, which passeth knowledge,*
> *that ye might be filled with all the fullness of God."*

> *Ephesians 3:19*

When I was a little girl, my older brother, Wayne, used to tease me that I *"wanted to, but more than likely would never be able to save the whole world!"* I didn't know it then, but I realize that in a way, at times, I've actually tried. Whether it was assembling kids who lived down the street, on the front porch of our little frame house, to play *"school,"* or pretending to vaccinate a line of neighborhood youngsters, with a plastic needle, from the nurse's kit I had gotten for Christmas, I was always trying to do something for someone else. I can remember collecting all of my dolls and distributing them to other kids in our neighborhood who didn't get anything for Christmas because I felt bad about that. Imagine that? It did not occur to me that I could not possibly supply every child I knew with a doll because I didn't have *that* many! In any case, I tried to give away the ones I *did* have! I have since learned better. Today, instead of dolls, I give out hugs. They're less expensive and in greater abundance!

I believe that the negative things that have happened in my life were each part of Satan's plan to completely destroy me. My destruction would make impossible the fulfillment of God's plans for me. I'm not saying that I am a rare or unique individual. On the contrary, this is true for anyone. We are all born into this world to fulfill a call upon our lives that exists upon our conception. God has a perfect plan for each and every one of us. Satan, however, has a plan, too! His plan is to overthrow God's plan! It's that simple! In order to prevent us from fulfilling God's call upon our lives, he does everything he can possibly do to stop us—to hurt, cripple or maim us! It is his primary objective! Once you realize that, you can recognize his handiwork—a mile off! Families and their members are his number one targets! If he can cripple a man, he has a chance to debilitate his entire family! That is why he is so bent on destroying males. Kill the male and you may kill his seed! No more fathers, no more sons!

I am convinced that what it takes for a man to know how to be a good father is that he must *first* love God with his whole heart! A man who loves the Lord will take care of that which God has entrusted to him—his wife, his sons, and his daughters. He will willingly provide the covering they must have in order to withstand the fiery darts of the enemy. When the father is absent, whether it is physically or emotionally, Satan tends to come and wreak total havoc on the lives of those *"fatherless"* children—especially if they don't know God for themselves! That is the crucial element—to know God for yourself!

> *"Behold, what manner of love the Father hath bestowed upon us, that we should be called the sons of God:"*
>
> *1 John 3:1*

It was a really hot, summer day. I was about seven years old at the time, but I can remember the day as if it were yesterday. We were living in Fort Dodge, Iowa, in a red and white painted frame house, next door to my paternal grandmother's house. Across the street, behind a row of similar framed houses, was a river that flooded periodically, after we had had a good rain. Billowing maple trees lined the streets of the neighborhood, their delicate blooms accentuating the seeming harmony of the scene. My memories of that time and place would become clouded by the sadness of later days, but those were days of imagination and childhood play. Those were days when we patterned our behavior after that of the people who affected our lives each day. We played house and simulated the mannerisms of the adults we had watched, all too unassumingly.

All of my father's brothers' and sisters' kids played together every day in a field behind our grandparents' house. Some of my uncles and aunts were very close in age to some of our cousins, so we spent most of our summer days together. After everyone had completed their chores, we were released to go and play, each having promised to stay out of trouble. While we played out back, my grandmother busied herself inside the house throughout the day. My grandmother, Tiny, was a soft-spoken and very tolerant, petite woman. She had to have been very tolerant to have withstood my grandfather's adulterous behavior. Just across the alley from Grandma's house, lived Granddaddy's mistress and her children, some of which looked remarkably like my father and his siblings! When Grandma died, the woman devoutly attended her funeral. At the funeral, I learned that they had been very close friends for a very, long time.

My grandfather, known throughout the small town where we lived as *"Bob Clayton,"* was huge, larger-than-life, and almost mythical to me. I don't ever remember talking to him or his talking to me. The only real remembrance I have of him is that of fear! He probably wasn't physically as big and frightful as I remember, but in my seven-year old perception, Ulysses' one-eyed Cyclops had nothing on him! When he came home from work, the children in the family usually scattered! We were careful not to get underfoot when he was around. And nobody, absolutely nobody dared do anything that might result in getting a whipping from Granddaddy!

Well, it was a very hot summer day and, as usual, we were outside, playing *"house."* Everyone had paired up, as it were, with their respective spouses. Once again, I was my Uncle Steve's wife. We were both in the second grade at a school at the top of a very steep hill, not far from where we lived. I **hated** being married to Steve because I **hated** cats! He **loved** cats, and he had a litter of them! Being his wife meant that I had to be mother to his huge pack of stinking, mangy cats! I'm still not fond of them today! Anyway, as usual, I found myself baking mud pies in the hot, muggy, summer sun and playing *"mama"* to Steve's cats. My brother Wayne and his *"wife,"* Shirley were busy in their space in the yard, making vacation plans or something. My cousin Peter and his *"wife,"* who was another cousin, Carolyn, were at *"home"* doing whatever they thought married folk did.

I *thought* that everything was going along well, but obviously, *somebody* was doing *something* they should *not* have been doing! Before I knew it, Granddaddy had summoned everybody into the house and, word had it, we were *really* in for it! **Nobody** wanted Granddaddy to spank them! He seemed to be a huge, unapproachable figure in our lives. We were all afraid to death at Granddaddy's summons! I'm not even sure why he frightened us so, but he did! Anyway, we all trudged up to the house and filed in, one-by-mortified-one! Granddaddy stood towering in the kitchen doorway and motioned for us to come in. He had *"heard"* that some of the bunch was outside playing house a little too realistically. I had no idea what he was talking about. As far as I was concerned, playing house simply meant baking mud pies, sweeping the dirt floor of my make-shift house and playing mama to Steve's feline kingdom!

Unbeknownst to me, several of the older kids had been *"making out"* in the backyard like *"kissing cousins!"* This, Granddaddy growled at us, was not the right thing to do! Cousins don't kiss and touch each other like boyfriends and girlfriends, he told us. We were never to do anything like that again, he warned, or else! Although Steve and I had not been doing anything like that, I was determined that I would *never* try it! It was not on my agenda to get whipped by my granddaddy. I had heard the bloodcurdling screams of those who had fallen victim to his strap! I was determined that I would never do anything to warrant my getting a taste of it!

Sometimes, I think about my granddaddy and his avid warning, and his instructions about what was *"right."* I am amazed that he was able to tell us to do-as-he-said, while we watched the lifestyle he maintained. I am convinced that parents who tell their children to do as they say, but not as they do are walking a very thin line with God. *"Train up a child,"* the Bible says, *"in the way that he should go."* How can you do that when your own image is tarnished? God has already instructed that we should lead by example. Whether my granddaddy knew it or not, that is exactly what he was doing . . . leading by example. My own father unmercifully abused my mother whenever he saw that other men gave unwarranted attention to her red-haired, hazel-eyed, fair-skinned beauty. Before her bruises could heal, he was usually hot on some other woman's skirt tail—time and time again!

"Train up a child in the way he should go: and when
he is old, he will not depart from it."

Proverbs 22:6

It was my mother, Almarine's birthday. I was about seven years old at the time. I rode with my father to pick her up from Globe Union, the factory where she worked on an assembly line, making small television parts. She almost skipped to the old Plymouth, carrying an opened package, a birthday gift she had received from some of her co-workers. Obviously excited about the present, she could hardly wait to show it to my father. Eagerly, I peered over her shoulder from the back seat, trying to see what it was that had her so elated. Inside the box were satiny pieces of red lingerie. Mama's favorite color was red and everyone who knew her knew that about her. She removed a shiny, crimson satin brassiere from the box and held it in her slender fingers of one hand while she lifted a matching slip out with the other hand. She smiled as she held the pretty undergarments in her hands.

My father glared at her and spat venomously, *"I KNOW you don't think you're gonna wear anything like that!"* Before she could even reply, he snatched the bra, the slip, and the box out of her lap and tossed the assembly out of the window!

Mama sat frozen, her mouth wide in amazement, but said nothing.

In the seat behind her, I, too, was in shock! *HOW* could he have done something like that? *WHY* did he do it? I didn't understand. She had been so happy, so delighted with the gift. It was her birthday! As far as I knew, he had given her nothing!

In a single heartbeat, my father had successfully ruined Mama's birthday! Without another word, he started up the car, put it in reverse, and backed out of the parking space. He sped out of the parking lot, burning rubber on the pavement, leaving the beautiful lingerie on the asphalt.

The ride home was the longest one I could remember. Daddy was silent and focused on the stretch of highway in front of him. Mama sat stoically, across from him, biting her bottom lip and fighting to keep the tears that had filled her eyes from falling. Behind her, I watched her shoulders heave from time to time and I knew that she was crying. I was convinced that my father was the *MEANEST* man alive. Next to him, Granddaddy was a *SAINT*!

The next evening, in an obvious attempt to make up with my mother, Daddy decided that they would go out to a local nightclub. It was the basis of every apology I had ever known him to make to her. After every abusive episode, he took her *"clubbing."* One would think that he would be ashamed for people to see his wife with fresh bruises on her face and arms. Perhaps it had some symbolic meaning for him that my brothers and I could never understand. The discolorations could have been his way of convincing himself and others that he was the one in control. If that was his intention, he could not have been further from the truth.

They got dressed and, as usual, Mama looked like a knockout, wearing her favorite red dress. As she stood in the full length mirror in the bedroom, the dress hugged her shapely Coke-bottle figure. She fussed with her soft, auburn hair until Daddy yelled from the living room that it was *"time to go!"* Mama's baby brother, my uncle *"Bear,"* stayed at the house to keep an eye on my three brothers and I. We always liked for him to stay with us because he usually got really drunk, and we easily got away with playing practical jokes on him. On more than one occasion, Mama and Daddy had returned home from an evening out to find him, asleep in the bathtub, with his curly black hair knotted up in her pink, foam hair rollers! Once or twice, they would find him, his hands and feet tied up, with some of Mama's old nylon stockings. He would awaken in a drunken stupor, and my brothers and I would already be in bed, still giggling at the success of our antics!

This particular evening, Daddy had taken Mama to a club, and three other women that he had been fooling around with were there, too. The women had become incensed that *"Tony"* had the nerve to bring his *"wife"* into their presence and the three of them jumped on him! It had taken the police to get the furious trio off of him! One of the women had had a knife and she had succeeded in cutting his face in several places. Mama had had to drive Tony to the hospital to get one of the cuts in his face stitched up before coming home. The other cuts had been bandaged. In the tussle, his stark white shirt had been ripped and covered in his own blood.

Mama walked into the house with an unusual look on her face. Staggering behind her was my father, his face a bloody mess! When I saw his battered, bloody face, I flinched! Without a word to us, Mama went straight to their bedroom. I hurried behind her, straining to get a glimpse of her face so that I could see if she had been hurt in any way. To my relief, she had not been touched. The women had only been out to get my father. I'll never forget that night. It was the one time I felt that he had gotten what he truly deserved!

When I think about the way my father acted, I cannot help but attribute some of that behavior to the examples he had had to follow. When he charmed my mother, sixteen and already carrying another man's child, he was not really concerned with her needs. He wanted her and somehow *"needed"* to possess her. That became clear after he treated her like an object, a trinket on a chain connected to a belt-loop on his pants. If anyone else gave her any attention, he flipped! He absolutely would not stand for another man to look upon her with desire, real or feigned! He often abused her as a result of someone else having looked her way more than once. I, too, felt the brunt of his obsession.

The church we regularly attended was having a *"King and Queen"* contest. I was in the running for queen and another little boy was running for king. Other than the two of us, the other contestants were much older. I didn't know it then, but those who would wear the crown were those who were able to raise the most money! I was very busy, diligently collecting contributions and selling raffle tickets for the contest. In the evenings, one of my aunts or uncles would walk with me through our neighborhood and nearby communities, door-to-door, in search of donations. Some people would just give me the money and not even take the tickets, exclaiming how *"cute"* they thought I was and telling me how much they hoped that I would win. I would smile broadly, say *"thank you,"* and traipse exuberantly to the next door.

One evening, one of my aunts and I returned to my house after having canvassed the neighborhood. We had just visited the nearby train depot and my collection envelop was bulging! When we walked into the house, I noticed that my father had company. A man whom I had never seen before was in the living room, sitting on the sofa. He was smoking a cigarette and drinking from a Styrofoam cup. When he saw us, he spoke to us both. Since I *was* running for the crown, I approached him, to ask him if he would make a contribution to the cause.

"Why sho', you pretty little thing!" the stranger exclaimed, jumping to his feet and thrusting his hand into his pants' pocket.

Before I knew what was happening, my father had jumped up and, with what seemed like a single fluid movement, leapt between his friend and I, and slapped me on the cheek! I was visibly stunned!

He glared down at me with angry eyes. *"Don't you ever ask any man for any money!"*

Confused and hurt, I felt tears well up in my eyes. *"But Daddy—,"* I began, in an attempt to explain that I wasn't asking for any money for me. It was for the church! For the *"King and Queen"* contest! Didn't he want me to win?

"Don't ever do that again! Do you hear me?!" he screamed at me.

I nodded, warm, salty tears running down my cheeks. I turned and ran to my room.

At the time, I didn't understand why he had become so angry with me. It later occurred to me that he never wanted me to depend upon anyone for anything, **except** him. I was his little girl . . . *his!* I realize that, had my father lived, I would have had a really hard time in my relationships with others—particularly with men. I could just imagine him staring down my prom date with cold, callus eyes. In most likelihood, no boys would have had the nerve to even express interest in me at the risk of facing my father. He was, in my estimation, the meanest man I've ever known!

I have said this many times before. I eventually felt sorry for my father. In his twenty-eight short years of living, he had lived a life full of pain and anguish, a life based upon a very low self-concept, insecurity, anger, hatred and selfishness. How many people do I know like that? Many times, I have had occasions to talk to people who were suffering some of those same symptoms. They were hurting. Hurt people hurt people! They tend to deal out to the people in their lives the same pain that has been dealt to them. It is what they know how to do best! Sometimes, they are unable to establish positive relationships with others because they look into the mirror each day and see the face of someone they have actually come to despise. They don't know how to love others because they have never been loved, nor have they learned how to love themselves! They physically and emotionally abuse the people in their lives because either they have been abused or grew up watching the abuse of someone they love. Then there are those who allow themselves to be abused because it is the primary interaction they have witnessed between their parents or whoever raised them. Like their parents, they become trapped in the vicious cycle and other people, who really don't understand, and wonder why and how they stay in such pain-filled relationships. Even the abused wish they knew the answer to those questions.

In *Opening the Door,* I talked about how important it was for me to forgive my father for the terrible wrongs he had wrought in my life. I have, indeed, forgiven him for the way he tore my life apart . . . for slapping me without reason, for trying to possess me unjustly, for abusing my mother, Almarine, and even for ultimately blowing her brains out on that very cold night in November, 1966. Some have found it hard to believe . . . that I could ever forgive him for that. Nevertheless, I have. I realized that actively performing the act of forgiveness was the only way I could rise out of the ashes of my own life and become the person that God had created me to be. I forgave my father because it was what God wanted me to do. If I loved Him, I had no choice, and I loved the Lord much more that I could have ever loved Tony!

I realize that my father had tried to walk in the shadow of his father, and what an awesome shadow that was! To a great extent, he was just as much a womanizer as my granddaddy was. He tried desperately to fill the shoes that Robert Clayton had worn so comfortably. They were too big for him, and alas, he struggled. Since he couldn't adequately maintain the life his father had lived, complete with another woman and another family in his possession, he tried to possess the women in his life. My sister, Debra, was living evidence of Tony's attempt to possess her then-fourteen year old mother Evelyn, by raping her. He tried to blind my eyes to the fact that there were not any other men alive, save he, by writing me *"love"* letters when I was eight years old that I would not even begin to understand until I was a young lady myself! He tried to possess my mother, at times being irrational enough to attempt to shield her beauty from others. To have her beyond his grasp, was to lose control of her. When he felt himself losing that control, he took her life. Before killing her, he even confessed to her that if he couldn't have her, nobody else could! He left this world without even realizing that she never even belonged to him in the first place. She had belonged to God!

Years ago, the city of Columbus, Georgia sadly reported another senseless act of physical abuse and unnecessary violence when a young, sixteen year old girl was brutally murdered by her nineteen year old ex-boyfriend. My heart ached as I realized that the girl's father was a former classmate and friend of mine. I grieved for him at the loss of his only daughter. Just as tragic was the fact that the boyfriend had also shot his former girlfriend's mother in the head and chest, and her life hung in the balances for weeks after the assault. The newspaper reported that the young man had murdered his ex-girlfriend when he flew into a jealous rage over a snapshot he had seen of her and another boy. The young lady was smart and had been very popular at her school. It was later divulged that the picture was not even a recent one, but instead, was a dated school superlatives picture. In his defense, the unremorseful young man proclaimed, *"See what women make you do?"*

What a senseless waste of human life with so much potential! It is so sad that the young man felt that he had somehow been *"forced"* to take my friend's daughter's life. I choose to believe that it was something that simply did not have to happen! I am convinced that there was another possible alternative, an answer he had not considered. I refuse to believe that anything she had said or done had given him cause to kill her. I do, however, believe that she had given him some claim of ownership. He felt that he *"owned"* her. He didn't know that she actually belonged to God! Why then, did he see the beautiful young girl as his possession?

The day after her funeral, I was talking to some students in the hall after school had ended, and I made an observation to them. *"When you give yourself sexually to someone, you know, they assume ownership of you,"* I said.

"What do you mean, Mrs. B?" one young lady asked, looking curiously at me.

"Well," I explained, *"When you give him YOUR 'stuff,' he begins to believe that YOUR 'stuff' is really HIS 'stuff.' After all, you gave it to him."*

Neither she, nor the three other students could say a word. I smiled compassionately at them and then continued on to my classroom. I knew that I had given them a morsel of thought worth considering.

It is true that once a young lady has given a young man the one thing that she can never recapture—her innocence—it is no longer hers. What most young ladies don't realize is that this most precious gift was intended for the one person they would live out the rest of their lives with. It is the one thing that, if preserved for marriage, fully consummates the blessed union between a man and a woman. I am convinced that one of the reasons that people seem so dissatisfied in their marriages is the fact they have so much to compare their spouses to! Just imagine . . . if you had never been with anyone else before and your new spouse had never been with anyone else before, when the two of you gave yourselves to each other, you would *both* believe that the other person was, as my youngest son, Chris, would say today, *"the bomb!"* After all, you would have nothing else to compare each other to! Unfortunately, by the time most people decide to marry, they have a lot of experience and, as a result, continually scrutinize their mates, become dissatisfied and shout *"incompatibility"* when the other person fails to measure up to their expectations!

What we have going on, even in schools today, are a lot of youngsters getting experience they really would be better off without! Youthful innocence is lost in musty locker rooms, in other isolated areas of schools, beneath the stairs after school hours, in deserted restrooms, or in the backseats of dark school buses on trips to and from athletic events. Little girls are becoming women much too soon and boys are trying to fit shoes into which they have yet to grow. With the present rise in sexual activity taking place in middle and high schools, and sometimes, even during school hours, there promises to be even more discontentment, more separations and increased divorces in future marriages! Even more importantly, if young people don't wake up and stop giving possession of their bodies to other people, there will be even more acts of violence as the recipients struggle to maintain their possessions!

> *"I beseech you therefore, brethren, by the mercies of God,*
> *that ye present your bodies a living sacrifice, holy,*
> *acceptable unto God, which is your reasonable service."*

> ### *Romans 12:1*

With so much permission and encouragement to freely explore sexuality being crooned in the words of popular music, demonstrated in movies, soap operas, television shows and talk shows, even plastered across billboards throughout our communities, it is no wonder that young people have been caught up in the sex craze! A simple search on the internet for chocolate chip cookie recipes will produce an astounding number of pornographic websites! All influential sources of media proclaim that it's okay to do whatever turns you on! Kids are listening to explicit lyrics which encourage them **to "whistle while you twerp,"** or to pursue women who wear thongs! High school-aged students walk the hallways of their schools echoing the conviction that rather than prepare themselves academically for the future, they should be looking for a *"hot"* boy or girl—not someone they can share a future with, but someone that can give them the ultimate sexual satisfaction, even if it *is* only temporary!

It seems that too few people understand what it means to preserve their bodies, the temple of the living God. My generation was different, but only minutely. We, too, were preoccupied with physical pleasure, eager and curious to experiment with physical relationships and, as a result, we, too, sacrificed our consummate gift to the undeserving. I have often told my students that it had to have been God's grace that preserved me and many other people I know. With the eruption of HIV and AIDS-related deaths reported in recent years, I *know* that He had to have had His arms of protection around us! If not, I, myself, might have never survived the carelessness of my youth and young adult years! There is no guarantee that the same grace and mercy extended to me will be extended to this generation. In that regard, I continue to encourage young people to practice the *only "safe sex"* there really is—*abstinence!*

What are we teaching our children? What kinds of seeds are we sowing? Are we aware of the perspective harvest? It will surely come! If fathers continue to lead by displaying the wrong examples or fail to lead at all, our children will continue to spiral downward towards destruction, as so many seem to be plummeting! I write this specifically with regards to fathers because God has given them such an awesome responsibility, and some seem to be unaware of the tremendous calling upon their lives! God created the first father, Adam, left him in charge of everything, and he messed it up! Since then, so many fathers have followed in his footsteps, neglecting the responsibilities that accompany the position. Much too easily, males have become *"daddies,"* some of whom never mature into *"fathers."* Proverbs 4:1 tells us that children are to listen to *the instruction of a father, and attend to know understanding.* Without the father's instruction, most children fail to get the principal thing spoken of in the seventh verse of that chapter: *wisdom.* Wisdom is that understanding that comes with knowledge. Without knowledge, people are perishing! Look at the news! Read the headlines! Our children continue to perish!

In our society, many men are more like the prodigal son spoken of in the parable than they are like fathers. Most worldly men live for the moment, wasting their lives on riotous living. They spend years in their own little *"far country,"* running away from their responsibilities, and seldom fulfill their purposes in life. Some, of course, come to themselves, but nowhere near the number who don't! They become one-half of the failed marriage, the missing link in the dysfunctional family, a statistic in the penal system, a crack-cocaine addict, an absent parent, an obituary announcement, a long, lost brother, or a prodigal son. If only the prodigal sons would come home and become the fathers that God intended for them to be! Then our children would have a better chance at survival in the world. More importantly, they would be better equipped to live in the world while they prepare for eternity!

One of my senior English classes trudged their way through *"The Tragedy of Macbeth"* amidst constant interruptions. Just as we began reading and discussing the events which led to the tragic hero's downfall, our progress was halted when I was scheduled to help administer the Georgia High School Graduation Test to a group of juniors at our school. After that was complete, there were scheduled assembly programs, a teacher technology training program and other unforeseen interruptions. It was already challenging enough to get high school students interested, much less excited, about Shakespeare! To keep them motivated enough to continue reading, I related the characters in the play to persons they, themselves, knew in real life. As a matter of fact, it was somehow simple to compare the likeness of treacherous *Thane of Cawdor* to people we *all* knew! I discussed with the students the fact that he had committed treason, a crime that was punishable by death in those times. They found it interesting that, at the point of death, he became an honorable man!

"Sounds like some people I know," one student remarked.

"Yes," I replied, *"me too."* I was at once reminded of the many people who lived their lives, either straddling the fence of salvation, or at the farthermost end, completely without Christ! Until they are met with crisis or a life-threatening situation, they fail to acknowledge the presence of God at all. How many guilty people stand before the judges' bench and beg for God's mercy to intervene and keep them from serving time as punishment they justly deserve? They have lived their lives without God, doing anything and everything they were big and bad enough to do. Then, when they get caught, they want Him to *"hook a brother up!"*

I always found it intriguing when my students saw beyond the words on the pages of their books and read between the lines to see the implications for their own lives. The *Tragedy of Macbeth's* Thane of Cawdor, they observed, was thought to have been honorable because at the point of his execution, he confessed his wrongdoing, asked for the king's forgiveness, and repented of his sins. Wow! Well, that's God wants us all to do!

One of my students posed an interesting question. *"If you confess your wrongdoing and ask God to forgive you, you're straight, right?"*

"What do you mean?" I asked, pivoting on my stool to look at him.

"I mean," the student, whose name was Anthony, said, *"Like, if I've done something to offend someone and then I ask God to forgive me for what I did, everything's fine. Right?"*

Understanding his dilemma, I replied, *"Wrong."*

He interjected, *"I always thought that if you asked God to forgive you, you were straight."*

"Well, that's the first step," I explained, *"but you're not finished."*

Everyone's ears tuned in on the conversation. I could tell, because every eye in the room was on me. I took a deep breath. I am all-too-conscious of the fact that teachers have to be careful about what they say within the walls of the public school classroom. I tried to keep the conversation geared towards the behavior of Macbeth's predecessor. *"You see,"* I explained, *"The Thane of Cawdor had sinned against the throne of Scotland. He committed treason against King Duncan. Of course, we have already read that the appointment to the throne was a position that was ordained by God. For the Thane of Cawdor to commit treason against the throne was the same as committing a sin against God. He had sinned against the authority that the king had been given by God! He must have realized this before his execution, so he carried out the idea of Christian ethics and repented. He first confessed that he had sinned against the throne and against God, he begged the king to forgive him, and then he repented."*

"What does that mean?" another student asked.

"What?" I asked, turning to the other side of the room.

"That he repented," she replied.

"That means that he made a vow never to do it again," I said, facing the entire class. *"Well, that part was pretty obvious. He was put to death shortly thereafter, so there was no chance of him doing anything again!"*

Anthony's face lit up. *"So not only did he confess to God that he had sinned, but he asked the King to forgive him, too?"*

"Yes," I answered. I knew he was trying to get somewhere. I just wasn't sure where that was.

"So, in other words," he went on, *"if I did something to hurt someone and I asked God to forgive me, if I haven't asked that person to forgive me, I'm not really finished?"*

I nodded.

"Wow!" he said and looked across the room.

Before I or any of my other students knew what was happening, Anthony was up, out of his seat. He walked across the room to the desk where a fellow classmate, Vernon, was sitting. "Man," he said, his arms outstretched, *"I'm sorry!"*

"Yeah, me too, man," Vernon said, standing to his feet.

The entire class watched as the two young men embraced each other. I was speechless!

After they had apologized to each other, Vernon turned to me and said, *"At the beginning of the school year, we got into it and I almost jumped on him, Mrs. Bryant."*

"Man, I was wrong!" Anthony chimed in.

They never revealed what it was that had brought them to the point of fighting. In fact, nothing else was said about the incident in question. They had gotten a revelation in their lives, after the example of Macbeth's Thane of Cawdor. God had used this infamous literary work to do a work in the lives of two young men who were about to embark upon the rest of their adult lives. I smiled and, within myself, I said, *"Look at God!"*

> *"Judge not, and ye shall not be judged: condemn not, and ye shall*
> *not be condemned: forgive and ye shall be forgiven:"*
> *Luke 6:37*

In high school, I had been very astute, determined to do my best academically. My grades always were pretty good, which allowed me to be inducted into the National Honor Society during my junior year at Columbus High School. Additionally, I was also involved in the Chorus, Drama Club, and Student Council activities. During my Freshman year, I had attended Jordan High School, and I had been voted Vice-president of the Freshman class. During my first dramatic endeavor, a Neil Simon trilogy of plays entitled *"Plaza Suite,"* I had landed a role in *"The Wedding,"* as the zany mother of the bride. For our troupe's performance, we won second place in the Regional 2-AAA District play competition. For my acting performance, I was awarded Best Actress in the District. Aunt Meg was as pleased as punch when my drama teacher told her the news.

All in all, I had a good high school experience. Aunt Meg was very involved in most of my activities. Likewise, she was at almost every one of my eldest brother Wayne's football and basketball games. He was an all-star athlete, both on and off the field and court, earning the love and respect of his teachers and his peers. I have always looked up to my big brother. I still do! He is an honorable man and a Christian. His pursuit of excellence landed him a full scholarship to the University of Tennessee at Chattanooga. Today, he still lives there with his wife Marnita and their family.

My middle brother, Michael, was on the Columbus High School Wrestling Team. Academically, he fared adequately, but his real love was on the mat! I can still remember his constantly spitting in an old Maxwell House coffee can, trying to lose body fat (that none of his family members could actually detect!) and achieve his ideal weight for an upcoming match! He was then, as he is now, committed to doing whatever is necessary to reach his goals. Aunt Meg was somewhat involved in his educational experience. I say *'somewhat'* because by this time, she was so busy catering to all of the tri-city area that she seldom had time for very much else. In fact, I don't ever recall her sitting ringside at any of Michael's matches.

By the time Ronnie got to high school, Wayne and I had graduated. Michael was there, but Ronnie was, for the most part, on his own. Aunt Meg was swamped in weddings and receptions, office parties, church dinners, and the like. In the mornings, she drove Ronnie to the steps in front of Columbus High and watched him enter through the heavy wooden doors. Almost every single day, he walked into and then through the school and went right out of the back door! By the time Aunt Meg found out that Ronnie had actually accumulated more days *out* of school that he had been in, he had failed the eleventh grade! I can still recall the day she received her awakening! It was Friday afternoon and I had come home from Atlanta for the weekend.

Upon hearing that Ronnie had been behaving like a juvenile delinquent, skipping school, not doing his work, and hanging out with undesirables, Aunt Meg hit the roof! What did he mean carrying on like that? How could he have been behaving so terribly? How could he have been skipping? Hadn't *she* driven him to school herself? Hadn't *she* watched him enter the building herself? Hadn't *she* been there to pick him up in the afternoons *herself?* I listened to her rant and rave and then, when she finally calmed down, I tried to talk to her.

"You know," I said, sitting at the kitchen table, *"you really haven't spent very much time with Ronnie."*

"What do you mean?" she shrieked, turning on me from the stove where she was busy preparing for yet another catered affair.

At once, I knew that I had entered dangerous territory, but there was no possible retreat. *"Well, you've been really busy—I mean, you've always been busy—but you took more time with me and Wayne than you've had time with Ronnie and Michael."*

"I've done the best that I could," she said, sounding like a martyr. *"I took you kids when you had nobody else."*

What she said was true. I knew that. *"We appreciate what you and Uncle Ben did,"* I said. *"The only thing I'm saying is that Ronnie has kind of been left on his own for a long time now."* I wasn't accusing her, but it probably sounded like I was. I tried to clean it up a little bit. *"I mean, you are so busy catering that you haven't even had time to go to the school, to meet his teachers, to find out how he's doing in class. When Wayne and I were in school, you were always around! All of our teachers knew you, personally! If we did anything, you knew about it before we could even get home!"*

She knew that I was telling the truth, and I could tell that she had been convicted. *"I can't be everywhere at the same time,"* she said, turning back to the stove.

I sat silently, watching her shoulders heave from time to time.

By the time Ronnie appeared in the doorway, all hell broke loose! Aunt Meg chastised him as she had never done before. Ronnie stood before her and did not say a single, solitary word. He just stood there, his head lowered. He reminded me of a lost sheep. He had had no shepherd to guide him, so he had simply followed the crowd of other lost sheep. My heart ached for him. He was the same little three year old curly headed boy that had looked into my eyes the night our mother had died and asked for her. He was the same little innocent child to whom I had pledged my life to protect and care for. He was only three years old when both of our parents died. He had not even known them! Aunt Meg had been the only mother he had ever really known.

"If you get into trouble," she screamed at him, *"don't call me!"*

With that, Ronnie's brown eyes filled with tears. It was hard for me to see whether or not he was crying because I was.

Before the month had ended, Ronnie had gotten into serious trouble. For the first time, he did as he had been told. From the holding cell at the county jail, he *didn't* call Aunt Meg. Instead, he called me at my apartment in Atlanta.

When I asked him whether or not he had alerted her as to his whereabouts, he reminded me of her instructions. *"She told me not to call her."*

"I know," I said, *"but I don't think she really meant that."*

"Well, that's what she said."

I hesitated for a moment. I had been there. I, too, had heard what she said. *"I'll call her,"* I said, finally.

Ronnie had become involved in something that was much bigger than he knew. He and some of his peers had become cohorts in a check-theft and check-cashing ring. Ronnie, in his youthful ignorance, had ended up taking the *"rap"* for the person in charge. He either could not or would not divulge the identity of the person for whom he had been working. He paid for his silence with incarceration at the age of seventeen. It was his first encounter with the legal system and the beginning of a lifetime of reeling in and out of jail.

That was just the beginning! Ronnie went from juvenile delinquent behavior and misdemeanor crimes to drug abuse. For most of his life, the demon of possession has been a stronghold. Like most addicts, he began with marijuana, enjoying the temperate *"high"* it provided. When weed was no longer able to take him as high as he wanted to go, he tried other street drugs. For a short time, he was able to escape reality, putting his problems, his issues, and his responsibilities at bay—at least until he came down. Satan was right there, watching and waiting. He knew that Ronnie was *almost* his! He was always in the right place at the right time, helping Ronnie get acquainted with people who could get him the *"hook up"* he began to crave. He would constantly remind Ronnie of the emptiness in his life, the hole that had been created that night in November. Yes, he would tell Ronnie, *"Get high and you won't even have to think about it—in fact, you won't even have to think about anything—not your mother, not your father, not your family, not . . . even . . . God!* Gradually, he migrated to crack cocaine. Since it was a more addictive and overpowering drug, it only took once to get him hooked. To get it, he would lie, cheat, and steal from his own family—from the people who truly loved him! Wandering the streets at all hours of the night, in search of a rock, Satan would convince him that his family did not even love him. The enemy would lie to Ronnie and tell him that nobody loved him, not even God. Once Ronnie was convinced of this, he would be able to find no reason to turn back!

I wrote him a letter once and told him that sometimes, things get so bad and you get so low that you end up flat on your back. When that happens, the only way you can look is up. One day, he decided that he had sunken as low as he wanted to go.

The first time, he made an honest attempt to get his life on track and off of drugs, he went, voluntarily, into a local drug rehabilitation program. He was to reside at the treatment center for thirty days, during which time he would undergo therapy and radical detoxification. At the end of the program, he would be released, back into the *"real world,"* where crack cocaine would be patiently waiting for his return.

On weekends, family members were allowed to come in and attend counseling sessions with their loved ones. Afterwards, we could visit with Ronnie in the courtyard or lounge on the premises. One Saturday, I went alone and decided to attend a session designed specifically for family members who wanted to help their loved ones beat their addiction. We were in a room that seated about twenty-five people comfortably. I sat down on a green leather sofa next to a middle-aged woman whose eyes were red-rimmed, as if she had been crying recently. I said *'hello'* to her and she smiled, but avoided my gaze. I directed my attention to a tall, slender African American man who had just made his way to the front of the room.

"Don't be fooled into thinking that your friends, sons, daughters, husbands, wives, brothers and sisters will be cured in here," the speaker, Mr. Elder, began. *"They won't. Alcohol and drug addiction is forever."*

What a startling way to begin, I thought! Forever? I was sure that I, nor anyone else present, wanted to hear that their brother, sister, or anyone else would be addicted forever! That didn't make me feel very optimistic. Oh, I already knew the consequences of drug addiction. I had already experienced the effects of it.

I recalled that when Ronnie had come to live with us, I had been very relieved. We had not heard from him in almost a year. In that time, Aunt Meg had passed away and he had not even been aware of it! When he called, nearly a year later, after her funeral, to ask how she was doing, I was a little ticked off. When I told him how she was doing, that she had been dead and buried a year earlier, he was silent. I had no idea what he was thinking or how he was taking the news. After he hung up the phone, we didn't hear from him for another two or three weeks. A month later, he was home with us to stay for what he said was a *"while."*

I did not know that Ronnie had a serious cocaine addiction. He had been working for a month or so, painting houses. Gradually, his demeanor began to change. Where he had been funny and sociable, he became sullen and distant, sleeping much more than usual. On his off days, he slept all day long, having come in very late the night before. When I questioned him, he was evasive and would not look me directly in the eye.

I suppose I should explain something here about my relationship with Ronnie. The night that our father murdered our mother, grandmother, shot our seven-year old brother Michael and our grandfather, and then killed himself, I was eight and Ronnie was three years old. That night, after all of the commotion had settled and the police sirens had been silenced, Ronnie, me and our ten year old brother, Wayne, were taken to one of our aunt's house nearby. I was traumatized, having witnessed the catastrophic ordeal just a few hours earlier. I was afraid to sleep near the window on the sofa bed that had been prepared for us. In my head, I kept seeing the bloody scene at Grandmama's house. I kept hearing the rounds of gunfire, piercing the darkness of that night. In my ears was still the constant blaze of police sirens. I could not get it out of my head that Michael had been shot through the window at our grandmother's house!

My aunt told me to lie down and try to go to sleep. Reluctantly, I laid my head down on a pillow. When she told Ronnie to do the same, he looked at her with the saddest eyes I had ever seen and said, *"No, I'm waiting for my Mama."*

To hear him say that filled me with more grief than my eight-year old body could endure. I cried uncontrollably. Ronnie, affected by my reaction, put an arm around me. When I realized that it was his arm around my waist,

I took my hands from my face and looked at him. The look of sadness on his little face prompted me to say, *"Don't worry. I'll take care of you."* We sat on the sofabed, embracing each other. I don't know how long we stayed like that, but I do remember my promise to my little brother. Throughout the years, no matter what it cost me, I have found myself trying to keep that promise!

So there we were, twenty-six years later, Ronnie and I—him, still looking for comfort from some kind of emptiness, and me, still trying to fill the void. I became angry with him for his sudden change of personality. I wanted to know what was going on with him. Before I could ask him again, he disappeared from home for three days . . . with my VCR. When he showed up again, the VCR was not with him. At first, he lied to me about it. He said that he didn't know where it was. Then, he changed his story and told me that he had pawned it. For reasons unknown to me, I asked him if he had a problem. He replied that he did. Then, I asked him what his problem was. When Ronnie told me that he was on cocaine, I was numb. I had just recently heard on the news about a young man who had shot and killed his grandparents because they would not give him money to buy cocaine. The commentator had stressed the fact that those in search of money to buy drugs would stop at nothing to get it! I thought about me, my son and my dad, living in the house. I realized that the person standing before me was not the brother I knew. It was someone else—someone who was addicted to cocaine!

I gave Ronnie three choices. He could go and get professional help, I could call the police and he could go to jail for stealing my VCR, or he could get out and live on the streets and take his chances with the other addicts out there. One fact remained—he could not stay in the house with us in his condition. He chose to go to treatment and ended up at the drug rehabilitation center.

Mr. Elder told the friends and family members who were present that Saturday that drug addiction was a vicious cycle for those who say they want out, but don't really mean it. *"Once you are an addict, you are an addict for the rest of your life,"* he declared. *"But you can learn to live without it! It is a matter of making a decision to commit to living without it and working to fulfill that commitment."*

Since that day at the rehab center, I have discovered that there is more to overcoming the demon of addiction than learning to live without drugs! The treatment program is good, but someone who really wants to get off of drugs and alcohol needs more than the radical medical and psychological treatment that is available in a structured rehabilitative program. What they really need is *Jesus!* In order for change to take place in the life of an addict, change must first take place in his or her mind! You can tell yourself anything you want. Without

Christ, that demon will stay right where he is, tearing your life completely apart! Not only *your* life, but the lives of your family members! That is why he is there in the first place! He is the reason for the addiction! He is the reason so many go in and out of treatment programs, only to be released and then return to their same self-destructive behavior! What is incredible is that I have heard so many addicts, like my brother, who really and truly do not *want* to do drugs! They say that they just can't help it! They don't know what to do, or how to beat their addiction! They don't have an answer to their problem, but I do—the answer is *Jesus!*

Ronnie has been a resident of the prison system of Georgia for most of his adult life. At this moment, in fact, he is once again incarcerated. Part of his problem has been his experimentation with and eventual addiction to crack cocaine. Not only has he suffered the devastation of the drug, many of our family members have been duly affected by his drug abuse on numerous occasions. We have all been at the end of our ropes with his drug addiction. Our breaking point came much sooner than his did, if he has experienced that revelation at all! Our knees have been bruised and worn while we prayed desperately for his deliverance from the demon of addiction. It *is* a demon! It has made him forget the God that preserved his life the night our mother was murdered. It has clouded his vision so that he cannot see the pain he has caused both himself and the people who love him. It has deafened his ears so that he cannot hear the words of reason from those of us who would tell him the truth. The demon has sought to destroy Ronnie and has almost done just that!

I have often wondered if the sins of our father have manifested themselves in Ronnie's life. According to Exodus 34:7, God declared that he *"would by no means clear the guilty; visiting the iniquity of the fathers upon the children, and upon the children's children, unto the third and to the fourth generation."* This tells us that, whether we like it or not, we will have to bear the guilt of our father—not only us, but our children and our grandchildren! When I read that, I was immediately amazed at the thought that I, or my children, would have to pay for my father's horrible sins! After all, he had sinned not only against God, but against us! And to think that we would have to pay the penalty for his actions?

Surely God would not hold us responsible. Would He? I was reminded of Christ's coming to make salvation available to us. Because of His ultimate sacrifice, our sins have been forgiven. I realized that because I have accepted Christ in my life as my personal Savior and made Him Lord of my life, my sins have been forgiven. Any sins that I bore, as a result of my father's transgressions, have been forgiven of me! Because I accepted Christ as my personal Savior, according to the Word of God, I am a new creature, old things have been passed away, and all things have become new! Thank God! I don't have to live under the penalty of Tony's sins—simply because I chose to serve God! My God! I hope and pray that whoever reads this will get that revelation! Unless we choose Christ, we live under the penalty of our fathers' and our forefathers' sins! Hallelujah and thank God for the blessed redemptive blood of Jesus Christ, the risen Savior!

Fathers must be aware that the penalty of their sins will not rest solely upon them. Their children will be affected by the seeds they have sown. It's the truth! We can see it happening in our society today, however children need to know that the cycle can be broken! Many young people are following in the same desolate footsteps of their fathers and forefathers. They don't even know why! When asked why they do what they do, they only know that something inside of them compels them to make the choices they have made. They cannot even verbalize what that *something* is. They don't understand that it began with the iniquity of their fathers.

Once, Ronnie commented to me that no matter what he does, trouble always seems to find him. Without as much as a thought, I responded, *"That's because you live at the wrong address!"* I was not referring to the hideous bright orange and blue painted frame boarding house on the west side of Atlanta where he was renting a room at the time. I was talking about the place where his heart resides! I'm not sure he understood what I meant, and as I recall, we didn't go into any great detail. He simply and blindly concurred with what I said. Where our heart resides determines our plight in life. It predisposes our condition and ultimately determines our disposition. It makes all the difference in our lives. It influences the choices we make. The next time he called me, I told my youngest brother that he didn't have to suffer the iniquities of our father any longer. He simply needed to make a choice to give his heart to God, and once and for all, be freed from the sins committed by our biological father—against us and against God. Only then would the terrible cycle be broken in his life!

He seemed to take this new revelation with some optimism. What if, by making a choice to give his heart completely to the Lord, he was able to change his life forever? He had superficially accepted the invitation to join the church before, walking timidly up the aisle and extending his hand to the pastor. Yes, he had even been baptized, symbolically burying the old man beneath the tepid water and emerging a *"new creature."* Unfortunately, it had only been an outward display, and no real change had ever taken place in his heart. I brought this to his attention, and he readily agreed that obviously, he had not been changed. It was true. At the time, he had continued to bounce back and forth, on and off of crack, in and out of jail, up and down in the spiraling tempest that had become his thirty-seven year old life!

I went on to tell him what the Apostle Paul had written in the tenth chapter of his letter to the Romans. He gave the key to salvation when he said that *"if thou shalt confess with thy mouth the Lord Jesus, and shalt believe in thine heart that God hath raised him from the dead, thou shalt be saved."* In other words, we just have to make a heartfelt confession in order to receive Christ into our hearts. Paul went on to say in verse ten that *"with the heart man believeth unto righteousness; and with the mouth confession is made unto salvation."* Just say it! I told my brother that the power of death and life was in his tongue. If he wanted life, apart from the dismal existence he had maintained for most of it, he needed to begin to speak it and accept that salvation that Christ freely offered to him. *"He stands,"* I said, *"at the door and knocks. He won't force His way in though. He waits for us to invite Him into our hearts and into our lives."*

The operator interrupted our conversation to tell us that the call would be disconnected in a minute. Before hanging up the telephone, I presented Ronnie the challenge to honestly and sincerely commit his life to Christ. I did not pray the prayer of salvation with him, although I felt strongly compelled to do so. I did, however, ask him to think about what we had discussed and, I told myself that when he called again, we would pray together. I felt that he needed a little time to absorb what God had given me to tell him. I had long discovered that before change could take place in someone's life, it had to *first* take place in his heart and mind. Hopefully, Ronnie had gotten that message. Only time would tell. In the meantime, I would continue to pray for the transformation to begin.

"And be not conformed to this world: but be ye transformed by the renewing of your mind, that ye may prove what is that good, and acceptable, and perfect, will of God."

Romans 12:2

SIX

O NE EASTER, MY three brothers and I could hardly sleep knowing that four chocolate bunny rabbits were just inside the door of Grandmama's old white refrigerator with our names' scrawled on the boxes which contained them! I was about six or seven years old, but the memory has stayed with me throughout the years. On occasion, when I tried to find some positive memories to think about amidst all of the unpleasantness that I have endured throughout the years, I have often thought about those chocolate rabbits. They were milk chocolate hollow rabbit shapes that tantalized us from the very moment they were brought into the house and removed from the Woolworth's shopping bag in my grandmother's hand! Carefully, she would place them in the refrigerator so that they would not melt in the kitchen warmth. She distinctly warned each of us not to touch them. They were for Easter, she told us, with a wink of her eye. With wide, eager eyes, we each nodded our consent and licked our lips with anticipation. On Easter Sunday morning, the wait would end, and each of us would finally get to hold Peter's chocolate pals in our hands!

As usual, we were sent to bed early that Saturday night. I can remember going to sleep, but some time during the night, I awoke to the sound of what I could have sworn was a tiny voice calling my name from the kitchen! Stealthily, I slid down off of the sofa bed in the front room of Grandmama's shotgun house. Mama was sleeping peacefully, my baby brother Ronnie tucked safely under her arm. My getting up had not stirred them. I tiptoed across the floor, careful not to step on Wayne and Michael, who were sleeping on a pallet in the center of the room. Wayne was sleeping in the peculiar way he has of doing so. His eyes were only partially shut, but the steady rhythm of his breathing told me that he was sound asleep. I went into the middle room and found Grandmama and Granddaddy, in their bed, snoring contentedly.

The kitchen was just beyond their room. Again, I heard the little voice, *"Nesi!"* My footsteps quickened in its direction. When I got to the kitchen, I saw nothing. For a moment, I thought my mind was playing tricks on me. Then, something told me to open the refrigerator door. *"Nesi!"* The voice was coming from within the heavy white door. As quietly as I could, I opened it. In plain view were the chocolate bunnies! One of them was calling my name! I could not tell which of Peter's pals it was. I only knew that, at least one of them was speaking directly to me! Before I knew what I was doing myself, I had snatched the nearest chocolate bunny from the shelf closest to me and pried the cardboard top off of the decorative box! *"Yes!"* the rabbit coaxed me. *"Take a bite!"*

I had no choice but to oblige him. Without further hesitation, I bit one ear completely off the chocolate bunny! As suddenly as I had done it, I knew that I was in trouble! Grandmama would most certainly notice a chocolate bunny rabbit with a missing ear! What could I have been thinking of? I stared at it, aware that my fingers were becoming moist where they touched the rabbit's hollow chocolate body. Then, suddenly, my adolescent mind had a great idea! No one would notice the missing ear, if none of Peter's pals had ears! Brilliant, I thought, with great satisfaction! Without another thought, I chomped off the rabbit's other ear, put him back in his box, and replaced the box on the refrigerator shelf! Then, carefully, expeditiously, I removed the other rabbits, one-by-one, from their boxes, bit both of their long ears off, and put each one of them back where they had been!

After the last of the four rabbits was put securely back in place, I tiptoed quietly back through my grandparents' room again, into the living room, carefully stepping around Wayne and Michael, and slid back onto the sofa bed, next to Mama. She was still sleeping soundly, Ronnie snuggled close to her.

Before the Easter morning sun could rise above our house and proclaim the resurrection day, Grandmama's strong, vibrant voice summoned the four of us to the kitchen. I had no reason to suspect that I was in any trouble. After all, the rabbits were just as uniformed as they had been upon their arrival at our house—of course, none of them had ears now, so they all looked just alike!

My brothers and I stood at attention before our grandmother. I plastered the most innocent look I could muster upon my face. Grandmama's eyes panned the line of pajama-clad children. When she looked at me, she cleared her throat. *"Ahem—what I'd like to know is—Ahem,"* she began, *"who ate the ears off of all of these rabbits?"*

My brothers looked at each other and at me. *"Not me!"* Michael and Wayne seemed to say, simultaneously.

Ronnie, who was around two or three at the time, chimed in after Wayne and Michael. *"Not me!"* he said, mimicking them.

Grandmama's eyes found mind. *"Nesi, do you know anything about these rabbits with no ears?"* Her left eyebrow rose. *"Humm . . . ?"*

I looked down at the kitchen floor and shifted my weight from one foot to the other. *"Ahm, no,"* I lied.

"Are you sure?" she asked, putting a golden-skinned hand on one hip.

"Well, . . . ahm no, I'm sure."

For a moment, no one said anything. Then, Wayne, my eldest brother, who always seemed to know just *who* had done *what*, made an interesting observation. *"Is that chocolate all over your face?"* he asked, looking directly at me.

My eyes widened! I had not even considered the fact that I might be wearing the evidence of the previous night's escapade! I put a hand up to my mouth and slid it across my lips. When I took my hand down and looked at it, sure enough, there was chocolate in my hand and on my fingers! I had been caught *"brown-handed"* and Grandmama had known that I was the guilty one from the moment I had entered the kitchen! Much to my relief, she began to laugh. My brothers joined her and started laughing, too. A little reluctantly, I, too, found myself laughing. Inside, I thanked God that Grandmama had found the incident so funny that she had not even chastised me, for once, for not telling the truth.

A devout, church-going woman, my grandmother, *"Miss Ruth"* Martin, was a very strong influence in my life. I did not realize just how great an impact she had had on me until I was a grown woman. On my way from the cross-country tour with my first book, at the end of the summer of 1998, I pondered that question. We had just left Shreveport, Louisiana for the second time. It was just shortly after my miraculous encounter with the woman at Pastor Williamson's church. We had stopped at McDonald's and gotten the boys some food to eat. They were eating noisily in the back seat of the car. Terri was dozing, her head propped up against the window, still warm from the afternoon sun that had begun to set on the road behind us.

"What's wrong?" Derrick asked, glancing over at me and then back at the long stretch of road before us.

"Nothing," I said. *"I was just wondering how I turned out to be the way I am."*

"What do you mean?" he asked.

I sighed, thoughtfully. *"I mean, why am I the way I am? Why am I not on drugs? Not a prostitute? Sane? Why am I still alive after everything that's happened to me?"*

My husband understood what I meant. We had often discussed how ironic it was that some people had gone through much less than I had and, as a result, had found themselves trapped in some sort of sad, self-destructive condition. So many times, I had met young women who habitually gave themselves to one man after another, trying desperately to erase childhood pain and neglect. I had also met young men who had fallen into the cycle of drug or alcohol abuse as a result of having grown up without a strong male role model in their lives. I don't know how many times I had met adults who were either abusers or the abused, perpetuating the vicious cycle of child abuse to which they, themselves, had fallen prey. Personally, I knew women who had found themselves locked into unhealthy relationships and either did not know how to leave or, for some peculiar reason, did not possess enough courage to even attempt to do so. If asked why they continued to stay with someone who abused them, they could not even answer the question.

Here I was, a survivor of violence. I had survived a childhood filled with pain and anguish at having watched my own mother killed. I had been sexually abused for seven years of my adolescent life by my caregiver. After I revealed this truth to my *"mom,"* I was subjected to her bitter resentment and gross animosity, which usually came across in the form of harsh criticism and verbal abuse. During my first marriage, I became a battered wife, eventually escaping to safety by running across the country with a thirteen-month old baby in tow. Some may find it hard to believe, but I do not now, nor have I ever had a drug or alcohol problem. And most of the time, I felt like a pretty sane individual!

"I was just wondering," I remarked to my husband, *"what it was or who it was that sowed such seeds into my life to cause me to grow up to be the person I am today—despite that dark cloud of misery that has seemed to hover over me for most of it."*

"Oh, I see what you mean," Derrick said.

"I don't know who it was, but I tell you what," I said, a weary smile on my lips, *"I sure do thank God for them!"* I closed my eyes and tried to let sleep overtake me. Little did I know it, but when we returned home the next day, I would have the answer to my question.

When we got home, a pile of mail that had accumulated during our trip awaited us. Our neighbors, an elderly couple, had been kind enough to collect it for us each day while we were away. When I sat down at the dining room table with the stacks of bills, letters, sales papers, etc., I began randomly opening and separating each piece. At the bottom of the stack was a large, manila envelope. I had saved it for last, and when I looked at the return address, I recognized the name as one that I had not heard for quite some time. It was from someone whose last name was *"Lumus."* As I recalled, my grandmother used to work for the Lumus family who had founded a mill in Columbus many years before I was born. She had worked as their maid for a number of years and, although I had never met any member of the prestigious family, I knew that my grandmother, Ruth, had been working for them when she died.

I opened the enveloped and extracted from it a letter and a cardboard folding picture frame. Before reading the letter, I opened the frame and was surprised to find a picture of my grandmother holding a little Caucasian girl in her lap! A light gasp escaped my lips. The picture had to have been taken a very long time ago. My grandmother's hair was jet black, wavy, and parted down the middle, with a coiled braid on either side. I vaguely recalled seeing her wear her hair like that. Who might have sent it to me, I could not help but wonder.

Derrick came into the dining room and saw me, seated at the table. *"Anything besides bills??*

"Yeah," I said, holding the cardboard frame open so that he could see it.

"Who's that?" he asked.

"My grandmother," I said. *"But I don't know who could have sent it to me."* Then I remembered the other contents of the envelope. I put the picture down on the table next to the stack of bills and opened the letter.

A man, whose name was Cam Lumus, had written the letter to me. In it, he shared with me that he had seen my picture in the newspaper and had read the article about the cross-country trip I had planned to take *Opening the Door* and share it with people all over the country. Mr. Lumus talked about my grandmother and the tremendous blessing she had been in the lives of him and his sister, Leslie, the little girl in the picture. He told me that she had come to work for their family at a time when they had needed her most and that she had impacted their lives. Then he gave me the answer to my question. This man, whom I had never had the opportunity to meet, told me that he had gone out and purchased a copy of my book, read it and, as a result, discovered that I was very much like my grandmother. He said that she had been kind, loving and forgiving and had taught those qualities to both him and his sister. Obviously, he wrote, she had taught them to me, as well.

As I read his letter, my heart swelled with a mixture of joy and grief to know that my grandmother had left her legacy with me. She had taught me the way to go, even though she had not lived long enough to see what I would do with the life she had sown good seed into! I hated that she had not lived long enough to see the fruits of her labor. My mind wandered back to the days when my brother Wayne and I used to walk, hand in hand, around the corner to Sunday school at Greater Peace Baptist Church where Grandmama was Youth Director. I remembered the way she chastised us for misbehaving and, when necessary, was careful not to spare the rod on our behinds! I recalled her admonishing us, as small children, to sit perfectly still in our little red rocking chairs, while claps of thunder and heavy raindrops stormed above us on the tin roof of her old shotgun house on Baldwin Street. *"Keep still,"* she would whisper. *"The Lord is doing His work!"*

I had not even realized it, but dedicating my life to working with youth in the church, in schools, and in the community had been an extension of the hands Ruth Martin had used to touch children within her reach! Certainly, lives had been touched by her! Two generations later, I was still trying to carry the torch! Immediately, I located the phone directory so that I could call Mr. Lumus. I wanted to speak with him directly, to tell him how much I appreciated his taking the time to write to me. Relatively easily, I found his phone number and sat down to call him.

The voice at the other end of the phone was overjoyed to hear from me. Although I was, for the most part, a stranger he had read about in the local newspaper, a special bond existed between us. That bond was an extension of the love that my grandmother had so abundantly heaped upon both my brothers and me and him and his younger sister during their childhood as well. The heart that had held so much love for her own children and grandchildren had been big enough to include space for the Lumus children. Mr. Lumus shared with me some of the details of his and his little sister's relationship with the loving woman they affectionately referred to as *"Foo-Foo."* She had come into their lives at a much-needed time and filled a void that had been created as a result of their mother's illness and difficulty in running the household. Foo-Foo had come in and kept things together for the Lumus family. She had kept their house immaculately clean, loved the children earnestly, and befriended a fragile Mrs. Lumus.

On the phone, Mr. Lumus told me that when he read the article about my having gone through so many traumatic experiences and risen, like an eagle from the ashes, he was reminded of my grandmother. In me, he said, he saw the same strength and determination he had seen in her! I was very much like her, he assured me, whether I had realized it or not. At the end of our conversation, I knew with certainty that my grandmother, Ruth Martin, had sown the seeds of love and determination deep within me when I was just a child, not yet capable of knowing very much about the qualities she, herself, possessed!

After I hung up the phone, I cried. My tears were a mixture of sadness and joy. I felt sad because my grandmother's life had been ended so tragically at the hands of my father. No doubt, had she lived, innumerable more lives would have been touched. Even though I knew the loss was great, I cried tears of joy at having been blessed by God to have had someone in my life like Ruth Martin! Her powerful influence upon me had been an anchor which kept me afloat during the times the tempests and storms of life had nearly destroyed me. She had taught me to love God and seek diligently for Him in my life. She had taught me to respect His power and might. She also had taught me to lean not to my own understanding, for there would be many things that I would not be able to understand. In a very short time, my grandmother had taught me well.

> *"The aged women likewise, that they be in behaviour as becometh holiness, not false accusers, not given to much wine, teachers of good things."*

> *Titus 2:3*

I knew my eldest son believed that Derrick and I were way too persistent about being kept abreast of the affairs of his life. He never said as much, but I got that feeling every time I asked *"Who are you talking to?"* or *"Who is she?"* or *"Who else is going to be there?"* I never tried to excuse my inquisitiveness or dismiss it as just plain nosiness! On the contrary, my husband and I explained to Tjai that we were genuinely interested in what was going on in his life, and since his life was an investment from which we expected great returns, we felt entitled to inquire. This usually brought a cunning smile to his lips and a twinkle to his slanted, hazel eyes. *"A lot of kids your age,"* I was quick to remind him, *"would be glad to have parents who cared about them as much as we care about you."*

"Ah, uh-huh" was his standard response after those kinds of comments. He was usually pretty wise when it came to this particular subject. He knew that the only sensible thing to do was to voice a somewhat audible word of agreement and smile—and then he could get back to his phone-conversation-in-progress much quicker!

I am very proud of Tjai. Although there were times that he disappointed me, like any other youth might disappoint his or her parents, he still made me happy that he was my son!

When I was an Education Major at what is now Columbus State University, tirelessly pursuing my degree in Secondary English Education, an occasion presented itself when I thought it was time for *"the talk"* with Tjai. At the time, my then-only child was seven years old, a second grade student at a nearby elementary school. During an Introduction to Education class, the instructor had stood before our class and informed us that it had been recently reported in the news that two second grade students in an urban city had been discovered *"making out"* in the school boiler room!

"Making out?" I and several others chimed at once.

"Absolutely!" our astute professor replied. *"Children are becoming more and more sexually active at younger ages!"* he added.

I was appalled! No, I was mortified! Second grade? Tjai was in the second grade! I made a mental note to have *"the talk"* with him that evening. I would much rather than he heard the truth of the matter from me than to learn from childhood friends on the playground!

That night, Tjai took his bath, got ready for bed and went to his room. As usual, I went in so that we could say his prayers together and so that I could, as I sometimes did, read to him before he went to sleep. That particular night, I planned to read to him alright, but not anything Dr. Seuss had penned. I planned to show him the colorful pictures sprawled across the pages of my Introduction to Education textbook. In it were graphic representations of sexual intercourse. I know, it probably sounded like a lot to lay on a seven year old, but drastic times, they say, call for drastic measures, so . . .

I went into his bedroom and he was pulling down his Sesame Street comforter so that he could climb between the matching sheets. *"Tjai,"* I said, sitting down on his bed. *"I want to show you something."*

He came and sat on the bed beside me.

I opened the book to the page I had bookmarked. On it was a picture of a man and a woman's body, intertwined. The picture was an external view of a couple engaged in lovemaking, the making of a life. In fact, the caption underneath said just that, *"The Making of a Life."* From their position, however, not very much could have been distinguished, no sexual organs exposed or anything like that. Tjai looked at the couple, a little puzzled expression on his face. He was probably wondering why I would show him something like that.

Sensing, his confusion, I was confident that turning the page would provide greater insight to him. So I did. I turned the page and on the next page was the *"internal"* diagram of the previous page.

Greater bewilderment shone on his face. After a couple of seconds, he asked, *"What is that?"*

"Ahm ... it's a man and a woman—no, a husband and a wife," I corrected myself, knowing that it would be much easier to explain. *"This is how babies are made,"* I said, calmly.

Tjai took the thick book from me and held it in his hands. He studied the diagram for a moment, his eyebrows scowling. Then, he turned the book upside down in his hands so that he could look at the diagram from another angle.

I couldn't help but smile at that.

After a moment, he sighed, *"I don't get it."*

Unsure of what I should say next, I stalled for time. *"Ah ... what do you mean?"*

He shook his head. *"I just don't get it,"* he repeated.

"Well, this is what happens when babies are made," I tried to explain. *"Mommies and daddies have to love each other and they .... they show their love for one another like this, and then the mommy gets pregnant with their child."* I said that last phrase as if it was a revelation.

My seven year old was not the least bit impressed. Once again, he flipped the book around. Holding it upright in his hand, again, he sighed. Then, to my surprise, he said, *"That's okay, Mommy. I don't think I want to do that."* He stood up, handed my textbook back to me, pulled down his covers further and crawled into bed!

I couldn't see it, but I was sure my face was tight! Convinced that the *"talk"* had not gone quite the way I had anticipated, I appreciated the fact that he wasn't the least bit interested in this *"sex"* thing. I wasn't naïve, though, to think that he would continue to feel that way throughout adolescence and the teenage years. I knew I could only hope that he would choose abstinence, at least until he decided to get married. There was still time. He was only in the second grade!

During the summer of that same year, Tjai attended Vacation Bible School at our church. Towards the end of the week, when the invitation to Christian discipleship was extended to the sanctuary full of youngsters, he stood up. I had been seated at the piano, playing softly as the pastor talked to the congregation full of youngsters about giving their lives to Christ. When my son stood up, I turned my head to look at him. My first inclination was to get up and go over to him and tell him to sit down until I could have an opportunity to discuss this important step with him. We had talked about many things, but I had not yet gotten around to talking to him about joining the church.

The Pastor, Reverend Tony Thompson, Jr., then asked those who had stood up to go home and talk to their parents about the decision they had made and then ask their parents to return with them to Vacation Bible School the following evening. He would not, he told them, receive them as candidates for baptism without their parents' permission. I was relieved. I needed to talk to Tjai first to make sure that he understood what he was doing.

On the way home, I asked him if he understood. Of course, he said that he did. He wanted to get baptized, he told me in a voice full of innocence. I told him that we would talk about it later, after I had a chance to talk to Pastor Thompson. I thought I might need to get some divine guidance about the issue. I called my pastor that night and shared with him my concerns about Tjai's wanting to join the church and be baptized.

Pastor Thompson told me that I should not question the desires of Tjai's heart on the matter. He reminded me of Matthew 19:14, in which Jesus said, *"Suffer little children, and forbid them not, to come unto me: for of such is the kingdom of heaven."*

"But I don't want him to do it just because he sees other people doing it," I said.

"Well," Pastor Thompson said, *"talk to him."*

So I did. The next morning, at the breakfast table, as I sat across from Tjai, I asked, *"Do you understand what it means to come to Christ, to be baptized and to accept Him as your personal Savior?"*

He said, *"Yes."*

I went on. *"But do you understand—it doesn't mean that you're going to be perfect—but you've got to strive to be the best you can be all the time?"*

Again, he said *"Yes."*

"But do you really understand that you have got to be loving towards other people, and you have to show them Christ all the time?" I asked, *"Do you think you can do that?"*

Then my seven year old, stopped eating his Fruit Loops, looked over the rims of his glasses, and said the most astounding thing to me. *"Mommy,"* he said, *"you do it."*

At that moment, I realized just how closely my child was watching me. He was looking at the examples I was setting! He was paying attention to my very footsteps! Parents must be acutely aware that children are watching them and listening to them! They are not pieces of furniture or some other inanimate object! They are adults-in-training! They are the fruit that will someday fall from our trees! They hear what you say and they see what you do! We cannot say *'do what I say'* and expect them *not to do what we do!* They might do what you say in front of you, but when they are away from you, they're going to do what they have seen you do and say what they have heard you say! We must be very careful that what we say in front of our children are things that we won't mind other people hearing!

I have sat in parent-teacher conferences with students who openly disrespect their parents in the presence of myself and their counselor. I have heard parents confess that they just don't know what to do with their child or that they don't know why their high school-aged child behaves the way he or she does. I have had limited opportunities to share with parents what I believe the motivating factors are in their child's behavior. I'm not sure people are ready to hear the truth of the matter. As a whole, people like to look at other people's children more realistically than their own. I'm guilty of that, too! Of course, we all want to believe that our children will and won't do certain things. We easily become defensive in their behalf, as well. Observe any little league sports activity where wide-eyed parents sit on the sidelines and you will see exactly what I am talking about!

My point is that the old adage that *"the fruit doesn't fall far from the tree"* is true! Adam's sin in the Garden was transferred to his children. He had to have been reminded of his broken covenant with God when his son, Abel's blood was spilled onto the ground. Surely Cain's transgression reminded him of his own his fall from God's grace! The Book of Genesis does not record every detail of the first family's life outside of the Garden, so we have no real way of knowing what Adam's children saw or heard him and his wife do or say.

About eleven years ago, Tjai went to a covenant party for one of the teenage girls at the church we were attending. Until I drove up in front of her family's house, I did not even know what a covenant party was! I felt a little silly after I found out. As I waited for Tjai to go and find out how long the event would last and come back and tell me so that I would know what time to pick him up, a young lady who also attended our church, walked around to my side of the car to say *'hello.'* She explained what it was all about. She told me that a covenant party was a celebration for a young person's commitment to remain abstinent until marriage. The celebrant was prayed for and received a ring from his or her parents to wear as a reminder of their vow. I had never even heard of anything like that before, but I thought it was a great idea! Tjai had turned sixteen a month earlier, and perhaps, if I had known about it then, we could have done something like that for him.

Later that night, when I picked him up from the party, Tjai told me that he, too, had just found out what a covenant party was. He was pretty impressed with the affair that had been given to celebrate the young lady.

"I think that's a wonderful gesture," I said, merging into the light highway traffic.

"Me, too," he said.

"If we had known about that, we could have done that with you when you turned sixteen," I told him.

"Oh, that's okay, Mom," he said. *"I already did it."*

"What?"

"I already made a vow myself to wait until I get married."

I was mildly surprised. *"Oh?"*

"Yeah. We all did it when we went with Aunt Luella on that Step Team trip." He had accompanied my friend Luella and the group of teens she sponsors on a trip to perform step routines as part of an HIV/AIDS education program in which they participate. Tjai used to be a member of the team, before his rigorous football schedule took precedence. *"We all signed a form promising to be abstinent until marriage and to be drug free forever."* He said it matter-of-factly.

"Oh," I said, smiling. For a moment, I didn't say anything.

He did. *"I'm going to do it, Mom."*

Again, I smiled. Inside, I thanked God.

"The just man walketh in his integrity: his children are blessed after him."
Proverbs 20:7

SEVEN

S ECOND CHRONICLES, THE seventh chapter and verse fourteen reads: *"If my people, which are called by my name, shall humble themselves, and pray, and seek my face, and turn from their wicked ways; then will I hear from heaven, and will forgive their sin, and will heal their land."* I don't know how many times I have read these words. In fact, when I was Minister of Music at St. Mark's United Methodist Church in Los Angeles, California, the choir periodically sang these same words in a song entitled *"If My People."* Even then, as I listened to the words that had been set to a beautiful melody, I realized that God surely must be trying to tell us something. After all that has transpired in my life, I am truly convinced that there is strong merit there. If we want our land, our communities, our families, and our lives to be healed, there is an answer. In a time when men have become lovers of themselves, in the calamity of it all, they have received acceptance and pseudo-validation of their chosen lifestyles from principalities, powers, rulers of the darkness of this world, and spiritual wickedness in high places! Surely, there must be an answer! In this day and time, when fathers have turned against their own sons and taken their very own lives, or sons have beat them to it, we desperately need an answer!

The words spoken in the Apostle Paul's second letter to Timothy have already come true, for perilous times have indeed come! Daily, in the halls of the schools where I taught, I was made aware that children had become disobedient to their parents, unthankful and unholy. At the grocery store, one could easily encounter those who were without natural affection, trucebreakers, false accusers, incontinent, and fierce despisers of those that were good. Don't take my word for it! Just think about the times when you forgot something while you were in line, in front of a couple of people and you had to go back for it! Today, channel surfing on the television will quickly reveal how far mankind has gone to become lovers of pleasures more than lovers of God. The perverseness has spilled over into houses of worship, as well. Within the walls of our churches, we find those who may have a form of godliness, but actually deny the power of the Almighty!

I once gave a journal topic to one of my senior English students that went something like this: *"What is the answer to the current condition of mankind?"* Two-thirds of the class usually responded that there was no answer. I shuddered to think that they really believed that! To think that in a time when we desperately needed an answer to the turmoil and wickedness of modern society, there was none? My God! I was quickly consoled with the truth that I knew was written in God's Word. He said that if those who are called by His name, Christian believers, who are called and committed to walk after the ways of Christ, would put themselves aside, decrease and allow the power within them to increase, and pray, something spectacular would begin to happen! A *"wave"* would begin! You know what a *"wave"* is? It's that amazing thing that happens at the football game. When one section stands up, all the people in that section raise their arms simultaneously, and then, as they begin to sit back down, the next section rises to their feet and does the same thing. The *"wave"* continues around the entire stadium! It's an exhilarating thing to watch, people synchronized together! That can happen outside of the stadium, too! Christian believers who humble themselves and pray could officially ignite it! The people around them, in their homes, in their schools, on their jobs, in their board rooms and conference meetings, in their churches, at their PTA meetings, on the playground, in the locker room, in the classroom, and yes, in their families—even at the family reunion—would be affected by those prayers! People would begin to turn from their wicked ways and seek God's face! That's what it's going to take to heal our land, our communities, our schools, our homes, and our families!

Although I know it would have a profound effect, I am not advocating that we break the rules that have been instituted with regards to prayer in schools. On the contrary, I don't believe that Christians ought to break the law. I am, however, saying that our public lives do reflect what is going on in our private lives. If fervent prayer is a part of our daily private lives, then the effects of it will be made manifest in our lives and in the lives of those around us!

"But thou, when thou prayest, enter into thy closet, and when thou hast
shut thy door, pray to thy Father which is in secret; and thy Father which
seeth in secret shall reward thee openly."
Matthew 6:6

As a child, I can recall hearing those senior mothers in the church getting up during Sunday morning worship service and telling the congregation with fervor that *"prayer changes things!"* I had no earthly idea just how true that was! It would take years of pain and suffering and eventual deliverance from that pain and suffering for me to really understand for myself! Prayer **does** change things, especially when the praying is done by one who has a heart that is submitted to God! The Bible tells us that the prayers of the righteous have the capacity to move the heart of God. That tells me that the righteous men and women of God, in this millennium, need to get together and have a serious *"prayer meeting!"* If children are to be reclaimed by their fathers and mothers, and the senseless killing of our youth is to be stopped, some sincere, heartfelt, praying needs to get underway! If wayward husbands are to find their way home to the wives and children who need them, the wave needs to be ignited! If right relationships are to be mended between mothers and daughters, fathers and sons, and brothers and sisters, God's people must humble themselves, turn from their wicked ways, seek His face and *PRAY!* That is the answer!

I am not sure how many people actually observe the World Day of Prayer. For that matter, I don't know how many people even know what or when that is, until, of course, it is mentioned on the evening news. I do wonder what would happen if the world went on a prayer vigil to ignite change throughout the world, or even a community of people who desperately wanted to change their community! What about a family severely in need of healing? What if that family decided to pray and fast together in order to heal their own personal brokenness? What an awesome idea! Imagine husbands and wives, fighting to save their marriages, going before the throne of grace together—not in the presence of an anxious pastor or congregation or a marriage counselor—but before God, Himself, the Healer of brokenness! What about brothers and sisters, who, instead of airing their dirty laundry on national television, decide to get together and pray, with sincere hearts, to God, who is able to heal the pain of thoughts, words and deeds used to hurt each other? Oh, this is bigger than a wave! I'm talking *mega-tidal wave!* You know, something nearly as unimaginable as the one caused by the meteor and depicted in the box office hit, *"Deep Impact!"* That is what would happen when the righteous get together and pray!

In Matthew 21:22, Jesus said *"And all things, whatsoever ye shall ask in prayer, believing, ye shall receive."* Just prior to having spoken these prolific words, Jesus shared with his disciples the principle of faith associated with the parable of the fig tree. *"If you have faith and doubt not,"* the Master said, *"you shall not only do this which is done to the fig tree, but you will have the power to say to this mountain, be thou removed, and be thou cast into the sea, and it shall be done."* Wow! What mountains in our lives reach higher than those we can see with our natural eye? What issues in our lives surpass Geronimo's mountain or Mount Everest? When I think about it on that level, our problems are like molehills. Some things we think are too painful to even think about are, by comparison, like huge sand dunes in the desert to us, but if looked at realistically, they are more like anthills in the back yard! If we have faith and doubt not, we can tell the mountains in our lives to move and it will be done! How do we do it? His answer: ask in prayer, believe it and you shall receive it. There is, however, a simple stipulation: *We must abide in Him and His word must abide in us!*

I was forced to grow up without my biological mother in my life. That catastrophic night in which my mother died became a mountain in my life. I underwent puberty and adolescence in a house where I was sexually molested for seven years. Another mountain. A pretty big one! When I went to my aunt, who had become my *"mom"* after my three brothers and I were orphaned, to get her help in stopping the abuse, she couldn't handle it. Instead of coming to my rescue, her inner pain was turned outward and more abuse was shoveled in my direction. The guilt within me was nourished, growing and developing into another mountain! In an attempt to find love in a life void of that emotion, I reached out to the arms of another adolescent, who was just as ignorant about real love as I was. In a desperate search to fill the raging void in my youth, I made some mistakes which left me filled with guilt and anguish and yes, another mountain in my life. Even as an adult, I made some very poor choices and ended up in a loveless marriage as a battered wife. Just when I thought the mountains were already closing in on me, another one popped up into view. Surrounded by towering hills on every side, I found myself in a deep valley, at times, wondering if I would have been better off dead! I can't prove it, but the words the of the Twenty-third Psalm must have been being spoken in my behalf, somewhere by someone whose heart was humbly bowed before the Lord. I know this because while I was walking in the valley of the shadow of death, God was with me! His rod and His staff gave comfort to me in many dark hours. Even when my carnal mind wanted to go otherwise, God, Himself, led me in the path of righteousness for His name's sake. At times, I realize, He had prepared a table before me in the presence of my enemies, and still His holy anointing rested upon me, filling my cup to overflowing!

I am convinced that if it had not been for the Lord on my side, I would not even be here right now! I can truly say that I owe Him my life! That is the reason that I have responded to His call upon it by openly sharing and making available the details of my experience with tragedy and pain, healing and deliverance, with people all over the world! It is the least that I can do to honor Him!

"Praise ye the LORD. I will praise the LORD with my whole heart,
in the assembly of the upright, and in the congregation."

Psalms 111:1

"I've done everything I could to teach my son right from wrong and still, he won't do right!"

I listened to my exasperated friend exclaim as we sat on the sofa one evening when she stopped by, unexpectedly.

"I just don't know what to do," Rhonda sighed. Her son, Terrance had been once again incarcerated. Another case of, according to him, his being at the wrong place at the wrong time. Rhonda had received her oldest son's phone call from the city jail in the wee hours of the morning.

"Well," I began, not quite sure what she wanted to hear me say, *"Sometimes, I guess, you have to wait for them to grow out of these episodes."* I thought about my youngest brother, Ronnie, who was in jail at that very moment . . . again.

"I'm just tired of it," she said. *"Some people say that no matter how well you raise your kids, they can still go wrong. I guess that's what happened to Terrance."* She seemed to console herself with that statement.

Inside my head, my thoughts began to churn. I, too, had heard that rationale for kids who went seemingly *"bad"* even though they had been reared in the *"best"* homes. It was societal influences, folks would say, or peer pressure. The latter seemed to get the greatest credit for those who had chosen to take the road most traveled. I listened to my friend make the same assumption, but something within would not let me go along with it wholeheartedly. Many parents had given their children what they considered to be the *"best"* of everything. They had purchased for them the *best* brand-named clothing, sent them to the *best* schools, surprised them with the *best* Christmas gifts, let them grow up in the *best* neighborhoods, and always saw to it that their children had the *best* life had to offer! What would prompt a child who had been so well provided for to stray from the path their loving parents had so carefully mapped out for them?

Before I could consider what Rhonda's answer would be, I heard myself say, *"I know you gave him what you thought was best for him, but can I ask you something without offending you?"*

"What?" she asked.

It was too late to reconsider, so I just went ahead. *"In all of your giving, did you ever try to give him Jesus?"*

At once offended, she sat straight up on the sofa and glared at me. *"What do you mean by that?"*

Quickly, I tried to soften the blow of what I had said. *"I'm not saying you didn't take him to Sunday School or to church when he was growing up,"* I explained. *"What I'm asking is did you show Christ to him in your lifestyle?"*

She looked down and studied her hands in her lap as if they belonged to someone else. The room became uncomfortably silent.

"Rhonda?"

She sighed again. *"I know what you mean."* Her voice was almost inaudible.

She didn't have to say anything. At once, I knew that I had spoken to the heart of the matter.

What I said to my friend was not a criticism of her or of anything she had tried to do in raising her son in the single-parent home she had maintained for him. I knew that she had done what she thought was best for him. From my own single-parenting experience, and in trying to care for and nurture my son, Tjai, I had met with the same challenges that faced every other young woman forced to do it alone. I knew, too well, how difficult it could be to be at home, giving your child the benefit of your time, when you were working two or more jobs, trying to provide a roof over his head and clothes on his back.

Many people had gone through the same thing I had. I knew that. Rhonda had been no different. She had tried to raise Terrance in a shadow created by his father's absence. Sometimes, she had had to work around the clock and many times, he had been left in his grandmother's feeble care. Rhonda had done the best she could with what she had.

When I asked her if she had shown Terrance Christ in her own lifestyle, I was primarily referring to the time she had spent with him. Had he seen her on bended knees, asking God for strength to be the best mother she could possibly be? Had she taken the time to teach him to say his prayers and to seek to know God for himself? Had she taken him to Sunday School and to church, instead of sending him or dropping him off? Had she been abstinent, to his knowledge, or had his young eyes seen an array of faceless strangers pass in and out of her door? Had he heard words escape her lips that God, Himself, would not be pleased with? Had her *"walk"* and her *"talk"* been the same? I didn't go into that kind of detail with her, but the look in her eyes told me that she had been convicted.

My friend and I belonged to a very unique, yet common, association of women who, for some reason or other, had found themselves raising sons and daughters alone. We had tried to be both mother and father to our children, desperately attempting to accomplish an impossible task! While we could be wonderful mothers, we could not remotely begin to fill the empty masculine void in our children's lives. I began to face that fact when I was trying to teach Tjai, at the age of two, why men and boys stood up to use the bathroom, while women, girls, and yes, mommies, too, sat down on the toilet seat. Although it was a challenge to tell him *how* to do it, I incurred a great deal more difficulty in explaining to him *why* he was supposed to do it that way.

The subject became a little more complicated when he came home from preschool, at the age of three-and-a-half, visibly upset that I had not told him that I was a *"girl."*

My eyebrows raised, I smiled, *"What did you think I was?"*

In a small, sweet voice, and tears in his eyes, he innocently declared, *"A mom."*

I took my little one in my arms. *"But moms are girls, too,"* I said, trying not to laugh.

That was the beginning of a new reality for me. For the first time, I realized that I was a divorced, single mother of a male child. Since his father had very little contact with him over the first seven years of his life, I was wholly responsible for the man that was developing out of that little boy. Before Derrick had entered our lives, I had to teach him the difference in right and wrong. I was the one who had to help him to develop a positive self-concept. The seeds I sewed into his life would determine his maturity, spirituality, credibility, compassion, self-esteem, and nature. How he treated other people was largely determined by the values I instilled in him. I was made immediately aware that the responsibility was innately mine and I knew that God would hold me accountable for how my son grew up!

At first, I was a little overwhelmed! After all, look how badly I had messed up my own life! There I was, in Los Angeles, California, alone and away from my family who were still on the other side of the country! I was struggling to pay more rent than my two-bedroom apartment in Hawthorne was worth. I was working two, and sometimes three, jobs in order to take care of the two of us. On weekends, I performed in various clubs in the Los Angeles, and Manhattan Beach areas. On Sundays, I played piano at a United Methodist Church in the vicinity. I had been maintaining an intimate relationship with a worldly young man who frowned every time I suggested that he accompany Tjai and I to church. I knew that this man was not right for me, but like many women who are desperately looking for *"Mr. Right,"* I felt that even though he was not a Christian, he was a *"good"* man and, just maybe, I could change him. Oh, I eventually woke up from that delusion, but it took a while. Today, I realize that if I had really trusted God while I was in the *"wilderness,"* I would not have had to stay there as long as I did, not that I was bent on taking the scenic route. On the contrary, I had no real desire to wander around as aimlessly as I did. In retrospect, I admit that it was the lack of focus on my part, but thank God for my deliverance!

"And thou shalt remember all the way which the LORD thy God led thee
these forty years in the wilderness, to humble thee, and to prove thee,
to know what was in thine heart, whether thou wouldest
keep his commandments, or no."

Deuteronomy 8:2

In my writing, I had shared with readers the day that I had no choice other than to live my life to the glory of God. The decision I made to walk after the example of Christ was a conscientious one. My life and the life of my adolescent son depended up on it! I am thankful that God was still there for me, even after I came out of my wilderness experience. Although I had not wandered about as long as the children of Israel, I had meandered long enough to realize that my life had been preserved for some greater purpose, some greater good. Many people are still wandering, trying to find meaning in their earthly existence. Every day, as they ramble, Satan shows up, to constantly remind them of the past they have tried to escape, the pain they have experienced, and the people who have hurt them. That's what he does best.

Satan knows that to remind us of our pain at every opportunity ascertains that we will always be bound by it. The remembrance of it keeps us in the wilderness. In the wilderness, human beings have a tendency to forget about God, His goodness and mercy. They begin to murmur against Him. Consider the children of Israel. Even after they had witnessed God's awesome power at the parting of the Red Sea, they had the audacity to doubt His ability to bring them out of the wilderness into the promised land overflowing with milk and honey! So what did they do? They murmured and complained that they would have been better off back in Egypt, enslaved by Pharaoh! They lost their faith in God. As a result, they spent forty years wandering around in the wilderness! Some never made it out, but died there! Some of those who were lost were entire families! They never made it to the Promised Land. No doubt, among them were husbands and wives, single mothers who had possibly lost their husbands due to conditions in Egypt, orphaned children, and broken families in the entourage.

Even today, many people are still wandering around in their own wilderness. Many are women who are in the same position as Rhonda, trying to raise their children alone. Some are former children from broken homes, who are now adults, trying to make some sense out of senseless situations. Others are former victims of childhood abuse trapped in a vicious cycle in which they have now become the abusers. Their wilderness is massive, full of confusion and void of understanding. They are looking for an answer. The answer is Christ! He is our way out of the wilderness! To know Him is to know the truth and no longer be deceived by Satan! To walk in His way is to come out of the darkness and into the light!

Proverbs 3:5 says *"Trust in the LORD with all thine heart; and lean not unto thine own understanding."* No matter what has happened to you in your lifetime, you must be confident that it does not have to destroy you! It does not have to set precedence for every relationship you encounter for the rest of your life. One reason that people have difficulty in relating to others in their lives is because of the past relationships they have experienced. Some women don't know how to properly relate to their husbands as a result of improper relationships they had with their own fathers. Some men don't know how to be good husbands because of the absence of good male role models in their childhood. Many marriages fail because neither party really understands their roles, rights and responsibilities in the relationship. Many people do not even know that the duties of the married state are contained in the New Testament Scriptures! A good pastor will counsel the perspective bride and groom and help them to understand what God expects from them as a husband and wife before they even consider getting married. It's sad to say, but many enter into the holy state of matrimony with unrealistic expectations. They end up in unhappy marriages, separations or eventual divorces—possibly preventable, had they first believed what God had to say about it and were able to get a clear understanding.

When Derrick and I got married, I was on the brink of spiritual maturity, but still a little *"wet"* behind the ears. I know this is true because even though our pastor at the time, Rev. Thompson, provided us marital counseling and discussed the duties of the married state with us in detail, I still had absolutely no intention on *"obeying"* my husband!

I had already surmised that phrase had been slipped into the nuptials by some man who considered the male sex superior and wanted to exert his authority over his female counterpart. You know, surely you've heard this before! Anyway, I nodded in faux agreement as Pastor Thompson sat across from Derrick and I in his living room and carefully explained the passage of scripture to us.

Having known me longer than I had known my husband-to-be, my pastor, mentor and friend asked with a sly smile on his face, *"Are you going to be able to do that?"*

"Uh-huh," I said, a little apprehensively.

"Nesi?" he said, tilting his head to one side. *"Are you really going to be able to do that?"*

Pastor Thompson knew that I had been a single mother and head of my own household for the past seven years. He knew how strong-willed and determined I was, too.

"I can do it," I said, although I was not fully convinced that I could.

The subject came up again, of course, during our wedding. Just prior to my bridal march, it had been raining cats and dogs outside the church! When the sun popped out, an awe spread across the church! Personally, I felt that it was God's blessings on our nuptials. As we stood before the crowded congregation on the fourth Sunday in November, 1992, Pastor Thompson led Derrick and I in our marriage vows. *"Repeat after me,"* he said. The smile on his face was nearly as bright as the sun that had suddenly began to shine and peer through the window as I walked slowly up the aisle.

"I, Denise Clayton Elder," he said.

"I, Denise Clayton Elder," I repeated, audibly.

"Take you, Derrick Dewayne Bryant."

"Take you, Derrick Dewayne Bryant," I said, looking up at Derrick. He was smiling and looking even more handsome than ever in his black tuxedo with the gold lame tie and cummerbund.

"To be my lawfully, wedded husband," Reverend Thompson continued.

I went on, repeating the words I heard him speaking, verbatim, until that *"obey"* thing surfaced.

"To honor and obey," Reverend Thompson said.

I fell silent.

He waited.

Derrick squeezed my hands in his.

"To honor and obey," he repeated, an amusing smile forming at the corners of his mouth.

"Ah . . ." I began, opening my mouth.

"Are you going to say it?" Reverend Thompson whispered, still smiling.

"What was it again?" I whispered.

Once again, Derrick squeezed my hand.

"To honor and obey," he repeated a third time.

I mumbled something that sounded like *"honor and obey,"* but between the four of us at the altar, Reverend Thompson, Derrick, me, and Jesus, we *all* knew that I had *not* consented to obey anyone!

By the time our first anniversary had rolled around, in the midst of our very first *"heated"* discussion, my husband confessed that he realized why I had not said those words during our marriage ceremony.

"Why?" I asked, whirling around to face him, with my hands on my hips.

"Because you knew you couldn't do it!" he yelled. With that, he turned and stormed out of the house! As much as I hated to admit it, he had spoken the truth. I never said that I would obey my husband. As I began to grow in the Word, however, and became more submitted to God, I found it easier to do so. It was as simple as this: if a woman is submitted to God, she will be submitted to her husband because God said for her to do it. I shared this insight with the women of Antioch at their 1999 women's retreat. Since then, I have shared it with many men and women across the country.

Wives, submit yourselves unto your own husbands, as unto the Lord.
Ephesians 5:22

Sometimes, when women hear that they are commanded by God to submit themselves to their own husbands, they become offended—particularly if they are married to men who do not have a real relationship with God themselves! A woman in Texas once confessed to me that she simply could *not* see herself being submissive to her husband. *"He is not saved,"* she cried! Not only that, he often made it difficult for her to attend church on a regular basis, starting silly arguments when she was preparing to leave for worship service. How could she submit herself to someone like that? How could she yield her own will to that of someone who seemed disinterested in getting to know Jesus for himself?

Earlier that day, I had shared with this woman and numerous others that I, personally, did not feel comfortable trusting a man who did not know the Lord. At the end of the final conference session, everyone was leaving to return to their respective homes. The woman, Etta, stopped me as I was about to leave the conference room. Somewhat despairingly, she told me that she had been having difficulties in her marriage. When I shared my views about this sensitive issue, she told me that she understood what I meant. In fact, she said that she felt the exact same way! The man she had married seldom attended church. How could she trust him to make decisions about issues that would affect them both? She deeply desired for her husband, as the Scriptures said, to seek God *first*. The fact that he failed to seek Him at all had been a great source of frustration to her.

Etta's situation was one that is shared by many women. Her concern was one that I have had myself. When I was married to Tjai's father, it was the primary reason that I knew he was the **wrong** man for me! I was grateful to the Lord that He had put Derrick in my life. He was a good man. Because he was willing to work with God, God could work with him! Because I knew this, I could trust him to make decisions for our family. It was easy for me to submit to him because I believed that he was submitted to God!

Some time ago, my husband came home from the fire station and told me that when he went in to work the day before, he had several messages from a woman he did not know. Before he could make any sense of the messages, this strange woman called him during his shift. Derrick told me that the woman had called him and said that she had recently read **Opening the Door.** She said that she had read what I had said about him being a wonderful man and she called him to ask him if he was really as wonderful as I had described him to be in my book! At first, he said, he was shocked to get such a strange phone call, but then, as she went on, he realized that she was actually interested in finding out how wonderful he was *"for herself!"* He said that he told her that he thought it was very improper for her to track him down after having read about him in his wife's book. Obviously, he said, she knew that he was married—to me! He also said that he told her that she should not call him anymore.

As I had listened to him, I leaned against the doorway in our bedroom and smiled.

"What are you smiling about?" he asked.

"Oh, I was just thinking," I said. *"I was thinking about how slick and conniving Satan is!"*

He looked puzzled, *"What do you mean?"*

"I mean, he is so slick and conniving, and so low-down that he wants to see if what I said about you is really true! If some woman calls you to see if you are as loving, committed and devoted to me as I said that you are, and you take the

bait and become involved with her, then Satan wins because he will have made a liar out of you AND me!" I explained.

"Humm . . . That's true" he said nodding his head.

"But you know what?"

"What's that?" he asked.

"He's a liar and the truth is not in him! Not now! Not ever! Because, first of all, I know that you love God. I also know that you love me and I know that you are devoted to me and the kids!"

"Uh, uh, uh," he mumbled.

"So if she calls you again, tell her something for me," I said. *"Tell her to be sure and read my next book, because she'll be in that one!"*

At that he laughed. Many years later, I discovered the reason why.

It has taken me fifty-one years to actually believe that the only way to truly please God is to live according to His Word. I am thoroughly convinced that men and women who really want to fulfill their purpose in life must live those lives according to the Word of God! It is the only way that marriages and other relationships will be successful, the only way lives will be rewarding, and the only means by which children's live will be righteous! The woman who seeks to know her purpose in God will be a good wife and mother, a successful woman, a virtuous woman! In Proverbs 31, there is a wonderful description of a woman who lives according to the heart of God! Even if she has suffered abuse and neglect as a child, she can *still* fulfill her purpose in the Lord! Even if she has been promiscuous in her past or has had unwanted pregnancies or abortions, she can *still* become a virtuous woman! Even if she has been in abusive relationships in the past, she is *still* beloved of God. Even if she has suffered with poor self-esteem or a negative self-concept, she can *still* rise out of the ashes and become a woman after God's own heart! If she learns to fear the Lord, she will be praised! God will give her a husband who will love and cherish her always! Her children will rise up and call her blessed! It is the reward of virtue! And *that* is the Word of God!

> *"Who can find a virtuous woman? for her price is far above rubies."*
> ***Proverbs 31:10***

It seems that we have so many issues in our lives, we can hardly stand up straight beneath the weight of them. We are suffering from past hurts that seem to hold us hostage throughout our lives. The amazing thing is that most people live their entire lives in pain. Someone hurt them a long time ago. They dealt with the injury the best way they knew how—either by giving somebody a piece of their mind, by attempting to get even, or by ignoring the hurt, hoping that it would eventually go away. The first method usually leaves people with a temporary feeling of satisfaction. They *"got it off their chest,"* or so they thought. Sadly, when you give someone a *piece* of your mind, you actually sacrifice your *peace* of mind. The anger and animosity is replaced by guilt at having spoken words you can never recapture! That's the *thing* about words; once they are spoken, they cannot be taken back! As a result, feelings are injured, relationships are severed, and ties are broken.

Getting even is a futile attempt to obtain reparation. First, and foremost, if you know anything at all about the Word of God, you know that vengeance is not yours to seek! It belongs to Him! When you try to get even, you try to take care of God's business. News flash: He doesn't need your assistance! Besides, you never really get even with anyone. If you do something to someone in retaliation for what they have done to you, you sink to the same level they were on when they hurt you. You don't have to be a rocket scientist to figure out that two *wrongs* do not make a *right!* There is *no* getting even! There is only getting ugly—by allowing yourself to wallow in sin!

The third strategy is trying to *ignore* the hurt. The tiny seed begins to grow, deep inside you, fed by the enemies' helpful reminders of the initial offense. Satan loves to remind us what someone has done to us. It keeps the fire of resentment burning! In fact, it will burn for so long, with flames that leap so high that it will consume anything that comes near it! Satan fans that fire with subtle reminders. He constantly puts that incident on your mind. He wants you to remember it always, to ponder it often. Oh he jumps with glee when you go so far as to talk about it—verbalizing your animosity towards the person who hurt you. He knows that the more you talk about what someone did to you, the more reminded you are. After all, *when you speak aloud, not only are you speaking, but you are also listening to yourself!* The Bible tells us that faith comes by hearing and hearing by the Word of God. Well, what do you think happens when you keep hearing about your hurt, your abuse, your injury, your bitterness, your hatred, your shortcomings, your failures or your fears? Your faith is channeled in the direction of that which you have spoken over yourself—the things you have been saying *AND* hearing yourself say!

You must believe that there is a way to deal with the hurt. It is not a secret, although it may seem to be because many people have yet to discover it! God has already provided the answer for any situation we could ever encounter in life. He has a word for you, your life, your situation, whatever it may be! He has given us the means of dealing with the things that hurt us in our lives. At the root of our pain is one very simple cause—sin. It is the cause that my father murdered my mother. It possessed his life. He was under the auspices of sin and did not even realize it. He did not live long enough to find it out! The devil tricked him, got him to do his dirty work, and then took him right on out of existence before he even knew what hit him! Sin caused my adoptive, father, Ben, to sexually molest me. He had a very real problem that he never dealt with. I don't know when it began, but it was most likely before I was even born. He could have tried to ignore it, thinking that the problem would either correct itself or go away. It did neither! Sin doesn't give up its residence without a fight! Ben allowed sin to possess him and provoke him to trespass against God *AND* me!

Sin has caused many to turn away from the plan that God has had for His children's lives. The effect is mind-boggling! On one hand, it makes one person do *something* to hurt another person. Now, the person who did that *something* has sinned. Do you know that Satan is not satisfied until, as a result, the person who has been hurt commits a sin, too? The man, woman, boy or girl who has been hurt, if they are not careful, will allow the sin that has been committed against them to cause them to sin, as well! The only way to keep this from happening is for the person who has been sinned upon is to do what the Word of God says—*FORGIVE!* More times than not, it is not easy to forgive the person who has trespassed against you. As a matter of fact, Satan has a way of convincing you that you *can't* forgive others for what they have done to you! What a liar he is! He would actually have you to think that you would be a fool to forgive someone for hurting you! Don't forget that he **is** a liar, has **always been** a liar, and will **always be** a liar! In actuality, you are a fool *not* to forgive someone for hurting you!

I have heard people say this so many times: *"I don't see how you could forgive your dad for molesting you! I couldn't do it!"* That is a lie from the pits of hell! You *can* do it! You *must* do it!

Unforgiveness will keep you from the blessings of God! It will cause your prayers to fall on deaf ears! God honors the prayers of the righteous! How righteous do you think you are if you are committing the sin of unforgiveness? Don't you want God to hear you when you call upon Him? When I recall those days that I lived in Los Angeles, wandering around, it seems, trying to find my purpose in life, I realize that I spent a lot of time praying futile prayers! I was praying for God to give me some direction, to show me which way to go and what steps to take. Many nights, I spent on my knees, on the side of the bed, while my toddler son, Tjai, lay snoring on his pillow. I prayed long and hard for an answer, but I did not get one—not until I forgave those who had hurt me in my life! If I had known then, what I know now, I would have done it a long time ago! I forced myself to wait *thirty-six years* to find out the truth of the matter!

If you want God to hear you, you must become His righteousness! I love what the Apostle Paul said in the tenth chapter of Romans. *"Brethren, my heart's desire and prayer to God for Israel is, that they might be saved. For I bear them record that they have a zeal of God, but not according to knowledge. For they being ignorant of God's righteousness, and going about to establish their own righteousness, have not submitted themselves unto the righteousness of God. For Christ is the end of the law for righteousness to everyone that believeth."* Can you understand what he is saying? His desire is that we all are saved, not just to have a way with words, but to have knowledge and understanding of *The Word!* Those who are without knowledge and understanding of the Word of God are ignorant of *His* righteousness! Instead, the Apostle says, they go around trying to convince themselves and others of their own righteousness! When they pray, God doesn't hear them, and He does not honor their prayer! They have not submitted themselves to God's righteousness!

He further goes on to say. *"That if thou shalt confess with thy mouth the Lord Jesus, and shalt believe in thine heart that God hath raised him from the dead, thou shalt be saved."* How? *"For with the heart,"* Paul says, *"man believeth unto righteousness; and with the mouth confession is made unto salvation."* Confession? What does that mean? It means that you admit that you have been living the life of a sinner and verbally confess your sins before God! It means confessing that you believe in the Lord, Jesus Christ as your Savior! You earnestly believe that He is the Son of God, who came into the world to die for your sins! He was crucified, died and buried, but He rose again, on the third day, with all power! That is the confession through which men are saved! Confession is made unto righteousness! God's righteousness! When you are saved, you put on the righteousness of God! No more bondage! No more secrets! No more sin! Righteousness!

That is some fantastic news! In fact, it is exhilarating! What is even more exciting is what Paul says in the eleventh verse: *"For the scripture saith, Whosoever believeth on him shall not be ashamed."* No more shame? No more shame for having been abused, abandoned or neglected? No more shame for having surrendered your virginity as a teenager? No more shame for having had an abortion? No more shame for having run away from home and devastated your family? No more shame for having mistreated your children? No more shame for having lied to and cheated on your spouse? No more shame for having lied or stolen? No more shame? That is some wonderful news—not for Satan, of course—but for you and me! Satan will not be very happy at all about your finding this out! It was his design to keep the keys to your deliverance hidden from you long enough to kill you dead! He wanted to keep you in the dark long enough for you to fall into a hole and die! It was his idea to keep you wallowing in a sea of regret and shame! But I will say it again—He is a *liar!*

> *"He was a murderer from the beginning, and abode not in the truth, because there is no truth in him. When he speaketh a lie, he speaketh of his own: for he is a liar, and the father of it."*

> *John 8:44b*

EIGHT

WE MUST KNOW, beyond a shadow of a doubt, that Satan's main and primary objective is to destroy us! From the very beginning, he set out to destroy man, God's greatest creation, in order that he might make mockery of the Creator, God Himself! Satan does not care about man! In his eyes, man is nothing, a nuisance, not worth time or effort and certainly not deserving of the world God gave to him. That is why the devil appeared to Eve in the Garden! He came to steal from mankind the world over which he had been given dominion! He came to kill mankind, eternally separating him from God! He intends to destroy the creation that was *good and very good* in the sight of God Almighty! He was not trying to give anything to Adam and Eve! Why would he?

He was still seething over being cast out of his eternal home in Heaven! He was still incensed over being ejected from his place among the heavenly hosts! He was furious that God would throw him out of Heaven and down to the pit of hell and then have the audacity to set a man up in paradise! He was jealous! Enraged! Immediately, he set out to get even! He is *still* trying to get even today! He doesn't just want to see us hurt; he wants to see us destroyed! In fact, he doesn't just want to see us destroyed, he wants to see us dead! Satan's goal is to sever the ties between us and God because if he can keep us separated from our Father, he can get us on *his* turf and have the home court advantage over us!

Just look at the prodigal son! When he left home, away from the love and care of his father, he found himself actually slipping and sliding away from life. The good life, a life of abundance and plenty, quickly became a fading memory for him as he wallowed in sin and degradation. From the dirt and grime of the pig pen, it became more and more difficult to remember how well he had lived when he was at home with his daddy. Because he allowed Satan to entice him to rebel and demand his share of his inheritance, his vision was clouded. Like many others have done since, he thought the grass was greener on the other side of the fence. Well, you know how Satan is, don't you? He knows how to dress up a lie! Oh yes! He can make what you don't have look fabulous, compared to what you already have!

Many young people have left the love and security of home to become runaways, living on the streets of urban cities, selling their bodies to survive and watching their lives go up in the effervescent smoke of a crack pipe! They have been tricked, by the wicked one into believing that their parents are the evil ones! They believe that their parents or guardians are unreasonable for demanding that they be respectful and abide by rules as absurd as coming home at a decent hour! Some believe in their own righteousness and totally disregard the authority of their parents! Most of these young people do not even know what the word *authority* means!

> *"For they being ignorant of God's righteousness, and*
> *going about to establish their own righteousness, have not*
> *submitted themselves unto the righteousness of God."*

> *Romans 10:3*

A short time ago, there was a notion up for discussion regarding whether or not parents should be held accountable for the crimes committed by their children. The idea was being entertained as a means of curtailing the impending wave of violence committed by youths. Opponents of the idea argued that no matter what a parent did or how well they raised their child, other pressures could influence adolescents, teens and young adults to behave ruthlessly and even, in some cases, commit murder! I discussed this with a group of young people and of course, many of them agreed that, sometimes, it didn't matter what a parent did, if a child wanted to misbehave, he would. One young lady admitted that she had been taught the difference between right and wrong, but still knowingly chose to do things of which she knew her parents would disapprove. Another young man said that he, too, knew what was right, but peer pressure was so strong that he could be persuaded to do otherwise, at times.

Derrick once said this about peer pressure: *"Peer pressure has little affect on young people if they fear the reprimand of their parents more than the ridicule of their peers."* I thought that was a profound thought! If young people were more worried about the consequences they would have to face with their parents than about what their peers thought about them, they would be less inclined to do wrong. I don't know, but somehow, the idea that *"If I do that, my mom and dad are going to kill me!"* is a bit more provocative than *"Latasha won't ever speak to me again if I don't!"* Why don't young people think like that today?

The Word of God tells parents to raise their children up in the fear and the admonition of the Lord. It is **not** a suggestion that parents do this, it is a command! I always told Tjai that if I allowed him to do whatever he wanted to do, God would hold me personally responsible for it! As his mother, I had been ordered by God to teach him the ways of Christ, to show him, by example, the way in which he should go, to demonstrate to him the blessings of God that were promised to those who are obedient to His Word. It was an important part of being a parent! It still is! How can I tell my children to do what is right unless they see me doing what is right? How can I tell them to do what I say, if they see that what I do is something to the contrary? I must lead by example!

Families, fathers, mothers, children, brothers, and sisters are under attack! We are involved in a serious warfare and it's really incredible that so many are walking around unaware of it! We have been told of our adversary, the devil, Satan himself *"as a roaring lion, walketh about, seeking whom he may devour."* It is true! Satan is turning young people against God, against their parents, against each other, and against themselves! He has set husbands and wives against each other, fathers and sons against each other and mothers and daughters at odds with one another! And my God, especially if they are unsaved, they can't even see what is really going on! He proficiently blinds the eyes of those who do not believe. According to John 12:40, *"He hath blinded their eyes, and hardened their heart; that they should not see with their eyes, nor understand with their hearts, and be converted, and I should heal them."* If he can keep men separated from God, in darkness, he can keep them from becoming heads of their households! They won't even realize their place in God or in their home! They probably won't even *be* at home! The woman who is separated from God does not know how to love her husband or her children as God intended! She cannot even see clearly enough to know that if she submits herself to the authority of God in her life, she can easily submit herself to her husband! The young man who walks in darkness does not realize that to rebel against his father or his mother is to rebel against the authority they have been given by God, and as a result, he rebels against God, destroys his promise of long life and guarantees his eternal home in hell! A young woman who attempts to live her life without Christ finds herself constantly yearning, yet never satisfying, the tremendous void she feels within. She tries to fill it by falling in and out of bad relationships, looking for the godly relationship that her spirit craves! She becomes hurt, damaged and broken. They are all broken. Broken families are full of broken people!

Sadly, these broken families of broken people generate broken extended families and the cycle goes on and on! Now we have communities of broken families and broken extended families. We have children from broken families and broken homes going to school and lashing out at whomever enters their paths—namely teachers and other authority figures. They don't respond well to authority because they have not been taught to do so at home. As I said, many don't even know what the word—*authority*—means! The children *"hook up"* with other children from broken homes and the situation goes from bad to worse!

When I was in school, no one I knew wanted the teacher to call their mother, father, or summon their parent to school, but many young people today could care less if a teacher or administrator threatens to contact their parents to discuss or resolve their behavior problem. Some don't respect their parents anyway and have no fear of anything their parents would do to them. Some truly believe that their parents don't care about them or whatever they do, so they think the parent probably won't show up anyway! Another group feels that their parents will uphold anything they do, because as long as the child is not at home bothering them, they are content. Still another group feels that their parents have no right to tell them what to do based upon their own lifestyles! Some of those students are quick to tell you that they hardly ever see their mother or father, much less talk to them. I have had more than one student to confess that they are allowed to *"get high"* or drink liquor, many, right at home *with* their parents!

This is not some kind of *"new morality"* as some have argued. There is, in fact, nothing new under the sun! Alcoholism, drug abuse, prostitution, promiscuity, juvenile delinquency, fornication, violence, homosexuality, or perverse behavior, are *not* new trends! Even in the Old Testament, Genesis13:13 tells us that *"the men of Sodom were wicked and sinners before the LORD exceedingly."* Even after the cities of Sodom and Gomorrah were destroyed by fire, the people continued to corrupt themselves and once again, became a crooked and perverse generation (Deuteronomy 32:5). Over in the New

Testament, Jesus, Himself, referred to the people of His day as a *wicked and perverse generation!* I dread to imagine what God must be thinking about us today!

Early one morning, during my daily Bible reading, I ran across a powerful message in the Apostle Paul's first letter to the Romans. In this epistle, Paul discussed the issue of ungodliness and unrighteousness. I was amazed that the words he wrote to the people of the church in Rome were so appropriate to the situation which exists in our world today! The Apostle said that even though people knew God, they did not glorify him as God! In other words, they knew who He was, but they didn't behave towards Him as though they truly believed who He was! Isn't that what people do today? Songstress Eryka Badu sings these words in a song entitled, *On and On: "Some people don't believe in God, but they fear him just the same."* The first time I heard it, I thought, if they really feared God, they **would** believe in Him. An African proverb states that *"He who fears something gives it power over him."* People don't fear God as they ought to. If they did, more of them would believe in Him!

Those people in Rome must not have really known God. If they had, they would not have *"changed the glory of the incorruptible God into an image made like to corruptible man, and to birds, and four-footed beasts, and creeping things."* They would not have worshipped animals and their images! They would not have dishonored their own bodies, or changed the truth of God into a lie, and worshipped and served the creature more than the Creator! Would they?

Paul goes on to say that because the people did these things, God gave them up unto vile affections. Women began to do those things that were against their nature, things that were contrary to the will of God, things that were perverse. Men and women began to act contrarily as depicted in the Scriptures which say that "*. . . the natural use of the woman, burned in their lust one toward another; men with men working that which is unseemly, and receiving in themselves that recompense of their error which was meet." (Romans 1:27)* In other words, they became perverse! They began to behave in a manner that was contrary to their very nature! They did not recognize God as the supreme, divine authority in their lives! As a result, they willingly participated in unrighteousness, fornication, wickedness, covetousness, and maliciousness. Men and women were full of envy, murder, corruption, and deceit. They became gossipers, backbiters, and haters of God! They were despiteful, proud, boastful inventors of evil and disobedient to their parents! The Bible tells us that these people were *without* understanding. They willingly broke the covenant of God! They had no natural affection or godly love and showed no mercy to others. They *knew* the judgment of God, yet they purposefully and willingly committed acts that warranted death! What is even more incredible is the fact that they enjoyed doing it and reverenced others who did likewise!

In our modern society, mankind continues to break God's covenant on a daily basis! Both those who are in the world, as well as those who profess to know God, knowingly and willingly commit all manner of sin and wickedness each and every day! People who claim to love the Lord and are called, according to His divine purpose, at times, so closely resemble worldly folk that it is difficult to tell them apart! The brokenness of individual families and their members continuously spills over into the pews of houses of worship. Not only is the social structure of the family shattered—the church family also suffers. At the center of the despair, Satan rejoices! He jumps for joy each time a marriage or a family breaks up. He delights in our trouble and hopelessness. He wants nothing more than for us to believe that all hope is lost . . .

Where is God in the midst of the brokenness? He is right where He has always been, like the father of the prodigal son, at the edge of the road, watching and waiting for us to return to Him and be restored . . . made whole. Many are just like the prodigal son and have their entire life wandering as well, out there, out of the arc of safety provided us, vulnerable, susceptible to each and every attack of the enemy! Not only us, but our brothers, our sisters, our children, our husbands, wives, mothers and fathers! No one is exempt from the vicious attack! No one! How young or old you are has nothing to do with it. Satan desires to sift you as wheat—the new shoots as well as the aged, weather-beaten stalks alike!

When I was twelve years old, during a revival at my family church, I accepted Christ as my personal Savior and stepped out on God's Word. At the time, I didn't even know the real implication of my profession, but God heard me and throughout the years, allowed my salvation to be the anchor that kept me, despite the frequent attacks of the enemy. I have always said that Satan has been after me for a long time. I believe he put my name on his rolodex the same day that I gave my heart to the Lord. In fact, the names of every born again believer is there, too! Someone's wife's name is there. Satan has her number and uses her husband to call it frequently. Someone's mother's name is there. The enemy has enlisted the aid of her wayward son or runaway daughter to keep her up nights, her pillow wet with tears. Somebody's sister's name is there. Satan has called upon her addicted brother to yank at the strings of her heart in order to keep her down, and unable to fulfill the will of God in her life. Can you see it? If you have confessed Christ as Savior of your life, your name is there, too! Undoubtedly, Satan has some agents close by, working on what you think is your *"last nerve,"* trying to get you to just curse God so that you can die! He has your name and your number. If he can just get you to answer his call, he can get your name *out* of the Book of Life and onto his list of those who are forever cursed!

Because of Christ, we have been given the opportunity to not only have life, but to have life more abundantly! That means that husbands and wives can have strong, beautiful, loving relationships when Christ is in the mix! Men will love their wives as Christ loved the church. Wives, in turn, will honor their husbands and find it easy to submit to them because it is the commandment of God! Together, they demonstrate obedience to the Word. Their obedience moves the heart of God. As a result, He blesses them—abundantly! It's the principle of reciprocity. You're familiar with it—you do your part, God does His part! That's how it works!

Mothers, whose lives are committed to Christ, are able to demonstrate virtue to their daughters. They can teach their daughters how to be strong women of God, based upon their own testimony of faith! Proverbs 31 says that *"the children of the virtuous woman will rise up and call their mother blessed among women!"* Just the other day, I watched some adolescent children and preteens on a popular talk show admit that they had commonly referred to their mothers with derogatory terms. The children were bitter, angry and resentful. The mothers of those children sat on the stage, weeping as the talk show host described, one after another, numerous accounts of the outrageous behavior their children had exhibited. I could not help but look at the broken, sobbing women and wonder what kind of behavior *they* had demonstrated to their children. As I watched, I prayed that God would help me to live my life as a virtuous woman because I didn't want my children to ever look upon me with disdain. I never wanted my sons to look at me and see a hypocrite, a liar, a cheat, a backbiter, a gossiper, an idolater, a dishonorable woman! On the contrary, I wanted to be the kind of woman described in Proverbs 31. My heart's desire is that my sons will rise up and call me blessed! But I am wise enough to know that children, for the most part, are honest and they will call it like they see it. We just have to be careful about what we let them see! We cannot afford to say one thing and do another. We must not be double-minded, behaving one way in the presence of others and another within the comfort of our homes, in the presence of our families. In other words, we must let our feet walk the same walk that our mouths are talking!

"But be ye doers of the word, and not hearers
only, deceiving your own selves."

James 1:22

People do not always receive the truth well. In the words of youngsters I've associated with over the years, *"People just can't handle the truth!"* That is a pretty accurate statement. Most people can't really handle it! It is human nature to shift the blame for our circumstances onto someone else. This holds especially true in relationships! We are very quick to lay the fault for the failure of our relationships in the lap of the other party. When things fall apart and the relationship ends, we are usually the victim, having been wounded by the other person. Well, if everyone feels that way, exactly who is doing what to whom?

Once, I shared this concept with a large group of men and women to whom I had been speaking. *"It's always the other person's fault!"* I screamed, adamantly. This drew laughter from the crowd of people sitting in the large fellowship hall. *"You know it's true! You know you haven't done anything wrong! Don't you?"*

"Amen, Sister!" a young man shouted from the rear.

Again, the crowd burst into laughter.

I spoke to the poised group of people for about an hour about the importance of healing past wounds in order to begin anew. Some people had not been able to get over things that had happened in their pasts. As a result, their present relationships were very much in jeopardy! A young lady shared with me that she had been in and out of relationships, one after another, never being able to establish anything meaningful with anyone she met. She could not understand what was *"wrong with men these days!"* I smiled as I listened to her account of putting new males in her life on alert from *"jump street,"* as she put it.

"I just tell them up front," the young lady explained, *"I don't have time for no trifling man! If they want to mess around, I tell them not to even waste my time! They can just get to stepping!"*

Several young women seated on her row gave others in their vicinity *"high fives!"*

What, I wondered, had happened in the life of this attractive young woman, whom I later learned was a flight attendant, to cause her to *expect* every man that she encountered to be the type of man that messed around? It had become a self-fulfilling prophesy in her life, and she did not even realize it! As soon as she had made her spiel, almost immediately, the brother probably realized what her expectations of him were and set out to make *sure* that she was not disappointed! Before they even had the opportunity to get to know each other, she had spoken ill-fated words over their relationship, setting the wheels of doom into swift motion!

After I had listened to what she had to say, I opened my Bible to a familiar passage of Scripture found in Proverbs 18:21: *"Death and life are in the power of the tongue: and they that love it shall eat the fruit thereof.*" A hush went over the crowd. I looked up from my Bible that rested on the podium in front of me. *"So exactly what delicious morsels have you been serving up for yourself?"*

"My God!" the same young lady exclaimed.

We have the ability to speak into our lives evil or good, poverty or prosperity, sadness or joy, sorrow or hope, animosity or love! We can prepare a delicacy of love and fellowship or we can dish up a plate of hostility and resentment—it all depends on our appetite, or the desires of our spiritual palate! What do you have a taste for?

In my writing I didn't just share the details of meeting my husband. I talked about my having surrendered my life completely to the Lord and trusting Him to give me the husband that He had ordained for me. When I met Derrick, I wasn't certain that God had heard me clearly because, for one thing, the man did not always agree with me! The nerve of him, telling me *'no!'* I must admit that, at times, I had questioned God about what He had done. Hadn't he heard me correctly? I thought I had been very *specific* in my request . . . a man who would love me and Tjai, one whom I could share God with, one who would grow spiritually with me . . . someone I could trust and depend on . . . a man who had a heart after God's own! Wasn't that specific enough? Oh yes, I did ask that he be nice to look at, too! Well, I could tell from looking at him, that the latter requirement had been satisfied, but what about all of that other stuff?

After we had been married for a little while, I began to wonder if he was *really* the husband God had for me. Like I said, he wasn't afraid to tell me *'no'* when he felt like it. That was kind of difficult for me to accept. I was not used to a man telling me what to do. After all, I did not even say that I would *'obey'* him when we got married, right? Why should I have to do it then? I had not yet run across the Scriptures that commanded me to submit myself to my husband yet, so I was still a bit willful in that area. I began to seek God's will in my life and when I did that, He began to reveal to me, in no uncertain terms, what he expected of me! I began to speak the Word into my own life. I began to see myself as a woman after God's own heart that was deserving of the man I had petitioned God for. Funny, when I was putting in my request, I did not even consider whether or not I was ready for a man like that! Nevertheless, I began to speak those words into my own life, selecting items to go on my plate, those things that would satisfy my appetite. When I figured it out, I was careful about what I verbalized to the Lord. An adage says, *"Be careful what you ask for . . . you just might get it!"*

When Derrick and I were in the process of correcting our very *"flaky"* credit in order to qualify for a home loan, the enemy began to throw a lot of darts our way! It seemed that every time we turned around, some hidden blemish on our credit was popping up on our credit report! On more than one occasion, my usually confident husband began to *"speak"* his mind on the subject. He would be just about to say something like, *"If this keeps up, we're never going to-"*

"Stop!" I would yell, interrupting him. *"Don't you dare speak that over our lives!"* I was determined that we would not stop our progress with the words of our own testimony! *"We will get our house!"* I would say. *"We are going to be in our home for Christmas! We will spend the New Year in front of our own fireplace! We will!"*

Derrick got the message and changed his testimony to match mine. We agreed that, under no circumstances, would we allow the enemy to thwart the divine plan of God for our lives. He had already promised us our home! We chose to believe His report! We chose that our dream of owning our own home would live. So we chose life! The dream caught up to our confession, and we were able to move into our new home in November, 1994, over the Thanksgiving weekend! I believe Derrick was finally convinced! Are you? Remember, you will have what you say. When you speak things into your own life, remember, not only are others listening . . . so are you!

> *"Let no corrupt communication proceed out of*
> *your mouth, but that which is good to the use of*
> *edifying, that it may minister grace unto the hearers."*

> *Ephesians 4:29*

It is time to heal! I am convinced that once individuals get this thing right, families will follow suit! Young people need to heal. They have been deeply hurt. They have tried to turn to mothers and fathers, but their pain has been ignored, unresolved. Not only is the pain still there, it has increased and compounded! It is the stuff within the bags of luggage they carry around with them all day long! They put it down next to them on the school bus. They step around it to get out of their desks to go to the pencil sharpener. When the bell rings, they pick it up and carry it out of the room to the next class. While they are carrying it, if anyone rubs them the wrong way, there is going to be trouble! Young people need to put their baggage down. If they don't do something about it, the weight is going to become heavier and heavier still! Before long, they won't even be able to carry it! They will drag it in and out of relationships with them. The relationships won't work because the other person probably has even more baggage! There is nowhere to put any of it! Both parties fight for space to keep their precious painful experiences! Both want to share their pain, but it is just too overwhelming! Remember: when one broken person hooks up with another broken person and they don't become *"one;"* they are still *"two broken people!"*

The woman who realizes that she is in need of healing must do the same thing. She must seek out the will of God in her life and totally surrender herself to it. There is no other alternative! Only then can she be content in her life and ready for a meaningful relationship. It is the only way she can draw close to her creator. She must do what Hebrew 12:1 says *"and lay aside every weight, and the sin which doth so easily beset us, and let us run with patience the race that is set before us."* Without the weight, she can rise up from her infirmity and mount up with wings as the eagles! Without the weight of excess baggage, she can become a virtuous woman, a loving wife, a complimentary and supportive helpmate and a good mother!

It's time for broken men to heal. They have tried to be strong, impenetrable and masculine! Real men! They bury the hurt within the deepest crevices of their hearts. They, too, used to be little boys whose lives were filled with disappointment and bitterness. They didn't understand why their own father wasn't around. They are probably still trying to figure it out, still trying to make some sense out of it. Unless healing takes place, their sons will have the very same issues! The cycle will continue!

I know how men are. As a child, I was the only girl in a family of four children. I grew up around my brothers, played football with them, argued and fought with them. Now, I have three sons! For a very long time, I was the only female in my house of five men, aged six to seventy-eight! As I said, I *know* how men are! It is extremely difficult to get them to take out the trash! Just imagine how hard it is for them to unpack and unload those negative experiences and emotions they've been holding onto all of their lives! Still, it *must* be done in order for healing to take place!

A man who truly desires to be healed of past hurts and move into the promise of God in his life, must be real with himself and with God. He must openly and honestly confess that he is human and capable of making mistakes. He must confess and ask God to forgive him for his wrongs. He must also make amends with those he has wronged and make a conscientious choice to forgive those who have wronged him. *Then,* the healing can begin! Only then can he begin to be the man that God has called him to be and the husband and father God has divinely ordained him to be!

I pray daily for my sons. I was always using them for examples, when I was teaching in high school. As I said, my students probably thought that I was an extremely strict parent, but I really was not. My husband and I sincerely tried to sow good, positive, and righteous seed into their lives, and we expected a good, positive and righteous harvest! *"I expect a lot from Tjai,"* I would tell my students. *"I put a lot in there, and I expect to get a lot out!"* Isn't that the way it should be? Doesn't the Bible say that you will reap what you sow? If that's the case, and I do believe that it is, I purposefully sowed seeds of love, kindness, mercy, determination, and diligence into their lives. Most of all, I was careful to sow seeds of faith in them.

My testimony is a seed of faith for my sons. They know that I have overcome great odds to become the person I am today, therefore, they know, better than anyone, that I don't expect them to make excuses! It is a waste of time! If they make a mistake, it is a mistake and they can and must learn from it! I am constantly telling them that a *lesson unlearned is a lesson returned!* If you don't want to keep making the same mistakes over and over again, learn not to do the same things over and over again!

My sons have seen me rise above my circumstances. I thank God for the testimony that He has given to me. Without it, I would not be able to provide proof of His goodness, mercy and awesome power! They don't have to take anyone's word for it! They have living proof in me, their mom! I must confess, however, that I would not have been able to show anyone anything if I had not put down the baggage that I had been carrying around with me most of my life! Had I not laid aside the weight that threatened to trip me up, several times, I would never have been able to rise up and be the woman that God created me to be. I had to unpack. I had to *"come clean"* with myself, with God, and with those who had hurt me in my life. It was the only way for me, and I promise, it is the only way for you.

I had to stop keeping secrets—secrets about myself, secrets about my past, family secrets! As long as I was holding on to them, Satan was holding onto me and holding those things over my head! That's what he does, you know. He gets hold of that *"something,"* and he uses it to keep you bent over, bowed down and bound up! As he constantly reminds you of your mistakes, he tightens the shackles on your feet! As long as you don't realize that it is a trick, he's got you right where he wants you! But as soon as you figure this thing out and you realize that *"greater is He that is in you"* than that old demon that is in the world, you are on your way up! Once I gave up my secrets, I began to walk in the promises of God—newness of life! Not just life, but life more abundantly! If that sounds like something you want, God is ready and waiting to help you unpack!

The concept of revealing family secrets is a two-fold one. It relates, on one hand, to the keeping of secrets that seem to threaten the very core of the family. On the other hand, it relates to those seemingly secret answers of healing that can be found in the Word of God. The actual remedies for our problems can be found in the Bible, God's Holy Word! The solutions have been kept secret, as it were, because the enemy has successfully clouded our minds and blurred our vision so that we cannot get through to the answer! He has kept people distracted so that they cannot see what is right in front of their faces, right within reach, on the coffee table, collecting dust, on the bookshelf, becoming a family heirloom. The *real* secret is that the we can be free, in an instant, from the burden of the issues we all possess! We can be free because the truth will do that—free us! The only truth is that found in the Word of God! You can just put *"two and two together."* Get the truth and be made free!

Satan would prefer that we stay as far away from the truth as possible, so he constantly feeds us lies! We will *never* be able to forgive others for some of the things they did to us. We will *never* be able to rise above our own circumstances. We will *never* be able to overcome the tragedies of the past. We will *never* be able to get off drugs and alcohol. It is *impossible* to find grace in the sight of God after we have sinned horribly. Our lives can *never* be mended. Our family ties are *forever* broken. These are all *lies!* We *can* forgive those who have done wrong to us! We *must* forgive in order to receive the blessings of God! Don't let the great deceiver fool you another minute! Forgive and be forgiven! Release and be blessed! We *will* rise above our own circumstances. *"Wait on the Lord and be of good courage,"* the Scriptures say, *"and He will strengthen your heart."* When you realize the truth in this, you will be able to rise above any tragedy you have ever experienced!

When we study God's Word, we are able to recognize the wiles of the devil—before he launches a full attack. 1 Peter 5:8 tells us that we are to *"be sober, and vigilant because our adversary the devil, walks about as a roaring lion, seeking whom he may devour."* Drugs and alcohol are just another weapon that Satan has used to divide and conquer God's children! The sin and the guilt that it produces is just another weapon that the enemy has devised to use against us! But the Word of God tells us that when we know the truth, no weapon that is formed against us will prosper! But we must be sober! We must be vigilant! Our broken lives can be mended and, as a result, our families will be restored!

"And ye shall know the truth, and the truth shall make you free.
If the Son therefore shall make you free, ye shall be free indeed"

John 8:32 & 36

I had been living in Los Angeles, since 1985. In October 1990, I picked up my things, packed up Tjai and returned to Columbus, Georgia. In 1991, I discovered that I did not know what in the world I was supposed to be doing! I admitted to myself that I had made so many mistakes in my own life that I could not even remember having ever been truly happy! I had made some very bad choices that I would have to live with for the rest of my life! When I reached that conclusion, I knew that I needed to start trusting someone who knew much more than I did! I had to let someone take charge of my life and oversee my tomorrows—someone who was already there! I concluded that the only person who could actually fill those shoes was Father God himself! After all, He was the one who was already there, in my upcoming tomorrows, just waiting for me to get there!

That was one reason that I could really relate to the woman in the Scriptures! I, myself, had been bowed down in my own infirmity for thirty years! I understood why as soon as the woman, discussed in the thirteenth chapter of Luke, straightened up and began to glorify God, she had been healed of her infirmity! She gave God the praise for her cure, to whom all praise is due! When cooked souls are made straight, they will testify by glorifying God! They have been delivered, and they have a testimony about that deliverance! They have found out how to let go of all of the stuff they have been holding on to for so long. They have discovered how significant it is to let God have His way in their lives, and the news is so overwhelming that they just can't keep it to themselves!

Today, many people need to know that although Satan is going about, to and fro, seeking whom he may devour, through Christ, they can be set free! Anyone who has been misused or abused in their lifetime needs to know that they can have that liberty through Christ Jesus, and they must hold onto that liberty and know that no weapon that is formed against them will prosper! I know that *NO* weapon that is formed against me is going to prosper! *NO* weapon that is formed against you will prosper . . . just *"standfast!,"* Hold onto the liberty wherewith Christ has made you free, and do not be entangled or caught up with the yoke of bondage—because *NO* weapon that is formed against *YOU* is going to prosper!

That message is one that I have tried to get across to men and women all over the country! Several years ago, when I founded *Healing Hearts Ministry,*

I was determined to try, as earnestly as I could, to address the needs of men and women who not been able to fulfill the will of God in their own lives. *Healing Hearts* targeted issues that had been developed in the lives of those who came out to the weekly meetings to address the difficulties of overcoming emotional, physical or sexual abuse they had experienced—or were currently facing! We addressed some of the unresolved issues of personal tragedy, mental anguish and traumatic experiences that many had not been able to overcome. Those who attended the meetings were able to talk about their own personal grief and spiritual brokenness with others who could relate to them because they, too, had *rocked in the same boats"* many times throughout their own lives! *Healing Hearts* was established upon the liberating principles of God's Word, and I could openly attest to that! I would always begin the meetings by telling the men and women who sat before me that God would *never* use their pasts to determine their futures! Mature Christians, I told them, let their pasts remain in the past! As a result, they don't have to react—they can respond! Week after week, I looked into the eyes of those who earnestly wanted to know *how* to respond. Without the question ever being asked, I would give them the answer: *Through forgiveness!*

At some time or other, every person has been separated from God because of their sins, but He has always been there to form a close relationship with them. He reached out to us in a personal way by sending Jesus Christ to live with us and teach us how to forgive others! Christ taught us just how vital it is for us to live our lives as much like Him as we could! Because Jesus died on the cross, God's forgiveness through His Son, Jesus Christ, became available to everyone!

In the 9th chapter of Matthew, we find remarkable instances of the power and majesty of the Lord Jesus Christ, efficient to convince us that He is both able to save the uttermost of all that come to God through Him, and He is willing to do that! He *is* indeed able! In this chapter, Jesus healed the sick of the palsy, raised a ruler's daughter from the dead, healed a woman who has been suffering with a bloody issue for numerous years, gave sight to the blind, cast the devil out of the demonically possessed and cured all manner of sicknesses and diseases! What a mighty God we serve, one who is able to restore not only health and strength, but life itself!

Some friends took some time out to bring the man who had the palsy to Jesus! Jesus saw the faith of the man's friends and because of *their* faith, He healed *him!* Even the lame could be brought to Christ by his friends, and they, themselves, were not rejected by Him. In the faith of the paralytic himself, as well as that of those who brought him, Jesus recognized the man and his friends' *faith!* That assures us that if we want Him to heal us, we *first* need to let Him *see* a display of our faith that He *can and He will* do it!

I Thessalonians tells us to *"Pray without ceasing."* That tells us that as Christians, we are to develop an attitude about prayer, one that will not allow us to give up! We are to *always* be in communication with God. Praying for a *"show"* is *not* praying with faith. A couple of years ago, when I was falsely accused of committing a crime I would *never* have even thought of committing and placed behind prison bars that I never expected to find myself, I realized that I *had* to have enough faith in God that He would hear the prayer that passed beyond my trembling lips and take complete control of the situation. I had no idea about what was going on, how I got there, or how or when I was going to be delivered out of it! A Hispanic man, one who was in the holding cell next to mine, tried to get my attention and talk to me. With tears trickling down my face, I turned to him and told him that I was sorry, but I just could not talk to him right then. I needed to talk to my Father, I said. Then I turned my face to the wall in that holding cell, and I remembered Job and the turmoil that he had found himself in. I knew that he had done nothing to bring it about himself! I believe that Satan was simply looking for someone to pick on, and Job just happened to be the target that he found! God, however, *knew* Job and the faith that he had! He *allowed* the situation to befall Job—the loss of his wealth, the devastating loss of his children, and the foolish suggestion of his wife to simply just *"curse God and die."* By comparison, Job had undergone much, much more than I had—even though I felt more down than I had ever felt in my life! The one thing that Job's wife said, despite the horror that her husband had undergone, was that he should just *"curse God, and die?"* Despite her suggestion, Job told her that in all the days of his appointed time, he would just *wait* until his change came. He had that much faith in God! Who was I then, I asked myself, *not* to trust God and let Him have His own way in my life and work the entire ordeal out Himself? I simply surrendered the situation to Him, wiped the tears from my eyes, and closed my mouth so that He could have His way!

Praying for a *"show"* is *not* praying with faith! We are expected to pray to the Father, in the name of Jesus, realizing that there are different types of prayer for different sets of circumstances. In Matthew 16:19, Jesus said that He would *"give unto thee the keys of the kingdom of heaven: and whatsoever thou shalt bind on earth shall be bound in heaven: and whatsoever thou shalt loose on earth shall be loosed in heaven."* That is a prayer that we would be loosed from or bound out of circumstances that we have found ourselves in—even those that we brought upon ourselves! In the prayer alluded to in Luke 10:19, Jesus told His disciples that He gives His believers *"the power to tread on serpents and scorpions, and over all the power of the enemy: and nothing, by any means, shall hurt them."* In essence, He gave them power over the enemy! According to James 4:7, the pre-requisite is that we are to *"resist the devil,"* but **first,** we must submit ourselves to God in order to do so!

Crack, cocaine, or other illicit drugs destroy the lives of men and women and their families. Matthew 12:29 tells us that a strong man's goods cannot be destroyed unless He *first* be bound to the enemy's strongholds! Those drugs are simply strongholds, weapons that Satan uses against God's creation—mankind! The only way that mankind can fight against him is to make a quality decision that he or she is going to act on God's Word and believe just what *He* says! That passage of Scripture also says *"Or else how can one enter into a strong man's house, and spoil his goods, except he first bind the strong man? And then he will spoil his house."* Crack cocaine is the enemy's strongholds! It is strong enough to take hold upon someone's life and utterly destroy it! To fight against it, we must pray a prayer of faith and a petition—a prayer that involves *none* of the five senses. It is a prayer that is done using the *sixth* sense! We must *first* make a quality decision that we are going to trust in God's Word and have enough faith to believe it! After all, according to Hebrews 10:38, *"Now the just shall live by faith!"* So, it is a way of living our everyday lives!

In Paul's letter to the Romans, in the 8th Chapter, he says that *"all things"*—good things, bad things, indifferent things, thing that hurt us, things that help us, things that make us and things that might even break us—*"work together for good for those that love the Lord, and who are called, according to His purpose!"* Down at the 35th through 39th verses, he mentions how important it is for believers to let **NOTHING** separate them from the love of God! Not hunger or nakedness! Not danger! Not unforgiveness! Not even the very threat of death! But nothing, Paul says, must separate us from the love of God! If we hold fast to that significant principle of faith, in **ALL** the things that come against us in our lives, we are **MORE** than conquerors! Why? Because He loves us! And we are not just victorious in battle—but **MORE** than conquerors in our very own lives! Paul goes on to say that nothing—not death or life, not angels or principalities, not powers, nothing going on right now, not things that happened when we were growing up, not issues of physical abuse, not issues of sexual abuse, not issues of rape, not issues of illegitimate pregnancies, not even abortions, not those lies you thought you were going to have to take to your grave with you, not those secrets that you've been carrying around with you all of your life as if they were Samsonite luggage—but nothing—**NOTHING** is able to separate us from the love of

God, which is available to us through Christ Jesus our Lord! Hallelujah! Isn't that a relief? It has certainly relieved me!

In *Opening the Door*, I wrote about going deep into a place where I had packed away every negative, hurtful experience I had ever had in my life so that I would never have to deal with them again. However, when I began to *"unpack"* those suitcases and dress bags, I realized that the weight had been so heavy, it had actually stunted my spiritual growth and development! I couldn't even be what God had intended me to be as long as I was carrying all of that extra weight around! Then, I read a passage of Scripture that said, *"Wherefore, seeing we also are compassed about with so great a cloud of witnesses, let us lay aside every weight and the sin which doth so easily beset us and let us run with patience the race that is set before us!"*

Lay aside every weight? What does that mean to you? It **SHOULD** mean that it is time to lay aside the grudges you have been holding onto! It is time to forgive that man or woman for misusing or abusing you! The time has come for you to even forgive yourself for the things you have done in your own life! It is time to let go of those boxes of bitterness and anger! It is time to lay aside every weight so that you can begin your life anew—as a new creature, holy and acceptable unto the Lord! It is past time to stop letting those things separate you from the love of God! They are all that have been standing between you and Him! I pray that by the time you reach the end of this book, you or someone you have shared it with will be able to do just that!

It has been some time since I sat down and seriously decided to do some serious writing, but I felt it was the time to do it when this work exploded within me! It would not be the first time I wrote, but it would be the first time I did so with genuine purpose. This book would truly contain a story—my story—one that would be told with sincerity and honesty that I had attempted to, but had been entirely unable to, tell many times before. This time it would be told for all to read and know the truth!

I had been disabled since May 2002. My mind had been affected by the grand mal seizures that I had suffered many, many times! In 2007, I had begun to feel a calm that I had not experienced since the day before the episodes had even begun! My story, I told myself, seated at the computer keyboard, would finally be told! I was ready to share it with the world!

As usual, one Monday morning, I woke up, and before I even climbed out of bed, I had begun to say my prayers. I had gotten pretty used to surrendering my days to the Lord before my feet even touched the floor each day. So with my eyes still closed from the slumber I had surrendered to the night before, I laid prostrate beneath the covers and quietly talked to my Father, thanking

Him for waking me up and keeping me and my sons safe from any more hurt, harm and danger than we had already experienced in our lives.

I confessed that I knew that He was well aware of the fact that most of the fifty years that I had lived had been filled with more pain and sadness than I would have ever imagined! Yet, through it all, I thanked God for bringing me through each and every one of them! Many tears had found their way down my cheeks more times than I could even remember. My heart had been filled with sadness more times than happiness, but as I had heard a gospel music artist sing many times, I confessed that I, too, *never would have made it without Him!* And here I was—*still* here, sad and alone, but *still* here! Much of the time disheartened, but I was *still* here! Literally broke, with just a few dollars in my worn, beat-up purse, but *still* here! Physically disabled, unable to do what I had gone to college and earned a Bachelor of Arts Degree to do—teach high school English Literature—yet, I was *still* here! In my second year of teaching, I was attacked by a student, for reasons that I have yet to understand, but nevertheless, I was *still* here! I had been attacked, a second time, in my last year of teaching, by another student that I had actually believed I might be able to help. At the end of that school day, I was arrested and put in jail, accused of my being the attacker instead—yet, I was *still* here! And now, here I was, undergoing a divorce from the husband I had truly believed that I would spend the rest of my life with—alone, but *still* here! Many times, I had actually asked the Lord *"Why was I still here?"* He never responded, so I had accepted the fact that it wasn't because He was too busy to answer my question. Obviously, I concluded, He was just not through with me yet!

So I decided that I would stop asking that question. Why shouldn't I? It was God who had started the whole era of the life I was living, so He could go on and have His way in the entire shebang! I had always inspired others to trust in the Lord to handle the problems that affected their entire lives. Funny, I had said the appropriate words to others to soothe their troubled hearts and somehow calm their minds, but I had never expected to have to use them on myself! And here I was—waiting to hear from Him what I was to do with the rest of the life He had given me. In Job 15:22, I had read about the man who had suffered much greater anguish in his life than I had ever imagined to experience in my own, but had concluded that, *"If a man die, shall he live again? All the days of my appointed time will I wait, till my change come."* After all of the pain and anguish he had endured, the devastating loss of his wife, his children and all of his material possessions, and the disappointment he experienced with his friends' lack of comfort or support, he was one who was *still* determined to wait on the Lord to fix things *His* way. I had no choice but to do my own waiting because after all of the suffering he had endured, Job 42:12 said that *". . . the LORD blessed the latter end of Job more than his beginning: for he had fourteen thousand sheep, and six thousand camels, and a thousand yoke of oxen, and a thousand she asses."* Even after his unbelievable losses, he was *still* blessed with more than he had ever imagined!

In my own suffering, I could not, in any way, compare myself to Job! He had suffered much, much more than I could have ever imagined! Many times, I felt that my agony was spectacular and unimaginable, but Job's losses were much greater than mine! How could I ever compare my own losses to those he had experienced? Honestly, I couldn't! I decided that I would have to take a deep breath, and get on with the days ahead of me. Besides, I reminded myself that God already knew what would come my way before I was born!

Since January 2000, I had been picking up my Bible each day and reading passages of Scripture, trying to hear from the Lord what He would have me do with the day He had given to me. One afternoon, I had began the ritual I had earnestly started and decided that I would go back to the very beginning of *The Word* and read about some of the miraculous things that God had done in the life of someone else. As I said earlier, I had actually asked God why in the world I was **still** here. Many things that had happened in my life had taken me to places that I never expected to go! In my fifty years of living, I had been beat on, talked about, misused, abused, molested, falsely accused and then arrested, and undergone just about any other negative experience that any person could endure! So why, after all of that, I wondered, had God allowed me to survive?

When I reached Genesis 2, my reading became slower and more intense, as I read about Adam, the first man that God had made. Verse 20 told me that Adam was busy, doing his work, the work that God had created him to do. In short, he was *"about his Father's business!"* Verse 21 described how God had put this man that He had made to sleep so that he could stop doing his own work for a moment and submit completely to Him. Sleep . . . the most helpless living state of human existence! While Adam was asleep, God took a rib from his side, not his head, not his feet, nor his back, but the place where the outcome would be a *man-made* with a womb! Verse 23 said that this woman that was made for Adam was *"bone of his bone and flesh of his flesh"* because she was actually taken *out* of him. Verse 24 went on to say that because of the way this woman was made for man, he would someday *"leave his father and his mother, and shall cleave unto his wife: and they shall be one flesh."* The newlywed couple was naked, but they were not ashamed. After all, they actually had nothing to hide!

As soon as sin entered the picture however, everything changed! *"Shame"* introduced itself! The serpent talked to the woman—*not* the man that God had put in charge of everything in the Garden. He talked to the woman that God had given to Adam. He knew that she had some spiritual intuition—unlike her husband. Her spiritual enlightenment had been given to her by God himself! Because she possessed it, she most likely had some desire to know things that she didn't necessarily have to know! Many women and I, myself, can attest to that! We are the ones who just *have* to know what's going on in every situation!

Genesis, Chapter 3 described the woman's encounter with Satan in the Garden of Eden. Most likely everyone knows the story, of course. Satan slid up to Eve in the garden, and he was looking pretty good! Today, women are easily attracted to *"pretty boys!"* My sons are handsome young men, who can easily fit the mode, so I can attest to that! I also know that a lot of people watch talk shows that come on all day long in most cities. Many segments are about some *"pretty boy"* who has abused or misused a woman!

Of course, Eve already knew what God had said. She knew that Adam had been told *not* to touch the tree that God had placed in the midst of the garden. She told Satan what God had said—*as if he didn't already know!* Satan replied an *"almost truth."* That's what he does well! He's the master of almost truths! But *"almost"* is like saying ninety-nine and a half and of course, that simply *just won't do! "Oh, no!"* Satan said, *"You won't surely die!"*

Now, Eve should have known what kind of talk that was! But since Adam wasn't around and her mind was idle, she was ready for the attention that Satan readily gave to her! He went on to tell her that God didn't want her to eat from the tree of the knowledge of Good and Evil because He didn't *want* her to know things that she didn't really *have* to know or necessarily *need* to know. And what kind of foolishness was that? He went on to tell her that God didn't *want* her to eat from the tree of the knowledge of Good and Evil because He didn't *want* her to know what He Himself knew! Satan told her that *"God doth know that in the day ye eat thereof, then your eyes shall be opened, and ye shall be as gods, knowing good and evil."* And he had a very good idea that Eve, being a woman, wanted to know things she didn't necessarily *have to* or really *need to* know!

So, Eve tasted the fruit and realized that it tasted pretty good—but of course, everything that is good *TO* you is not necessarily good *FOR* you! She tasted the fruit and gave some to her husband, Adam, and he tasted it as well. The Scriptures never tell us how Eve was able to get Adam to do it, but as soon as he had eaten the forbidden fruit, both of their eyes were opened and they realized that they were both naked! In their efforts to hide from God, they sewed figs leaves together and made aprons for themselves. They tried to *"cover up"* what they had done by covering themselves up! But, it was too late! The first man and woman that God had made and put in the Garden were ashamed! That was what Satan's goal was—to make them ashamed! Today, he is *still* at it—trying to make you and I ashamed so that we can separate ourselves from God, our creator, our Father! Satan actually tries his best to keep you from doing what God *initially* created you to do! He broke up the first family that God had created and he is still doing the same thing today—breaking up families! I can attest to that myself!

In our society, there is a visible downward trend of the family, a loss of distinction between men and women, and a broad acceptance of a *"unisex"* society. God, however, made a distinction in His creation. He made no mistakes about it! He had a purpose for everything that He created! When are we going to realize that we must forego our traditions and deal honestly with the Word of God? We attempt to make His word fit our culture—but God did not speak His Word to fit a specific culture. He rendered principles which mankind is *still* expected to live by!

God had formed Adam, gave him a place to live, a job to do, and a commandment to keep—the responsibility of leadership! From Adam's side, God created Eve—for him! She was a *helpmate*, one who was created to *help* Adam carry out the vision, the dream, the assignment that God had given to him! If a man has no vision or dream, or feels that he has no assignment, no purpose, no reason for being here, why on earth would God give him a helpmate to carry out that *"nothing?"* Both male and female *must* fulfill their responsibilities—they *must* carry out the assignments that God has given them! The original intention that God had for man was for him and woman to rule and govern the earth that He had created together! The fall ultimately moved the reflection off of God and onto Christ and the Church! Husband and wife were equivalent to Christ and His Church! It was the fall that *temporarily* changed things however! It was what Adam had done, not what his helpmate, Eve, had done. That proved that the curse came about as a result of Adam *not* fulfilling *his* responsibility! If he had not eaten *after* Eve, *perhaps* Adam could have even died for Eve and taken away her sin, just as Christ died for the church!

It will probably shake the rafters off of the roof all over the place that it is *not* actually true that men and women are to rule together! But we will remain as we are today, struggling for leadership, men against women and vice versa, under the curse, until Christ comes back again! Genesis 3:16 says *"Unto the woman He said, I will greatly multiply thy sorrow and thy conception; in sorrow thou shall bring forth children; and thy desire shall be to thy husband, and he shall rule over thee."* The woman's desire may be to seek control over her husband, and no matter how submissive a woman is to her spouse, her innate desire may still be to control her husband! And he is going to want to rule over his wife, but several times, I have told many men and women both, the Bible says that men are to be a *"covering,"* not a *"lid!"* Unfortunately, Adam actually listened to his wife, rather than to God, and she actually listened to the voice of Satan.

God intended for man to be the *"head,"* but somewhere, somehow, society became imbalanced! Eve usurped her husband's authority and he usurped God's Word! And in 2010, it is difficult to determine just who is the wife or husband because men are being allowed to marry men and women are being wed to women! We should be careful about disobeying the Word of God because we will have to pay for that disobedience when Christ returns! In the meantime, we must find balance in the Word of God. Just like Satan went through the woman to get to the man, society must realize that he was able to do that because the woman *was* the weakest link! 1 Peter 3:7 says *"Likewise, ye husbands, dwell with them according to knowledge, giving honor unto the wife, as unto the weaker vessel, as being heirs together of the grace of life; that your prayers be not hindered."* That does not mean that the wife is the physically or emotionally weaker vessel! Because women are more spiritually sensitive than men, they do sometimes pick up on things that men don't seem to have a clue about! Emotionally, women seem to react to things that don't even faze men! At times, that can be used for or against us! Women's sensitivity makes them more vulnerable to the attacks of Satan. However, God arranged that man provide stability for his woman! 'Looks like some of us are being a bit *short-changed!*

Nowadays, Satan is very busy finding new ways to get the man that God created on his side! Some time ago, television aired a minister admitting his homosexuality over the airwaves. Publicly, he shared with viewers all over the country—possibly all over the world—that he had a *"live-in"* homosexual partner. What really amazed me was that having shared this information with the entire world, his admission of homosexuality was now somehow being *accepted* in his church, and this man was now being ordained a priest! That simply proved that Satan was still throwing every stone he could into every believer's path! In the Garden of Eden, it was Adam and Eve—today, relationships of *"Adams and Steves"* are being accepted all over the place!

I cannot help but wonder if Christians, who are born again, baptized believers and profess to be filled with the Holy Spirit, are actually paying attention to what is really going on in the world around them! Everybody should just go back and read for themselves what happened in Sodom and Gommorah as a result of the lifestyle that was being practiced in **those** cities!

> *"Then the LORD rained upon Sodom and upon Gomorrah brimstone and fire from the LORD out of heaven; And he overthrew those cities, and all the plain, and all the inhabitants of the cities, and that which grew upon the ground."*

Genesis 19:24-25

If you take a look at Hebrews 13:8, you will find that Jesus Christ was the same yesterday as He is today, and will continue to be the same forever! And if you need a little more assurance, you'll find it in 1 John 5:7: *"For there are three that bear record in heaven, the Father, His son, Jesus who is the Word, and the Holy Ghost which are three in one!"* None of these words are written based upon my opinion. They are found in the Holy Bible, The Word, and you can read it for yourself!

1 Peter 5:8-9 says *"Be sober, be vigilant; because your adversary the devil, as a roaring lion, walketh about, seeking whom he may devour: Whom resist steadfast in the faith, knowing that the same afflictions are accomplished in your brethren that are in the world. But the God of all grace, who hath called us into His eternal glory by Christ Jesus, after that ye have suffered a while, make you perfect, establish, strengthen, settle you."* Those words stand out, like a brilliant light—especially at the times in my life that I realized that no matter what had happened to me, I had to be reserved and attentive! The devil had been doing his thing, going about, roaring like a lion in my life, for what seemed most of it! He had been actually walking about, forwards and backwards, up and down, as if he had some privilege—as if he had some right! I realized that Satan had really been trying to thwart the plans that God had for me. I confessed that I *would* do what God had called me to do, no matter what! I would *not* let anyone do or say anything to me, no matter how much their words might hurt me, that would separate me from my Father's love and divine will for my life!

Many times, I have found myself writing about trials and tribulations, struggles and strife that I have endured in my own life, from my childhood up to the present. I have stood and lifted upon the Lord's name in spite of my personal trials. I have shared with many others the goodness of the Lord, in spite of Satan's attacks against me! God was still in control of my life, no matter what the devil had tried to do to destroy me! Then, in May 2001, I became ill, like I had ever been before. Doctors could not even explain what on earth was happening or why it was happening to me! The only thing they said was that something was wrong with my brain. I underwent a brain surgery so that they could find out what that *"something"* was, but they still could not figure it out!

After suffering the grand mal seizures that began in May 2001, I began to feel better than I had felt in months! I thanked God every day for the health and strength that He had graciously given to me! I had undergone a brain surgery so that my doctor could find out cause of the seizures. Although I had not been able to understand why I had been stricken with something that my doctors could not explain, I *still* trusted God, and I knew that He would see me through the ordeal! When the results of numerous tests I underwent came back, my doctors had looked at the results with puzzled expressions on their faces. They actually had no answers! They did not know where the two lesions on my brain had come from, why or how long they had been there, nor where they had gone! They were simply fading!!

Derrick, was so relieved that he shouted for joy that the two spots had virtually begun to disappear! He and the doctor at Emory Hospital in Atlanta were both overwhelmed! Derrick clapped his hands and a broad smile spread across his face. The doctor happily said, *"Thank God!"* and grinned broadly. It *was* good news! After months of waiting, months filled with so much confusion and anxiety, the results had finally come in. I, too, was happy to hear those words from the doctor. Right then, I thanked God for the work He had done in my life! But—I also knew that there had been a purpose for the unexplainable illness and months of devastation that it had caused me and my family! I also knew that a new testimony was being given to me, and God was *still* not finished with me yet!

Behind a frozen smile, I thanked the doctor. He had been more than kind to us each time we had visited him at Emory! After Derrick and I left his office, I stood blankly in front of the receptionist as she gave us an appointment for a return date six months away. My husband and I walked out of the hospital and approached the attendant at a curbside stand to retrieve our car. With a broad smile upon his face, he took a slip of paper from Derrick and told us that it would be just a minute and our car would be brought around to us.

It was October and the weather was steadily changing. A brisk wind was blowing, so we walked back inside the hospital waiting area to stand behind the glass doors to wait for our car to arrive. Derrick told me that he had to go somewhere nearby to find a restroom, so we were left alone for a few minutes—just me and the Lord! There were some other people in the area nearby, but they quickly began to disappear. I realized that I was alone, so I began to talk to my Father. I needed some answers that I knew only He would be able to provide! *"What in the world was going on,"* I asked. *"What had I done to deserve the tumultuous things that had happened to me?"* I knew what the doctor had told us upstairs, that the lesions were disappearing from my brain. What in the world had been the cause of their unexpected appearance? No one seemed to know the answer to that question. I really wanted to know it myself!

Although there were times that I couldn't see or think straight, I knew that God was still there! I had no doubt that He was still in control! He had kept me through my trials and tribulations throughout my entire life! He had not left me then! And He was there right then! How did I know? Because I was still there! I am still lifting Him up and praising His name! I was confident that He always had it all under control! Because I trusted Him, I could love, in spite of being mistreated! Because of my willingness to love, even those who had attempted to hurt and abuse me, God had given me joy! I could have peace in the midst of my trials! Oh, I knew that long-suffering had taken longer than I expected, but it was alright because God had taught me how to have gentleness, goodness, faith, meekness and temperance! God was expecting you and I to do what *HE* had given us the strength to do—*no matter what!*

All the way home, my mind wandered. I was really puzzled! What had really happened to me over the past few months? Overjoyed, Derrick talked about the way things had turned out. He was quite elated that we had made it through the terrible ordeal! He was thankful that God had kept me *sane* and had enabled us to take care of our boys and our home! Seven months had passed since I had first began having grand mal seizures, and those days and nights had been difficult for him, me and our boys! I knew that all too well!

As we tread the miles from Atlanta to our home in Fortson, my mind went back to the beginning of my experience with seizures, the first day of what had become a series of unexplainable ordeals for us! That day had begun as an ordinary one. There were just three weeks to go before the end of the school year at Kendrick High School in Columbus! My students' minds had already just about shut down! It was a struggle, keeping them interested in school work, with the sun shining so brightly outside of our classroom and the birds chirping at the windows! The students' attire had already been altered to include culottes, shorts, and short sleeves. Some even attempted to wear halters underneath light jackets and blouses which they thought the teachers wouldn't notice. Each day had begun with beautiful mornings and bright sunshine!

That day, my son, Tjai, and I had hurried to the car and quickly backed out of our driveway. The clock was ticking, and we had an eighteen mile drive before us. I was teaching English Literature and Dramatic Arts at the high school where he was a junior, overjoyed with the realization that at the end of that school year, he would be a senior! Tjai would be the first of my brothers and my children to graduate from high school! Three more weeks and we could start planning for that big day! We pulled onto the highway at the end of our driveway and the *"soon-to-be-graduate"* got comfortable for the ride to school. As usual, Tjai slid down in his seat and closed his eyes. I remembered looking over at him, shaking my head and smiling. And then, at that moment, for the very first time, my lights went out!

I will never be able to describe any of the ride to school. The awesome God was behind the steering wheel, guiding my son and I over the eighteen miles away from our home in Fortson, Georgia to Kendrick High School in Columbus! I **do** however remember that once we had reached the campus, I had somehow flicked on my signal light to the left so that I could pull into a parking slot in front of the building. For a moment, I could see a car that was already there, parked sideways and sitting still, in front of me. God directed my foot to slam on the brakes to avoid hitting it! Suddenly, Tjai awoke and saw the car in front of us, and I heard him yell *"Mom!"*

Quickly, that car sped away. Almost automatically, I pulled my Expedition into a vacant parking space. Once parked, I turned off the car. Thinking that everything was alright, a relieved Tjai did his **normal** thing. He hurriedly opened his door, grabbed his bookbag, sent a quick *"Have a good day, Mom!"* in my direction, and jumped out of the car. Quickly, he closed the door and trotted off in the school building's direction. Everything seemed to be normal, so it had not occurred to him that anything out of the ordinary had happened to me. Somehow, things were not quite the same as usual though.

I don't know how long I had been sitting there, but amazingly, I got out of the car and stumbled into the building. Once inside, several students passed by me, many tossing a *"Hey, Mrs. B!"* in my direction. I could not say a word of response to them. With the hustle and bustle of the morning, things seemed no different to the students who were busily hurrying to various classrooms. Miraculously, God directed me to the front office. Inside, my principal, Mr. Carey, was standing at the front door of his office. It was somewhat unusual that he was there because he seldom stood around the main office before the first bell rang each day. He was usually walking through the halls, smiling and saying *"Good morning!"* to the students, letting them know that he was around.

"Good morning, Mrs. Bryant," Mr. Carey said, peering over the top of his reading glasses, as usual, a warm smile on his face.

I, however, could say nothing. Somehow, I looked *through* him, and felt my head shaking, from side to side.

"Mrs. Bryant?" Mr. Carey said, *"Are you all right?"*

I shook my head again—this time, indicating *"no"* in response to the question. The lights in the office began to flicker.

"Is there anything wrong?" he asked, stepping towards me.

I looked at him, a strange expression resting upon my face.

Mr. Carey guided me to a chair behind the secretary's desk. *"What's wrong?"* he asked, helping me into the seat.

I still could not verbally respond.

"Is Tjai at school today?" he asked. *"Is Mr. Bryant at the Fire Station? Station Four, isn't it?"*

My eyes found his, but still, I couldn't say anything. I could feel my body slouching down in the chair.

"It's all right," Mr. Carey said. *"Everything's going to be all right. I'll find them,"* he said, trying to assure me. Quickly, he rushed to the loud speaker and summoned Tjai to the office. A few other teachers had begun to enter the office. *"Call Mr. Bryant at the Fire Station,"* he told one of them. *"I think he is at Station Four. Tell them to tell him he needs to get over here to the school, right away!"* Then he was on the telephone, on another line, dialing **911**.

I turned my head to the left. Carolyn Randolph, one of the high school's Math teachers and a very good friend of mine, walked quickly towards me. I could see her lips moving, but I couldn't hear anything that she was saying. Then, at that very moment, the lights went out again!

Several days later, I woke up and found myself in a different, unfamiliar place. I was alone in a room in the Intensive Care Unit at St. Francis Hospital. Later, Derrick told me that he had only gone home to check on our sons, Tjai, Little Derrick, and Christopher. They were at home, alone and still devastated by what had happened to their mom! Their dad, too, seem to have been shaken up a bit by the sudden, unexpected occurrence! I, myself, was afraid because I had no idea *what* had happened or *why* it had happened to me! I had always been in good health and had suffered very few illnesses in my forty-three years of life! I had always been clear minded, and I usually had the answers to not only my problems, but those suffered by many others! What in the world, I couldn't understand, had happened to me?

With a broad smile upon his face, Deacon Brown, my good friend and confidant, came to see me after they had taken me out of Intensive Care and put me in a room at St. Francis Hospital. I recognized him, but I couldn't say anything to him. Each time I tried to speak, I was confused by the words that came out of my mouth! His visit was a short one, but something that he said stayed with me long after he had left me in that hospital room. *"God is going to take care of you,"* Deacon Brown said. *"He's not through with you yet!"* he assured me. In later days, it would be important for me to remember that!

Little did I, or anyone else who knew me, know that Satan had waged a war against me, but many years ago, I had already been equipped for the battle! The Scriptures tell us that Satan is constantly trying to *be* something. He is *as* a roaring lion, not that he *is* one! He is a *"wanna-be!"* Roaring lions scare their prey and thus gives them the opportunity to flee! He only roars when he thinks he has the advantage over them! He can, of course, possibly cause destruction, unless he is restrained by the righteousness of God! He is adamantly against us and will do anything he can possibly do to destroy us or at least, set us up for destruction, *BUT* God always provides a way for the faithful to overcome! We must have faith that He *WILL* see us through!

I realized that my mind was *my* battlefield for *my* fight of faith! I would have to hold on to my faith. I had been stricken with something that doctors could not even explain! I would have to remember the words that God had already spoken to me years ago, and I would have to be strong enough to rebuke the devourer, letting him know that I would, in one of the most difficult and challenging times of my entire life, rebuke Him! At times, I could almost hear Satan lying to me, trying to control my thoughts, so that he could eventually destroy me! He and I both knew that if I took to heart what he said, he would be able to do that. But God had already done so much for me that I could not ignore the many blessings that I had already received from Him!

During what I realized what was my own fight of faith, Derrick and I talked often. He constantly reminded me that I was stronger than I had begun to think that I was. He also told me that he had never before known anyone else like me, his wife, before! When I questioned his reasons for saying that, he simply told me that in spite of everything that I had undergone in my lifetime, I was *still* here! Since he met me, I had not been able to give up my fight of faith, and he could not help but admire that quality! A strong woman, my husband called me, as tears had rolled down my cheeks. A woman of God, he said I was, even when my legs wobbled beneath me, and I had difficulty standing up by myself! He had seen me standing upright and he knew that it had to have been God alone holding me up!

At that time, Derrick's encouragement helped me to see through the dark clouds that Satan had placed around me! I realized that God had created me for His own purpose, and Satan had known about me since I came into the world! My childhood experiences had been so overwhelming that it had been amazing that I had been able to overcome them! Others had shaken their heads, amazed that I could think clearly after having witnessed the brutal night in which my father killed my mother, my grandmother and himself! This simple little girl, Satan thought, would surely be destroyed! But adamantly, God had said, *"No!"* because there was still ***much*** that He had for me to do!

Since that horrible night in November 1966 didn't destroy me, Satan knew that he had to try something else—so he did! With both of my parents gone, my three brothers and I went to live with Aunt Meg and Uncle Ben. The family would not know it, but Satan would plant a seed of destruction in that little house of Twenty-second Street. In that house, I would be sexually molested by the uncle, who became my "Dad," until I was fifteen years old! Surely, that would do it, I believe the devil had presumed! So many lives have been destroyed because of molestation! Numerous others, some who could have been used to do great works for the Father, had been *"cut-off"* in their childhood! Surely, I realized, I had been on his list, too! But then, during my sophomore year of high school, things had come to a screeching halt! Something inside of me had risen up! One day, behind the wheel of the car that he was using to teach me to drive, I told my uncle that he must not ever touch me again! If he did, I swore that I would kill him! I actually don't think I could have even tried to do anything like that, but my uncle believed that I meant it, so he never touched me again!

That didn't even stop Satan from his efforts to destroy me though! So since that didn't work, once again, he decided to try something else! As a teenager, I began to receive attention that I had never gotten before. At home, I was disliked by my aunt as a result of the attention that she was not getting from her own husband. To tell the truth, I felt pretty miserable there, but high school presented some relief! I enjoyed being at school every day! My teachers were good and kind, and the atmosphere was wonderful! I had found many girlfriends who were *"growing up"* along with me! They and I had discovered that boys were *"different"* and *"unique!"*

The fruits of the Spirit spoken of in Galatians 5:22-23, *"love, joy, peace, long-suffering, gentleness, goodness, faith, meekness and temperance,"* are the ones that we are able to take part of. They are the things that we are able to experience because of the goodness of the Lord! You see, God has set these fruits out before us and they are available to all believers who will *"standfast in the liberty wherewith Christ has made us free, so that we cannot be entangled with the yoke of bondage!"* Well, you know what this *"bondage"* is? *"Bondage"* refers to the things that tie us up! These are things that happen in our lives and get us *"off course!"* These are things that the devil himself puts in our paths to throw us off! That's what bondage actually is!

Oh, I know that it is not easy to get back on your feet, after you've been knocked down—especially when you are faced with pain and affliction each and every day of your life! But God already knew that it was going to be a challenge for His children when He created us! Undoubtedly, He knew that we would have trials and tribulations in our lives! He also knew that we would have sicknesses and injuries! He was right there when things were not working out for you and I! He heard us when we cried out in the midst of our hard times! He was right there for us, just like He was with Job, when all of his children were slain! No matter what is going in our lives, Job's experience showed us exactly how *important* it is to just *trust God and keep the faith!*

I have trusted God everyday for my sons' safety while they are at school, and I've tried to make sure that they knew Jesus for themselves. I've always encouraged them to take Him wherever they go each and every day! Should Satan stir up *"stuff"* in my community, I want to make sure that the gift within me is stirred up so that I can take a stand upon the Word of God and not just walk around saying *"I rebuke you, Satan, in the name of Jesus!"* but I plan to depend on God to give me the wisdom, the strength, and the faith in Him that He will cast his butt out!!! I realize that the main thing to do is *not* focus on what I've been through. Jesus saved me so that I could show somebody else *how* to depend on Him so that they, themselves, can get through!

I can't help but to look at the story about the woman in the 13th Chapter of Luke, a woman, who after eighteen years of suffering, was miraculously healed of her own infirmities! I have talked about her many times, and recently, I discovered that she and I have very much in common! If the truth be told, you or someone you know can very likely relate to this woman! Jesus was teaching in the synagogue on the Sabbath Day and she just *happened* to be there. As it *happened*, He performed an act of charity, or an act of love, for her. The Scriptures tell us that this woman had a spirit of infirmity and had had it for eighteen years! She had an infirmity, an evil spirit, by divine permission, of course, that was so overwhelming that she was bowed down by strong convulsions and the Scriptures say that she *"could in no wise lift herself up!"* She had had this infirmity for a very long time! It was, by social standards—incurable! She could not stand erect, which is something that places man above beasts! Her illness was a dehumanizing one! Not only was she deformed by it, but it was painful for her to even move! Yet, she went to the synagogue on the Sabbath Day! Now, some people wake up with a slight headache and decide to stay home from church! But I must reiterate that if you are sick, the wise thing to do is to get to the *"doctor"* as quickly as you can!

Well, this woman went to church, despite her agonizing pain, and the Bible tells us that she did not appeal to Jesus! In other words, she didn't just go up to Him, fall down, and ask Him to heal her! Her condition had been going on for so long that any hope that she could have had that she would be cured had possibly long ago left her! She simply went to church to worship! Imagine that? Before she could even call upon Jesus, He answered her! She had come to be taught, to get some good food for her soul, and as a result, Christ gave relief to her bodily infirmity! When I read about this woman and her experience, it occurred to me that this is what is meant in Matthew 6:33 where it says that we are to *"seek ye first the kingdom of God and His righteousness; and all these things shall be added unto you!"* Christ, in His gospel, invites us to come to Him to worship, and when He calls us, He will undoubtedly heal us when we get there! That is something to think about, isn't it?

As the woman's story continued, Christ laid His hands upon her and spoke a powerful word of healing to her. He simply said, *"Woman, thou art loosed from thine infirmity,"* and she was *immediately* made straight and began to glorify God! Though it was a spirit of infirmity, an evil spirit that she had been under the power of for eighteen years of her life, Christ displayed a power that was superior to that of Satan's! Although she could *"in no wise lift herself up,"* Christ not only lifted her up, *but He enabled her to lift herself up!* The woman who had been bent over, crooked for eighteen years was *immediately* made straight!

Many of God's children are under a spirit of *"infirmity"* in our world today! When I say *"world,"* I mean the world in which we live, in our homes, in the places where we work, where we go to school—and even where we go to church! That spirit of infirmity is a spirit of bondage; through prevailing fear and grief, souls are cast down and disquieted within and people are troubled! They are bowed down with infirmities which are capable of undoubtedly destroying them! Some people have already lost the battle! Many lives have already been lost because of this evil spirit that has overtaken many of them! Young people are dying by the thousands because so many are bowed down and can in *"no wise lift themselves up!"* Their lives are being snatched away as they are *NOT* making their way to the church so that they can be healed of their own infirmities! Some parents are sleeping off affairs of Saturday night's events, and many of them are unable to get up and get those children to Sunday School or take them to morning worship!

People need to know that although Satan is still going about, *to and fro, seeking whom he can devour*, through Christ, we can be free! Anyone who has been misused or abused in their lifetime needs to know that they can have liberty, through Christ Jesus, and they must *stand fast* in that liberty and know that *NO* weapon that is formed against them shall prosper! That assures us that no weapon that is formed against you and I shall prosper, doesn't it?

Some years ago, I admitted to myself that I had virtually made so many mistakes in my life, I could not even remember having ever been truly happy! Like so many other people I knew, I had made some very bad choices that I would have to live with for the rest of my life! When I reached that conclusion, I realized that I needed to start trusting in someone who knew much more than I did! I needed to let someone take charge of my life, put me in the right direction, and oversee my tomorrows! I concluded that the only person who could do that was Father God Himself! If I trusted Him, I knew that I wouldn't have to worry about tomorrow—after all, He was already there, waiting for me!

The Bible tells us that *"he whom the Son sets free, is free indeed!"* You have to know that Satan will not be happy about your being set free. He is still ticked off about many deliverances that have occurred in the lives of numerous others! Oh yes, I know it! He does not want us to be delivered because he knows that we can't keep anything to ourselves! We just have to tell *EVERYBODY!* And when people begin to overcome by the blood of the Lamb, the Word of God, and the testimonies of others who have overcome, that is certainly something to shout about!

Job enters my mind and my writing quite a bit because I am one who can just about relate to the way that brother must have felt. I have felt very much like him myself! I could understand his confusion, wondering where the Lord was, wondering if He was really looking at the situation, and asking if He realized what was going on in this life of his! Haven't you been there at some time in your life? I know I can remember when I felt that what I was going through was too much for me to handle! I felt that the pain was too great for me to bear! It felt like I was all alone in my misery, so I called upon God, and asked Him if He was aware of what I was going through. *"Lord,"* I asked, *"Can't you fix this thing? Will you make things better? Won't you make this thing right?"*

We all have trials and tribulations in front of us! There is a door that we need to open and walk on through in order to experience His goodness! God is right there, on the other side, waiting for us, you and I, to open that door and walk on through! He already knows we can do it! He made us! He knew it would get hard sometimes! Many times, it hurts so bad that we become discouraged, but Galatians 6:9 encourages us to **not be weary in well doing!** That's what it says, isn't it? In due season, we shall reap, if we faint not! So we just have to hold on! Keep the faith! God is good, and He will do just what He says!

"And not only so, but we glory in tribulations also: knowing that tribulation worketh patience; And patience, experience; and experience, hope: And hope maketh not ashamed; because the love of God is shed abroad in our hearts by the Holy Ghost which is given unto us."

Romans 5:3-5

Many, many times, I have thanked God for saving me! But I know that He did not save me just for me! I have realized that after all of the trials and tribulations that I have undergone, I did not overcome them for myself! Somebody else needed to know just how good God is! Somebody needed to know just how wonderful He is! You might be going through some trials and tribulations of your own right now. You need to hear from people like me, an overcomer, because to do so can help you, give you courage and increase your faith, so that you can come on through! I willingly glorify God for using me and others so that somebody else will be encouraged! Someone will be enabled to **stand fast** in the liberty wherewith Christ has made them free!

We have all heard the story of Jesus' death on the cross for most of our lives. The Scriptures tell us how Jesus of Nazareth, born to a virgin woman named Mary and her espoused husband, Joseph, immaculately conceived by the Holy Spirit, was sought after, tried, and made to carry his own cross up Golgotha's hill to be crucified for sins that He had not even committed! According to the Gospels of Matthew, Mark, Luke, and John, when Jesus stumbled and fell on the way, he was aided by a single black man by the name of Simon. I'm not sure that very many people know that, but it's true!

Many Christian ministers recount the passionate story of Jesus' being chosen, of the known criminal Barabbas, to be put to death by crucifixion. *Webster's Dictionary* defines crucifixion as being **"put to death on a cross."** So, as the story goes, Jesus was nailed at his hands and feet, to a wooden cross, or stake, if you will, and hung between two criminals, while Barabbas, a well-known murderer, was set free! And what had Jesus Christ done to deserve such a fate? Well, they said that he healed the sick and raised the dead, gave sight to the blind, set the captive free, fed the multitudes who anxiously gathered to hear him speak *(some of whom were the same people who were later shouting that he should be crucified)*, and dared to stand up for righteousness' sake. That meant that He had to tell the truth—something which people were then, as they still are now, not prepared to acknowledge—especially when it was contrary to their way of doing things! The Bible says that Jesus told his followers that He was *"the way, the truth, and the light."* He said that the way to salvation was through Him, following after His ways. We would have to have, in other words, the mind of Christ!

The words of Christ are found in John 8:32, where He said *"And ye shall know the truth, and the truth shall make you free."* That being so, men and women in America should understand whom the Scriptures prophesied would be in bondage for four hundred years, in a land that was not their own—this people, the seed of Abraham. In John 8:37, Jesus spoke to the Jews and told them that He knew that they were Abraham's seed, but that He also knew that they sought to kill him because His word had no place with them. He told them that He spoke of that which He had seen with His father, God, who sent him, and they, on the other hand, did the things which they had seen with their father. In verse 39, they answered Jesus and said *"Abraham is our father."*

Jesus replied, *"If ye were Abraham's children, ye would do the work of Abram. But now ye seek to kill me, a man that hath told you the truth, which I have heard of God; this did not Abraham."* In verses 41-44, he clearly states, *"Ye do the deeds of your father. If God were your father, ye would love me; for I proceeded forth and came from God; Ye are of your father, the devil, and the lusts of your father ye will do."*

It is apparent that Jesus realized that the people whom He had come to deliver truth and knowledge to were *not* the people whom He had assumed them to be. They did not even want to *know* the truth! They abhorred it, and ultimately, tried to destroy it by killing Him! Many times, since that day, others who have fought for freedom, justice, and equality—the truth—have been slain! When Dr. Martin Luther King, Jr. stood up to proclaim that he had *"been to the mountain top and seen the promised land,"* he had a message to deliver. He declared that he had actually stood where Moses stood and heard the voice of God himself! He had come into the knowledge of the truth and what real freedom was all about. So he stood up to tell *all* men and women, little boys and girls, the truth! And *"they"* shot him down—still trying to kill the message by killing the messenger!

At one time, during slavery, Black people were given the Bible as a consolation. They were forced to take the name of their slave owner, their *"master."* They were told to believe in the Word of God, even though they were not allowed to read it for themselves. It was simply a matter of belief in what they were told and having faith that it would come to pass. The consolation given provided that although folks might suffer here on earth, when this life was over, they would get their reward in *"heaven"*—that is, of course, if they behaved like good *"Christians"* and were faithful servants! They were not told that according to the Scriptures, man could not serve God *AND* man, however they could not and *were not* allowed to read about it, so they didn't know anything about that. Some served faithfully and died—still awaiting their reward, and still in bondage. Some tried to escape and were lynched or beaten when they were captured. Some did escape and some who did, like Harriett Tubman, even came back for others. Many died in the fight for freedom—something which you will remember, is a reward for those who know the *truth!*

Once, I heard a young lady, recently having graduated from high school, say that she believed that Jesus was just like *"us"*—*"Black folks,"* she meant. Not only was the Savior *not* accepted by the publicans, He was a virtual threat to the officials because He told them, in no uncertain terms, that it was *not* their want, but *God's will* that would prevail! His boldness made them uncomfortable because they realized that He was capable of spreading the truth to others. They even accused Him of blasphemy, and I suppose, He did blaspheme—against their god, who obviously was *not* a god of truth. And his sentence was death—on the cross.

Some time ago, Mel Gibson's movie entitled *"The Passion of the Christ"* was shown in theaters across the country. It made its way onto VCRs and DVDs in numerous homes. Derrick and I went to see it before we took our sons to see the movie because we wanted to know what exactly was going to be shown to its viewers. Almost throughout the movie, I sat quietly beside my husband, with warm tears streaming down my face. I knew that I, myself, and others had read about it or heard about it, but to see it for myself was nearly unbearable for me! Jesus went willingly to the cross to die for me! For you! For people who continue to profess not to even believe in God! I could not help but think about that! Jesus' death on the cross was symbolic in that He was made to die a painful death, just as slavery was for those who were enslaved. He was made to suffer, for the Scriptures say that they *"pierced him in the side and placed a crown of thorns on his head."* In slavery, it was a common practice for the master to beat his slaves into servitude. And finally, Christ *"gave up the ghost."* That's a unique phrase. Black and white men and women in America, should have been encouraged to do as did Jesus did and *"give up the ghost"* as well!

Jesus' resurrection, or raising up from the dead, by definition, means *"no longer alive; benumbed; obsolete, extinguished; lacking luster or movement or vigor."* Furthermore, death means *"dying; end of life; and extension; annihilation; personified power that annihilates, kills."* A lot of people have been near death for a long time! Right now, there are many forces in our country trying to annihilate its citizens—poverty, oppression, homelessness, drugs, gang warfare, and let's not leave out welfare, designed to demolish the family unit, self-respect, independence, pride and dignity!

It is way past time for us to be *"Christ-like,"* and I am not sure that those who profess to be Christians understand that in its truest meaning. The Bible says that He arose from the dead. If that were to happen to Americans, there would surely be a change that would be so dramatic that it would literally shake the earth! That is because it would mean an awakening to the truth of who we are and what God wants for us—His people!

Can you remember hearing or reading about members of the Ku Klux Klan who rode upon Black neighborhoods, hooded to hide their faces, harassing Blacks in an attempt to run them out? The organization supposedly was a *"religious"* one whose members attended *"Christian"* churches and were upstanding members of their communities. They gave the impression that they were *"righteous"* people who were doing no more than what God had ordained them to do by terrorizing Negroes, who they felt were not their equal! To further convince Black families of their inferiority, they would leave a reminder in their front yards, a burning cross, to let them know that they were neither wanted nor welcome! I have often wondered how a people, who professed to love God and His Son, Jesus Christ, who suffered death upon the cross for redemption's sake, could take that cross, a symbol of Christ's death and His resurrection, and not only set fire to it, but use it to terrorize a people that they themselves taught the concept of Christianity! Perhaps they didn't really know what the cross truly represented—the resurrection of that which Jesus stood for—*THE TRUTH!* It was the truth that they set afire and their admission that they opposed it, just as they did in Jesus' time! Of course, they obviously had no desire for Blacks to know the truth. They knew that if that knowledge was acquired by Blacks, they would be able to overcome—and finally, be free!

That should prove to Black *and* White men *and* women that we have really missed something! Somehow, many have missed the significance of the parable of the death and resurrection of Jesus Christ! Some folks wear a cross around their necks—mostly, a gold or silver crucifix. But do they really know what the cross signifies? It means that God, our Father, lets us know that He wants us to be resurrected! It is He who dwells within each of us, but cannot rule until we know the truth! He said that it would make us free! The time is now for us to be raised up in the knowledge of the truth. The cross did not destroy it. It must be, just as Jesus was—resurrected!

The manner of love that God bestowed upon us was encouragement that we should be called the sons and daughters of God! He gave His only begotten Son, that we should become His sons and daughters! Ephesians 2:11: says *"For both he that sanctifieth and they who are sanctified are all of one: for which cause he is not ashamed to call them brethren ..."*

An astronomical number of lives have already been lost because of this evil spirit that has overtaken so many in our society! Many young lives have already been lost! During the last year of my teaching career, I had many students in my classrooms who professed to be *"antichrist"* or non-believers! The first time I heard young men and women say that surprised me. As that school year went on, not only did I come to believe their claims of disbelief in Christ, but their behavior convinced me that Satan was having his way in the lives of many of the youngsters I was trying to teach! Each day, I drove to the school confessing my faith in God and His goodness! When I entered the school house each morning, I asked the Lord to guide me and see me through the school day. On my way home, I would thank Him for His goodness, and His having kept me from any hurt and danger. My last year of teaching high school English Literature really taught me just how important it is to keep my faith in God in tact! I can attest to the fact that a lot of young people are dying by the thousands because for some reason, they, and so many of their friends, are so bowed down that they can *"in nowise lift themselves up!"* Their very lives are being snatched away by others, some, who are, and others, who are *NOT* surrendering their lives to Christ so that they can be healed of their own infirmities!

Ecclesiastes 12:1 tells us that it is vitally important that people seek God while they are *"young,"* and that term has a two-fold meaning. The word *"young"* can actually be interpreted in two ways. First, it can mean that you are to seek the Lord in the days of your youth, or while you are chronologically young, before you become encumbered with the cares of the adult life or the real world! In other words, we are to seek God while we are youthful, innocent and impressionable, as empty vessel that have not yet been corrupted by the sins of the world—before the age of accountability!

Another way to look at the word *"young"* is in reference to the salvation experience . . . when you are newly converted! That refers to the day when you initially accept Christ as your Lord and Savior—when most new believers get *"on fire"* for the Lord! You know, when you're so excited about God that you just want to tell everybody who will listen about your born-again experience! Oh, you know, when nobody had to wonder why you weren't at church because you were **always** there! Nobody had to tell you to pray about anything because not a day passed that you didn't talk to the Lord yourself! Then, the *"newness"* began to wear off and Satan recognized his opportunity to start messing with your mind! He began to make you doubt the reality of your salvation and question your relationship with God. That's just the way he is! He usually begins to remind new believers who they *"used"* to be, and the fun they *"used"* to have when they did the things they *"used"* to do! They first stop reading their Bible everyday and when the enemy sees that, he charges upon them—full steam ahead! He recognizes their *"youthfulness"* in the Lord, and he is known to set out to take full advantage of the situation; and his intent is to destroy!

Satan puts men and women up high on his agenda when they are set on doing what God brought them into the world to do, or when they are trying to do what they've realized that he or she was created to do. Remember, Satan even tried to get Jesus to take some pride in Himself by attacking Him! He began dealing with his physical appetite. Well, that's how he deals with us, isn't it? We have to be familiar with the Word of God in order to recognize that! The Word must become life and it must dwell within us! Each and every day, we must ask God to speak to us so that we can live each one as He created us to live them!

According to the words found in Ecclesiastes 12:1, we are to be ever mindful of God, our Creator, while we are young, because the day will surely come when the enemy will launch his attack on us! Well, here's another newsflash: *"It doesn't matter how old you are or how young you are! Satan wants you destroyed! He wants you devastated and out of control! Let's just face the facts . . . Satan wants you dead! He wants your faith, peace, strength and joy to "drop out!"* However, we must stop moaning and bewailing the trials and tribulations that he uses to accomplish the task! We simply have to know that we are not going to do anything without some opposition because it is part of our *"servant-hood!"* *Satan really wants to stop you and get you to turn around so that he cannot only STOP you from receiving your blessing, but he wants to destroy the blessings of those who God wants to use you to be a blessing to! (If you don't get that, read it over and over until you do!)* That is why it is so vital that we do not focus on the buffering of the devil. Instead, we must focus on the blessings of God! We must not let the storms that occur in our lives keep us from giving God our praise! We must remember just where He brought *us* from! I have had to remind myself as well!

In II Corinthians 10:3-4, Paul reminds us that although we are mortal beings, clothed in flesh, our battle is *not* with the flesh! In other words, our enemy, our adversary, is *not* a man, a woman, a boy or girl. Our adversary is none other than the Satan—the devil himself! Therefore, Paul says, the weapons of our warfare are not carnal! Guns and knives are not effective weapons for this battle either! That enemy cannot be physically killed or destroyed! So . . . since the weapons of our warfare are *not* carnal, we are going to need more than knives or guns to fight! We *must* be armed with weapons that are *mighty* through God, Himself, who enables us to pull down the strongholds that face us each and every day of our lives!

You see, we are dealing with some very *real* strongholds and that word means *exactly* what it says! A stronghold is some power, some force, or some issue that seems to have a *"strong hold"* on you. Once, I was guest speaker in a youth service. In a church filled with young people, I encouraged them to take a stand against some strongholds in their own lives. Note cards and pencils were passed out to the youth who were seated in the congregation. I encouraged each of them to take a card and write on it the things that they felt were keeping them unable to succeed in their youthful lives. The moment that they wrote on the note cards the issues that had been binding them up for as long as they could remember, the youths left their seats and walked up to the altar to deposit their cards in a trash can that had been placed there just for that service. That was exactly when Satan went to his *"Plan B"* on them! I told the young people that, too! When Satan witnessed their outward display of faith that night, he notified his agents that they needed to *"get on their jobs"* and get the youth back to where they were—or possibly in a worse condition than they had been in before! So, I told them, they were fortunate because they had come to the right place where they could find out about some weapons that are *not* of this world, but *mighty through God*, for the pulling down of those strongholds! I saw some smiles cross the faces of many of the young people in the sanctuary.

The weapons, which *can* and *will* help you withstand Satan's attacks in these last and evil days are found in the sixth chapter of the Book of Ephesians. In that chapter, Apostle Paul had addressed the Ephesians as *"children."* After all, we are **all** children, sons and daughters of the most high God! He is our Father, and our obedience to Him works the same for us as it does with earthly mothers, fathers and their children! We are to obey the Apostle's words because God said that it was *right* to do so. So Paul began by letting the Ephesians know that they must also see themselves as *"children."* Those who are chronologically young are under their parents' authority—or they are, at least, supposed to be. They are children of God who live under His divine authority! When you honor Him and His Word, the Scriptures say that *life will be well with you!* You are guaranteed not only of a long life, but a life that will be more abundant!

> *"Finally, my brethren, be strong in the Lord, and in the power of His might. Put on the whole armor of God, that ye may be able to stand against the wiles of the devil, For we wrestle not against flesh and blood, but against principalities, against powers, against the rulers of the darkness of this world, against spiritual wickedness in high places."*

Ephesians 6:10-23

NINE

IT IS 2010, and our world is still bursting at the seams with souls that are crooked! The result is virtually astounding! Crooked souls perpetuate crooked thoughts, crooked words and ultimately, crooked deeds! Just turning on the television or listening to the radio each day, we see and hear stories about them. We come to church, on our way to worship, to receive a Word from the Lord, a touch from the Master, but inside, as well as outside of those walls, are people whose infirmities are so great that the moment that they walk outside of the doors, the churchgoers' lives are being affected! Well, we cannot help but be affected! After all, we are in this world together, the strong and the weak, the just and the unjust, the saved and the unsaved!

I have made some very bad choices that I will have to live with for the rest of my life! I realize that I need to start trusting someone who knows much more than I do! I am determined to let someone take charge of my life and oversee my tomorrows. The only person who could actually fill those shoes is Father God himself! After all, He is the one who is already there, in my upcoming tomorrows, just waiting for me to arrive

That message is one that I have tried to get across to men and women all over the country! Several years ago, when I founded *Healing Hearts Ministry*, I was determined to try, as earnestly as I could, to address the needs of men and women who had not been able to fulfill the will of God in their own lives. *Healing Hearts* targeted issues that had been developed in the lives of those who came out to the weekly meetings to address the difficulties of overcoming the emotional, physical or sexual abuse they had faced—or were currently facing! We discussed some of the unresolved issues of personal tragedy, mental anguish and traumatic experiences that many had not been able to overcome. Those who attended the meetings were able to talk about their own personal grief and spiritual brokenness with others who could relate to them. They, too, had *"rocked in the same boats"* many times throughout their own lives! *Healing Hearts* was established upon the liberating principles of God's Word, and I could openly attest to that! I would always begin the meetings by telling the men and women who sat before me that God would *never* use their pasts to determine their futures. Mature Christians, I told them, let their pasts remain in the past! As a result, they don't have to react—they can respond! Week after week, I looked into the eyes of those who earnestly wanted to know *"how"* to do that. Without the question ever being asked, I would give them the answer: *Through forgiveness!*

Every person has been separated from God because of their sins, but God has always been there to form a close relationship with them. He reached out to us in a personal way by sending Jesus Christ to live with us and teach us how to forgive others! Christ taught us just how vital it is for us live our lives as much like Him as we could! Because Jesus died on the cross, God's forgiveness, through His Son, became available to everyone!

In the 9th chapter of Matthew, we find remarkable instances of the power and majesty of the Lord Jesus Christ, efficient to convince us that He is able to save the uttermost of all that come to God through Him . . . and He is willing to do that! He **is** indeed able! In this chapter, Jesus healed the sick of the palsy, raised a ruler's daughter from the dead, healed a woman who had been suffering with a bloody issue for numerous years, gave sight to the blind, cast the devil out of the demonically possessed and cured all manner of sicknesses and diseases! What a mighty God we serve, one who is able to restore not only health and strength, but life itself!

When I graduated from Columbus High School in Columbus, Georgia, like many of my classmates, I had gone away from home to go to college. I had attended Mercer University in Macon, Georgia, which was located about eighty miles away from Columbus. I was a Mercer University student for all of one semester, until I was overcome by what I interpreted as *"massive confusion"* in my life. One morning, I had awakened and simply had no clue about what in the world I was doing there! Supposedly, I was set on pursuing a degree in Political Science. I had flatly refused to pursue one in music because obtaining a degree in music would probably mean that the only area I could seriously consider going into would be that of Music

Education. Me, become a teacher? No way, I thought! *(That would turn out ironically when I actually became a high school English teacher about nine years later!)* I had always been music-orientated though. I had been writing songs and playing the piano since the age of eight. I had written my first song, *"What Now?"* when I was nine years old, taking piano lessons from a man that everyone called *"Smokey."* I think that playing the piano somehow came naturally to me. It has taken many years for me to realize that it actually was a *gift* that God had given to me! Everyone, and I do mean *everyone*, assumed that I would make music my career! While in high school, I had turned down a scholarship in music, because I did not want to go that route, and I realize that I felt that way because everyone *expected* me to do it. My adoptive mother, Aunt Meg, used to say that I always did the opposite of what I was expected to do. I guess she was somehow right about that. She also said that I always seemed to be somewhere that I was not supposed to be. Retrospectively, I believe that has been the case as well, more often than not. In any event, I had no intention of tapping out the years of my life with a baton, keeping time for some enthusiastic mother's *"wanna-be"* prodigy!

In the Spring of 1977, I had enrolled at Columbus College to pursue a degree in Political Science. All of my classes were in the evening. I tried diligently, but I just could not keep myself away from the Fine Arts Hall. When we were given a break in class, I would find my way over the campus to the building where many pianos were located. Sometimes, I would not even return that night, playing the piano and writing songs about the emptiness that existed in my life. I was dissatisfied with school, with life, and above all, with myself! At that time, I thought that my dissatisfaction was the result of everything *but* me! Nevertheless, I kept tapping away until October 1978, when I dropped out of college, for the *second* time, and moved to Atlanta, Georgia, in another attempt to *"find myself!."*

In Atlanta, I had found everything—*but* me! For some time, I performed as a lead vocalist and keyboardist with an Atlanta based rhythm and blues band and held down a job as Director of Music at a Methodist Church in East Point. These conflicting occupations were quite challenging—especially when the band would be out of town, on the road, on Friday and Saturday nights. We would have to pack all of our equipment up and speed back to Atlanta, before dawn, on Sunday morning, so that I could *"make it to the church on time"* for the morning worship service! The other members of the band never complained though. They all thought that I was a *"good Christian girl"* and never offered me any of the marijuana or cocaine they themselves were consuming between sets! They never let anyone else offer it to me either! Many times, I had sat in dressing rooms and watched them and other entertainers *"get high"* between our performances on Friday or Saturday nights. On the follow Sunday morning, I would sit upright at the piano and play the *"Songs of Zion"* with partially closed eyelids. Some people actually thought that I was *"in the Spirit"* when my eyes were closed like that. My good friend, Cheryl, who was a member of the choir, knew that I was just exhausted from the previous night's *"gig"* that my band and I had performed in a city not very far away! It didn't take very long for her to discover that my eyes were closed because I was suffering from exhaustion, having performed in a nightclub the previous night!

One evening in January 1982, I had received a call from one of my aunts who lived in Iowa. I had not spoken to her in a number of years. She called to tell me that my father's mother, Grandmama Tiny, had passed away. I had been very upset to hear the news. About a month earlier, I had intended to go and visit her the following Summer, having not seen her since I was eight years old! Because of the terrible things my father, Tony, had done, the aunt who assumed custody of us would not permit any of his family members to even talk to us. Periodically, they would call just to see how we were doing. Aunt Meg would say that we were *"getting along just fine"* and quickly end the conservation, before they could even ask to speak to any one of us. That routine continued throughout our childhood. In fact, I do not ever recall talking to any of my father's family members while living with Aunt Meg.

When I dropped out of college and moved out on my own, at the age of nineteen, one of the first things I did was to call my grandmother. I didn't even know her telephone number, so I called information to get it. I asked the operator at the other end of the line if she had a listing for a *"Tiny Clayton."* She told me a couple of things: first, she said that the number was *"unlisted"* and secondly, she informed me that my grandmother's name was not really *"Tiny,"* as I had always believed it was! She did not tell me what Grandmama's real name was, but she did, however, know her and she offered to contact her and have her call me, if I wanted her to. I was in shock! I didn't even know my grandmother's real name! I didn't know which feeling was stronger—embarrassment and stupidity—or my ignorance!

A few moments later, my grandmother called me back. She was very surprised that I had tried to reach her, after all of those years, but she was extremely glad that I had! During our conversation, I promised her that I would try to come and see her during the Summer. For whatever reasons, the Summer of 1978 had come and gone, and I had not returned to Iowa yet. In fact, for the next three New Years, my brother Michael and I would resolve to make the trip and end up not going for various reasons.

On New Year's Day in 1982, Michael and I vowed that we would definitely go to Iowa to see our grandmother during the Summer. He was as eager as I was to go! Well, Grandmama Tiny *(again, I have to reiterate that I never found out what her real name was)* couldn't wait for us any longer. That winter, when I did make the trip to Iowa, I did get to see her, but she was lying still in a grey casket, wearing a pink dress, her hands folded in stiff white gloves. Looking down at the face I barely recognized, I realized that she was not even aware that I was there.

At the cemetery, I could hardly see a thing! In that part of the country, the weather was awful that time of year. It was snowing and the wind was fiercely blowing the frosty substance into everybody's face! Not accustomed to it, I finally gave up and went back to sit in the car. I don't think anyone else could see either, but perhaps they were used to it, so they stayed around the grave site until the final words were spoken and the casket was lowered into the frozen ground. As I sat in the car, waiting for the service to end, I felt very much as if I was trapped in some kind of time zone or something. The dreariness of the snow billowing around the limousine, the sadness of the occasion, and the distance I felt from the other members of my family all served to thrust me further and further away from them. I felt as though I was alone, standing behind a brick wall.

The next day, the snow had stopped falling so one of my uncles took me around the city to take a look at Fort Dodge, the place where I had lived as a youngster. *"Where's that house we used to live in?"* I asked my uncle, as we turned down a street lined with bare elm trees.

"That red house?" he asked, his eyebrows raised.

"Yeah," I replied. *"The one with the wall in front of it."*

I remembered falling off of that wall one day when I was very young. My cousin Elaine and I had been playing, pretending to be tightrope walkers, stretching our arms out for balance, as we walked cautiously across the *"beam."* The wall was as high as I was tall at the time, I remembered. I was pretty tall for a seven year old, too. Somehow, I had lost my balance, tumbled off of the wall and landed on the ground in front of it.

When I looked up, the same uncle that now chauffeured me around the city had stood over me with squinted eyes. *"You okay, Shortcake?"* he asked, helping me to my feet.

"Yeah," I said, although I felt a little dizzy. My head had begun to hurt.

He helped me to his car, at the edge of the driveway. We got into the car and rode downtown. My uncle had some errands to run, and since he was supposed to be watching my cousin Elaine and I, he had taken us along with him. When we arrived downtown, he got out of the car and went into one of the buildings that lined the busy street. While he was away, I became ill, and began throwing up all over the back seat! Later, my mother said that the fall from the wall had *"shaken me up a bit,"*

For some reason, I was anxious to see that *"wall"* again. We turned down a street that was no more familiar to me than my grandmother's face had been.

"There it is," my uncle said, a broad smile spread across his face.

I was aghast! The wall that I had remembered being at least six feet tall was no taller than a step up on the walkway! I could hardly believe how tiny the red brick structure actually was!

"Are you sure that's the same house?" I asked him.

"Yep, that's the same house," he replied, nodding his head.

"That's unbelievable!" I whispered, not even looking at the house. I was too baffled about the wall!

It's strange how walls have a way of tampering with your perception of things! When you're walking on top of one or standing on one side of it, the wall definitely affects what you see! Most of the time, walls are quite threatening, especially when you don't know how you're going to get over them or what is on the other side of them! I do think that walls are necessary though. Without them, our perception would either be too narrow or too wide. Besides that—without them, we would be much too vulnerable! Sometimes, we need the walls for protection. At others, we need to be able to lower them when it's safe to do so. Life has taught me a lot about walls. Whenever I have looked back and taken a second look, I realize that they were never as high as I thought they were, nor as dangerous as I suspected them to be. They were just sometimes necessary—helping me to become the person that God created me to be in the first place!

> *"Nay, in all these things we are more than conquerors through him that loved us. For I am persuaded, that neither death, nor life, nor angels, nor principalities, nor powers, nor things present, nor things to come, nor height, nor depth, nor any other creature, shall be able to separate us from the love of God."*
>
> *Romans 9:37-39*

A lot of things changed for me in the years between 1978 and 1985. For one thing, I left the Rhythm and Blues band that I had been playing with for almost a year. The other members, all male, seemed to be more interested in the female following than the future of the group. Their goals and mine were no longer the same—not that I *knew* what my goals actually were! I was convinced that I wanted more out of the music business than they were after though. So, one day, I just quit! Then, I made the first of many big mistakes I would make in my entire life—I married someone who was very much like my father! I have written about him before, but I have to reiterate that I really thought that my father, Tony, was a horrible man! I had openly shared with others his having killed my mother and my grandmother, wounding my grandfather and my seven year old brother Michael, and then turning the .38 on himself. You would think that I would be able to spot his likeness a mile off! But no, I was still looking for myself—and instead, I found a husband! Our union was disastrous and after a year and a half and an eight month old son, I finally escaped, divorced what I had determined was my father's clone, and returned to Columbus, Georgia.

I know that people say that you can always go back home, but it is really never the same, and neither are you! Unfortunately, the people who have raised you don't seem to be aware of that. They expect you to somehow slide back into your *"slot"* and keep your curfew! You just want them to leave you alone and do whatever it is you *think* you want to do. I came home and found that I could not stay there very long. I realized that I was no longer *"at home,"* and that was somewhat devastating! I spent many hours trying to figure that one out! If that wasn't *"home,"* where in the world where was it then? Filled with a new urgency to find my place in life, I packed my little boy and my possessions up in a U-Haul trailer, hitched it to the back of my Chevrolet Cavalier and struck out west to California!

What I found when I got there was the ocean! The ocean is a very beautiful creation! God had to have made it because man was not capable of such perfection! Even the waters of the Pacific, dirty and polluted by mankind, appear to be pretty, tantalizing shades of blue the further out you look! For long hours, I sat on the beach, stared out at the waves, and wondered what I was supposed to do next! Some days, I sat, just meditating, hoping that God would have pity on me and send me a message in a bottle, washed up on the shores of Long Beach! I kept one eye on my son, frolicking at the water's edge, and the other on the white, foamy tide, looking for the message, hoping it would turn up soon—in the bottle! It never appeared. I would collect my things, shake the gritty sand from my feet and legs, and carry my squirming, most times crying, protesting toddler to the car. After a while, I stopped looking for the bottle and just enjoyed watching Tjai play in the water.

In September 1987, I had had the unique opportunity to perform in the stage production of the play entitled *"A Song for My Brothers."* The play, which was about several people who had contracted the AIDS virus and some who had died as a result of it, ran for a few weeks at the Los Angeles Inner City Cultural Arts Center. The experience was one that I know that I will *never* be able to forget, as long as I live! Steve, who was my manager at the time, had asked me if I would be interested in auditioning for an opportunity to sing the theme song for the play. The play was already being rehearsed in a theater that was located in West Hollywood. I asked him what the name of that song was, to which he replied, *"They don't have one yet."*

That was just like Steve, I thought. I, myself, had no idea about any lyrics that would address such a subject like AIDS! Like many others, I knew absolutely nothing about that or the HIV virus! Nevertheless, I undertook the challenge—to write *"the song"* which I would be expected to sing on the opening night of the play, if I was selected to do so. A couple of days later, I called Steve and told him that I had come up with something that he might be interested in hearing. A few hours later, he came over to my apartment and listened to me belt out the lyrics to *"Somebody Needs Your Love,"* a song that had to have been inspired by God and played on my antiquated upright piano. Upon hearing it, Steve was overwhelmed! Right then, he called the play's director and told him about it! The director, E. Lloyd Napier, listened to the song for the first time, over the telephone, and anxiously invited me to come to the auditorium in West Hollywood, where the cast would be rehearsing the next evening. I told him that I would be glad to come, so I went.

When I walked into the auditorium, I was immediately fascinated by what I saw on the floor level stage! Talented men and women, transformed into HIV-infected or AIDS-infected people, delivered lines that I swore must have been written with some actual victims in mind! I sat, spellbound, listening to monologues that were filled with so much pain and agony, that I felt I had been in the presence of people who were familiar with the real victims being portrayed!

By the time E. Lloyd spotted Steve and I standing in the back of the auditorium, he called for a break in the rehearsal and asked me to come up on the stage. The action I had just witnessed had humbled me so much that I found myself feeling a bit timid about facing people in the room to whom I had not yet been introduced! To one side of the stage was a *"banged up"* piano which was desperately in need of tuning. Anxiously, E. Lloyd introduced me to the group of actors as he led me to the piano. He told them that he had heard the song over the phone, and he had already fallen in love with what he had heard! He was very eager to hear it *"live,"* and he was anxious for the cast to hear the song as well.

There was no stool, chair, or bench, so I stood, slightly hunched over the chipped and peeling keys and played the introduction. It kind of amused me that my hands were shaking. I was not usually nervous, but at that moment, I could actually feel my knees quivering, as well! When I began to sing, the room was quiet. *"You know what's going on. You don't want to talk about it, but it's still happening. And it's happening to someone that you love. That's why everybody's got to get involved."* I began to feel the words, the music that I had written, and the meaning that God had intended for me to compose, but I realized that it had not been just for me. As I sang *"Somebody Needs Your Love,"* I was filled with an emotion that I had never experienced in my life until then! I realized that *"somebody"* was *"everybody"* and the truth was that we were *all* in need of love and compassion!

When I finished the song, not a single eye in the room was dry! For a moment, nobody said a word. Moments later, applause rose up and literally echoed throughout the place! Not only did the cast love the song, but E. Lloyd loved it so much that he wrote the *song and me* into the script of his play! Every night, during its run, I opened the play by walking out from the darkness to the center of the stage singing *"Somebody Needs Your Love."* Two other songs were added to the play—*"There's Always Hope,"* which I wrote, and *"You Don't Die,"* a song to which E. Lloyd had written the lyrics and I had penned the music. The play ended each night when, after the death of the main character, *"Sammy Lee,"* I strolled out onto the stage and sang our collaboration, *"You Don't Die,"* lyrics that were filled with so much emotion that I could hardly finish it without tears filling my own eyes!

I learned a lot about AIDS from that experience. Most importantly, I learned that it doesn't just affect homosexual males, but it claims heterosexual males and females, children, and even infants! Nobody is exempt! We are all at risk! Little did I know it then, but the illness would affect my very own family in days to come. I suppose that's why I had found it so ridiculous that the people the ostracized the elementary school boy who had AIDS tried to have him put out of their children's school. For all they knew, they could become HIV positive at any time, if they hadn't done so already! AIDS is something that has affected us **all** in one way or another! In spite of that or anything else that seems to divide us, what the world still really needs is love!

> *"And now abideth faith, hope, love, these three;*
> *but the greatest of these is love."*

1 Corinthians 13: 13

TEN

CONFESSION IS NOT just *"good for the soul."* It is the essence of salvation, and that is freedom from bondage! According to Luke 4:18, *"The spirit of the Lord is upon me, because he hath anointed me to preach the gospel to the poor; he hath sent me to heal the brokenhearted, to preach deliverance to the captives, and recovery of sight to the blind, to set at liberty them that are bruised."* How? Sometimes, through redemptive conversation! Romans 10:8-10 tells us that *"But what saith it? The word is nigh thee, even in thy mouth, and in thy heart; that is; the word of faith, which we preach; That if thou shalt confess with thy mouth the Lord Jesus, and shalt believe in thine heart that God hath raised him from the dead, thou shalt be saved. For with the heart man believeth unto righteousness; and with the mouth confession is made unto salvation."* Yes, even from abuse!

When I began doing some sincere writing, I talked about abuse because I could relate to those who have been abused. I shared with readers my memories of *"The Color Purple."* I wrote about having cried all the way through the movie, when good things happened and when bad things happened to the sisters, Celie and Nettie. I remembered feeling sorry for Celie for having been sexually abused by the man that she *thought* was her father. But I could really understand the character, Sophia, that had been portrayed by Oprah Winfrey. Sophia had had to fight off sexual advances of her uncles and her cousins and had become willing to kill her own husband, Harpo, before letting him beat her! My heart really went out to her, because she was very much like me! I confessed that I used to *be* Sophia! It was an admission that I made, not only to myself, but I had made it to the whole world! At the time that I said it, I had not realized that there were many more *"Sophias"* out there! Writing about my own experiences opened many doors for me, but I was determined to help other people around the world open their own doors and obtain healing in their own lives!

It doesn't matter how our wounds are acquired. We all need the good news of the healing power of redemption! It is true that evil is intended to destroy us! What we have to know is that God will take those negative experiences and use them for our good! Healing in our lives is not the resolution of our pasts. In fact, healing uses our pasts to draw us into deeper relationships with God, the Father, and His purpose for our lives! We have to understand how to deal with past hurts and acknowledge the damage to the human spirit while charting a path towards the abundant life God promises us! It took me about thirty-eight years of my life to discover that God never intended my past to determine my future. Mature Christians have learned to let their *pasts be pasts.* They have learned that when they do that, they have the ability to handle pressures in their everyday lives. They don't *react*—they *think* first, and then they *respond!*

One morning as I was reading my Bible, the words that were written in the fourth chapter of Mark crossed my eyes. Many, many times I had read about Jesus leading his disciples over to the other side of the sea and sharing with them parables that could not be understood by those who had not truly given their lives to God. I had already read the previous chapter, but when I reached the one in which He told the disciples to pass over to the other side of the sea, away from the multitude that had come to hear Him, the words stood out to me like a brilliant light! Beginning at verse 35, I read *"And the same day, when the even was come, he saith unto them, Let us pass over unto the other side."* I understood that Christ had taken them *away* from everybody and everything that they had become accustomed to. Verse 36 said *"And when they had sent away the multitude, they took him even as he was in the ship. And there were also with him other little ships."* Verse 37 says that *"And there arose a great storm of wind, and the waves beat into the ship, so that it was now full."* Humm . . . I thought, like the storm I had been undergoing for *most* of my lifetime? Many times, I had felt as if I was in the midst of a storm, just as many others had, that I had not done anything to bring it into my life. In fact, at that very moment, that storm was raging all around me each and every day of my forty-seven years of living! When I reached verse 38, I found that Jesus was *"in the hinder part of the ship, asleep on a pillow: and they awoke him, and said unto him, Master, carest thou not that we perish?"* Christ knew everything, so I was sure that even in his sleep, He *knew* what was going on aboard. The disciples were upset about being in the midst of the storm, but He didn't seem to be bothered at all by the raging wind and waves. Verse 39 says that *"And he arose, and rebuked the wind, and said unto the sea, Peace, be still. And the wind ceased, and there was a great calm."*

Even though the disciples were probably going out of their minds, thinking about what was going on around them, maybe even thinking that their lives would possibly be coming to an end, Christ was not unnerved by the wind or the waves at all. In fact, in verse 40, He asked them *"Why are ye so fearful? How is it that ye have no faith?"* Those words told me that no matter what is going on *in* or *around* you in your life, no matter how wild the storm is raging, no matter what has happened to bring about fear or confusion, or even ironic things that have happened to you or your family members, Christ expects you and I to have a sense of *peace* about it! After all, peace is the result of *trust!* When we trust Him to take care of whatever it is that comes about us, no matter how strong the winds are blowing, no matter how high the waves are rising, no matter how anyone or anything confronts us in our lives, we *must* have peace about it, because to do so is evidence of our trust in God!

I didn't intend to return to the school where I had taught in 2001-2002. My first year in that school had been a trying one, to say the least, so I had decided to return to the previous school system at the beginning of the next school year. The day I received paperwork from the school district to complete and send back to the main office, I had been sitting at the kitchen table filling it out. Tjai came into the kitchen and announced that he needed to go out to the center where he had been working during the Summer and pick up his final pay check. I told him to hurry and do so, but he needed to get back home as soon as he could. I was going to be leaving the house, en route to the grocery store to do some shopping. I had decided to put the paperwork aside and take a trip to a nearby grocery store. I didn't know why, but at that moment, I felt that I needed to go and purchase a few things. Tjai told me that he would be back as soon as he could, and he left the house. Shortly after that, I told Little Derrick and Christopher that I was going to be leaving home, going to the grocery store. I told them that Tjai was going to pick up his pay check, but he would be back shortly. Before I could get out of the house, Christopher came into the kitchen to tell me that he and Little Derrick, were in the midst of a game of football on their Nintendo station, so they would probably be wrapped up in it until Tjai returned. He went back into their bedroom, and I left home, on my way to the store.

While I was shopping, I picked up items that I really had not intended to purchase. Actually, they were not things that I had come to the store to buy, but I picked them up and dropped them into my shopping cart anyway. By the time I arrived at the cash register, my basket was overflowing! It even amazed me that so many items had found their way into my cart—especially since I had had no intention of doing so much shopping! By the end of that day, it would be evident that I had purchased things that my sons would need to care for themselves in my absence from home.

The flashing lights began to reappear in my mind after I had paid for my groceries! I had not suffered any Grand Mal seizures in an entire year! What in the world, I wondered, was happening to me? I pushed my shopping cart out of the store, into the parking lot where my car was. The wind and waves had, once again, begun to rise in my life! I could hardly see the lock that I needed to open the trunk of my car, but God enabled me to get my key into it, open the trunk and put all of my bags into the car. When I had put the last bag of groceries in, I closed the lid and pushed my shopping cart to a nearby stall. The flashing was becoming brighter as I found my way back to the car, opened the door, and climbed into the driver's seat.

"Oh Lord," I said aloud, *"I don't know what is happening to me, but I know that you do! So I'm going to ask you to take care of me! Please don't let me kill myself today! I have children at home, and I need to get back to them! I'm not ready to die yet! Please don't take my life today! Now, I'm going to start this car up, and I need you to help me get home!"* I must have sounded like those disciples in the midst of the storm! Distraught, they had awakened Jesus from His sleep and asked for His assistance. I put the key into the ignition and started up the car. That was the last thing that I would be able to remember. Later, I would only be told of the forty miles I drove down the road, from Columbus to LaGrange, passing the street that I lived on—the street where my three sons were at home, playing Nintendo and waiting for my return from the grocery store.

Days later, when my husband brought me home from the hospital, the papers that I had been trying to complete before that incident were still lying on the kitchen table. He encouraged me to just get into my bedclothes and lie down for a while. He said that I should not worry about finishing them up or anything else until I got better. I shook my head and told him that I was not going to do anything with them. I said that I intended to call the principal at the new school and let her know that I would not be coming back to that county to teach.

"Why?" he asked.

"I just need to let her know that I'm not going to be able to come when the new school year begins," I said. *"I believe that God wants me to just sit still and let Him have His way."*

"What?" Derrick asked, a puzzled expression having crossed his face.

"I believe that He wants me to stay where I am right now." I didn't need to ask anyone what to do or where to go next. I realized that after Jesus had caused the wind to cease and brought a great calm upon the sea, the disciples had asked one another who He was, able to calm the wind and have the sea obey Him. On the other hand, I *knew* who He was. I had been introduced to Him when I was twelve years old.

"Why?" Derrick asked, knowing that I didn't really want to continue teaching at that school.

"I don't know why," I said. *"I just feel that He wants me to wait and let Him take care of it . . . Anyway, don't you think that it would be safer for me to stay where I am, rather than to drive myself all the way over to Victory Drive and back each day?"*

Slowly, he nodded his head.

The next day, I called the principal at the new school and told her that because of the unexpected things that had occurred, I would not be coming to teach at her school. I thanked her for the offer, but I believed that, it would better if I stayed where I was at the moment. I told her that I had decided to just *"be still, and let God have His way."* So, that was exactly what I did!

When the next school year began, things were a bit different from the previous one. Everyday, I would have to sit in another teacher's classroom, during my planning period, while her students were gone to lunch. I didn't feel unsettled because having to spend my planning period in another teacher's classroom was not the newest position I had found myself in lately. Everything seemed kind of unfamiliar to me, but I thought that was because I was recovering from the brain surgery I had previously undergone.

In my head, healing was still underway! It had been a year and doctors had told Derrick and I that it would take some time for me to get well. He assured us that healing was indeed taking place, and I believed that! Even though I had found myself, several times, asking God to make the process speed up somewhat, I was still facing the fact that that would only occur in *His* time! I would have to wait, patiently trusting *Him* to heal my mind, my spirit, my body and my soul!

Every day was a new day! I had always known that God ordered each and every step we took! I had always trusted Him to do just that! When I thought about how far He had brought me, I had to attribute my success and having overcome the obstacles I had faced in my lifetime to Him alone! When I had traveled across the country, sharing with others, the goodness of the Lord, I had never talked about things I had heard about. Openly, I had shared with others who had landed in the midst of their own despair, just how good God had been to me! I talked about how He had made a way for me and the others whose lives I had been blessed to encounter! Constantly, I had encouraged others to trust Him like I believed that I had learned to do, so that they too, would have a testimony of their own about just how they had *"made it over!"*

Many years ago, I had realized that Jesus had come to teach mankind the importance of *"counting the cost"* of living a Christian life. He had His disciples to surrender everything that had significance in their everyday lives and follow Him. Living life as a *"Christ-ian"* meant that those who did so would be willing to do just that! To follow Jesus would cost them *much more*—just as it costs us today—to live their lives differently from the way many others did! According to Luke 14:26, in the presence of great multitudes, Jesus had turned and said *"If any man comes to me, and hates not his father, and mother, and wife, and children, and brethren, and sisters, yea, and his own life also, he cannot be my disciple."* Jesus had deliberately made the statement to let His followers know that to serve Him meant even more than abiding by *"family ties."* Understand that *"hate"* did *not* mean the same thing then that it means today! God has never advocated hatred. It was an act of their will, or a decision of their own! In the Scriptures, *"hate"* meant to *"love less"* or to *"prefer less than."*

Jesus had come to bring a sword to, to sever, or to bring a distinction about where our commitment is to be. Once, I heard a minister refer to a *"ham and eggs"* distinction. The chicken, he told the congregation, lays an egg for the farmer, thus indicating his commitment to him or her. On the other hand, the pig loses his life for the farmer when he is slaughtered, so that we can put ham on the table as part of our Thanksgiving and Christmas dinners! They must, Jesus told his disciples, be dedicated, willing to give their very lives to follow Him! We, too, must be dedicated, willing to give our very lives to follow Jesus! Matthew 10:35 says that Jesus came to *"set a man at variance against his father, and the daughter against her mother, and the daughter-in-law against her mother-in-law."* That meant that *"Christians"* would be willing to go against their own kin or members of their own households, if necessary, to follow Him. Following or discipleship *often* brings about conflict among family members—particularly in *"religious"* families!

The moment that His followers embraced what He had called them to do, the conflict began! However, Luke 14:24 indicated that we must put Christ *first*—even before ourselves! *Even the "called" must die before they can live!*

Everyone must give up their *own* ministry and serve one whom God has called until God calls them out to do *His* ministry. After all, no one has the right to be put in God's place. We must **_first_** seek the kingdom of God! Likewise, we must love our neighbors and ourselves! Jesus' hands and feet were nailed to the cross *for* me! It took me almost forty years of living to understand that as a Christian, I must be willing to bear my own cross! It is the test of a Christian's obedience to do the will of God! Verses 28 through 30 talks about the Christian getting into the middle of his or her own test and not being able to finish it. The problem is that they have not counted the cost! We have to be willing to follow Christ, no matter what befalls us! Of course, there will be times that we will get off track, but the key is finding our place, catching it very quickly, and getting back on track right away! I heard another pastor say that *"If the going gets easier, you're not climbing!"* We can get stronger! The trials and tribulations may become harder, but if you keep that faith in tact, they will *not* overtake you!

Although I had gotten to know many of the wonderful students and teachers at my new school, because of the negative behavior of the principal towards me, I had not wanted to return there the following school year. It seemed that as a result of my having experienced seizures the previous year, he had tried numerous times to get me to resign from my teaching position at that school. In my first year there, he had come into my classroom to evaluate me. During the evaluation, he had written several *"untruths"* about my teaching. In fact, he had actually written *lies* about what had gone on in my classroom the day he visited! I would not even sign the evaluation because of the lies it contained. Instead, I went home and typed a five page response to the evaluation, questioning his reasons for the things he had written about my teaching in his review. It had taken me an entire evening to respond to the review, but it took him a whole week to summon me to his office to discuss that response. He had called me to his office to discuss it with him. One of the and the assistant principals, a Black woman, sat quietly with her head bowed most of the time. He asked me *"why"* I had said certain things in my response. I told him that the reason that I had *"said"* those things was because they were *true!* I had no reason or cause, I told him, to lie!

He leaned back in his leather chair, somewhat ambiguously, and lowered his eyes as he told me that I would be *"happy to know that he had every intention of having me back at that school the next school year!"*

Staring down at the vacant space in front of me, I had silently vowed that I had no intention of returning to that school under that man's principalship! I would have to find a job teaching in another district! After the meeting, I returned to my classroom. I looked at the walls that I had covered with various pictures of instructional items and my students' work. It saddened me that I would have to leave the district at the end of the school year, because I had come to know and care for many of my students and several of the teachers at the school.

Missy Woodard was one of the teachers that I had known for many years. I had met her when I was a student teacher at a high school in Columbus. We were now teaching in the same district! In fact, when I came into the district, she was one of the first friendly faces I saw! When I returned from my leave of absence, she had volunteered to let me ride with her to and from our school daily until I was completely well. Each day, we had talked about our school, our students, our families, and most of all—our Jesus! We had prayed together many times, as we sat, in her car parked in my driveway, at the end of the school day! She had shared with me her dissatisfaction with the new principal at our school. Verbally, she had voiced her sadness that he had taken away from her many of the things she had been doing prior to his coming into the system. Time after time, tears had streamed down her face as I prayed with her, asking God to give her the strength she needed to endure the situation! Many times, I had encouraged her to be strong and not lose her faith that God would see her through the school year! She must hold on, I had told Missy, with tears running down both of our faces! God would see her through, I told her. She must keep her faith in tact!

The new school year began in August 2002. I realized that Satan had been bent on trying to beat me down, destroy my hopes and dreams, devastate my family, and turn me away from God my entire lifetime! I realized that he had put many obstacles in my path so that I would possibly be too discouraged to do what I had realized God had given me to do! I thought about my positive attitude at the beginning each morning. I would wake up, thanking Him for the night of peaceful rest He had given to Derrick, me and our sons! Each day, I had asked Him to guide my footsteps and direct my path. *"Lead me, oh Lord,"* I would pray, so that I would know to go where He wanted me to go, say what He would have me say, and do what only God would have me do throughout the day.

At the time that I had included those words in my prayers, I had no suspicion that I would be in an even greater battle than I had ever been in before! Until that time, I truly believed that witnessing my mother's and grandmother's brutal murders in 1966 was something that God had miraculously enabled me to overcome! Almost unbelievably, I had reached the point of being able to forgive Uncle Ben for sexually molesting me for seven years of my youth, and many times, I had thanked God for enabling me to minister to people all over the country, encouraging them to get beyond their own trials and tribulations! I had been able to actually prove to others that as a result of the faith that I had and the love I had for God, I had been able to overcome my own obstacles and press on towards the mark of the high calling that He had given to me!

One day, I stood before my class of juniors, and talked to them about the poor performance they had done in a test that I had given to them the previous day. The night before, I had spent a couple of hours trying to grade the papers, becoming more and more disgusted with my students. They had obviously not been prepared for the test—although they had known it was coming a week before it had been given to them! One after another, I saw the numerous mistakes the students had made on their tests. I had almost given up grading them because they were *all* failing! I had seven or eight tests remaining to be graded when I put my pen down on my desk. I wouldn't even attempt to grade another paper filled with errors that I already knew they would contain. I put all of the papers in a neat stack and paper clipped them together. I reared back in my chair and closed my eyes. What was I supposed to be doing? How was I supposed to teach young people English Literature when their minds were obviously outside of my classroom? What was in the loads they were carrying up and down the halls of the school every day? I realized that the students were entering my classroom and putting their burdens on the floor beside their desks each day. While I attempted to teach them the words of William Shakespeare or Waldo Emerson, their minds were already crowded with issues that they themselves were dealing with outside of the classroom—possibly, outside of the school building! I sighed heavily, got up from my desk, turned out the ceiling light and left my office.

The next day, I stood before my class and told them that after so many students had received an "F" on their test paper, I had stopped grading others. Looks of surprise covered the faces of many of the young people as I told them that I had come to the conclusion that the class had not paid very much attention to the material I had been teaching them prior to the test. I went on to confess that I had not graded all of the papers, nor did I intend to. Therefore, I told them, I dropped the stack of papers into a nearby trash can. No one said a word!

"What is on your minds when you wake up each day?" I asked.

Still, no one answered.

"Do you feel that you have so much on your minds each day that there is no room for English Literature or anything else?"

Two or three students nodded.

"Well," I began, *"what can I do to help you turn that 'stuff' off, when you enter this classroom, so that you can learn what I am trying to teach you?"*

"Mrs. Bryant?" the school secretary's voice sounded out of the intercom.

"Yes," I replied.

"Mrs. Bryant, would you please go up to the Teacher's Lounge and call the front office?"

"Alright," I said, in the intercom's direction. Then I turned to my students. *"I'll be right back, so please remain quiet until I return,"* I said to them. *"And don't let me forget where I was before the interruption, because I'm not finished!"*

Some of the students smiled. A couple of them chuckled. They had already become familiar with my mannerisms since the school year had begun. They knew that because of the Grand Mal seizure episodes that I had undergone, my memory had been affected. Many would always be helpful by reminding me of things, words or expressions that I had used since school had began two months ago. As usual, they would quietly talk among themselves during my absence.

When I reached the Teacher's Lounge, I opened the door for another teacher who was leaving out of the room. Then I went to the small desk upon which the telephone rested. I sat down, picked up the receiver and called the front office.

"Mrs. Bryant," the secretary began, *"some people from one of the city news stations are coming to your room to interview you and some of your students."*

"What?" I asked, genuinely confused.

"Some people from Channel 3 are coming to your classroom."

"Why?" I asked.

"I don't know," the secretary lied. *"They said that they want to come to your classroom to interview you and some of your students."*

"But why? Why do they want to come to my classroom?" I was a little irritated because it really wasn't a good time for newsmen or anyone else to come to my room. I was in the midst of chastising my students! *"Can't they go to someone else's room?"* I asked.

"No," she said. *"They are coming to your room, and they are already on their way, so just be ready!"* And with that, she hung up the telephone!.

I was appalled! She had hung up in my face! If I had had time, I would have called her back, but since the newsmen were en route to my classroom, I felt that I needed to get back down the hall to my students.

I hurried to my classroom and opened the door. The students appeared to be sitting quietly in their seats. I wasn't sure that they had been that way while

I had been away from them, but I was relieved to find them that way when I returned.

"Alright," I began, *"a reporter from one of the local news stations is coming down to our room in a minute for an interview or something."*

"From which station?" a young man asked, his eyebrows raised.

"I think it's Channel 3," I replied.

"Why?" a female student asked.

"I don't know why, but I do know one thing," I said. *"You all had better be on your best behavior while they are here!"*

"Or else?" another student asked, a sly smile across his face.

"Or else you all will be very sorry!" I said, and then I smiled.

Regardless of my smile, my students knew that I was serious. No one else said a word.

My door opened. A young lady and a male cameraman entered the room.

"Hi, Mrs. Bryant," the young lady, who was the TV reporter, began. *"We're from Channel 3."*

"Okay," I replied. *"And you are here because . . . ?"*

"We've come to present you with the Golden Apple Award!" she said, smiling.

The cameraman turned on his camera and lights filled my classroom. My students, the same ones that I had been chastising before I had left the classroom, and planning to resume my reprimand for their poor performance on yesterday's tests, began to loudly applaud! Some of them even yelled, *"Hey, Mrs. Bryant! Alright!"* *"Way to go Mrs. B!"*

"What?" I asked, astonished. *"You came to present me with what?"*

"The Golden Apple Award," the reporter replied.

I knew what the **Golden Apple Award** was. It was usually presented to teachers who had positively impacted the lives of their students and made them actually **want** to learn! It was an award presented to the teacher who made a difference! And there I was, fussing at my students about the low grades they would have received as a result of their poor testing performance! And those same students were now applauding my being rewarded for my teaching! I was speechless!

A couple of days later, I noticed that Krystle, one of the students in my fourth period class, was obviously having some of her own problems outside of our classroom. More and more each day, I had heard her voicing negative opinions about *everything* we talked about in our English class. Almost every day, our class was begun with the students doing some writing in their own journals. Sometimes, the topics were assigned, and at other times, the young people were given the opportunity to express themselves about whatever they chose to write about. The youngsters had eagerly agreed that this time to do some *"free-style"* writing on their own was great! They said that it gave them the opportunity to express themselves freely—readily agreeing to observe the one stipulation that I had given them—they were not allowed to use profanity in their writing! Nevertheless, they seemed to enjoy the opportunity to do some free-style writing when the assignment written on the front board indicated that it was time for them to express themselves! This also gave me an opportunity to personally get to know each of them. After all, I was openly willing to give my students the chance to know me, as well. I had long ago acknowledged that my teaching in the public school system was not the only reason that God had allowed my path with high school students to cross!

One day, since the students had more to share in their writing than time would allow, I made it an assignment that they were to complete at home and bring back to class the next day. When I took up the writing the next day, I told the students that I would take it home because I wanted to read what they had written. No one really objected, but many wanted to read their writing out loud the following day so that they could share what they had written with their classmates. I promised that I would bring their writing back the next day so that they could do just that.

That evening, in my office at home, I closed the door so that my boys wouldn't disturb me while I took a look at the students' writing. As I opened one after another journal, I read what the students had written, which allowed me to take a deeper look into their hearts and minds. As I sipped a glass of iced tea, I sat at my desk and read silently what each students had written. One student wrote that since he was born, his life had been one mistake after another. He wrote: *"My Mom did all types of drugs. She used to leave me with people she didn't even know to go off and do drugs. We didn't have a house, so we had to sleep in the back of a car."* As I read what the young man had written, I felt the tears begin to form in the corners of my eyes. *"At the age of one,"* he wrote, *"I was left in a drawer at a gas station over in California. I was found by the police, and they turned me over to the State. They gave me to my dad, who later ran away to get away from the responsibilities of having a family."* As I read the words, warm tears made their way out of the wells of my eyes and slid down my cheeks. *"A couple of months later, my mom died in a car crash. I don't really miss her,"* he wrote. *"I blame her for my immunity to feelings though. Later on in my life, I turned to drugs, but my grandparents turned me in to a center for drug abuse and a suicide attempt I had made because of the use of Prozac."*

As I read down the wrinkled page, line after line, this student shared, in his writing, the effects his parents had had on him—the mark they had made on his life, whether they even knew it or not! *"I lost all my faith in God,"* he wrote. *"I don't believe in Him anymore, and because of that, I feel that people look down on me. I can't help the way my life has been, but all these events lead up to who I am today."* I put the paper down on my desktop and took a deep breath! At once, I realized that I was now in the school where *He* had sent me, teaching the students that *He* had brought before me and I was doing exactly what *He* had given me to do!

Krystle, the student whose actions would later prominently lead me to stop teaching high school wrote: *"When I was in seventh grade, I have no clue what happened, but I turned into a "pothead" and started to hate everyone, but they were mean anyway."* When I read what she had written, I was deeply saddened. This young lady was bringing the bitterness and anger that had been developed in herself into my classroom each and every day!

Although I was careful to not fill my classes with talks about God and His goodness, I was always able to use the works contained in our Literature books to share what other writers had written in them. Teaching Literature gave me the opportunity to do that, as well as offer to them time, kindness and concern that a lot of them were not being given elsewhere! I was reminded of the task that God had given to me every day! Another student, I would simply call *"Amanda,"* revealed that to me in her journal writing that same day.

"When I was little, I thought my life was boring," she wrote. *"I was soon corrected. When I was six, my parents got divorced. A few years after that, my mom got cancer. When I was eight, she died. When I got to high school, I smoked pot, took EX and acid. I also drank alcohol. That caused me to hate school and fail easy classes. I rejected my family, too. I was always unhappy."* I could hardly believe the young lady whose writing I was reading was the same student that I had come to think very much of! I continued reading.

"One Sunday," Amanda wrote, *"I went to visit my old church. I ended up giving my life to Christ. That was the only way to be happy. I couldn't keep looking for this answer that wasn't there. My tenth grade year, I got this teacher named Mrs. Bryant. She helped me to look at life in a new way. She is awesome because she doesn't judge you! Instead, she helps you! I admire her because she has been through so much, but she is so strong. I know that is because she relies on God, and I want to be just like her! She inspired me to want to teach."* As I read Amanda's journal, a light came on above my head! I realized that God had allowed me to go to **that** place, at **that** time, for **His** purpose! Isn't **that**

what He does? Sometimes we don't even realize that He is moving in our lives, when He truly is!

I remembered the day that I was sitting on the beach, out in Long Beach, California, perched on a boulder, looking out at the Pacific Ocean, asking God to lead me, guide me, and have His own way in my life. Aloud, I had told Him that I would do whatever He wanted me to do. I just desperately needed some direction! I had been a computer operator at a large aircraft company in Los Angeles, not a teacher! In fact, on numerous occasions, I had sworn that I would **never** become a teacher! And here I was, actually having told the Lord that **whatever** He wanted me to do, I was **willing** to! As I sat on that rock, looking out at the deep blue Pacific waters, I had no idea that I would soon return to Georgia, reenroll in the college that I had dropped out of twelve years earlier, and actually become a high school English teacher!

When I had first begun teaching, I had gotten a job in a school system that was about twenty-five miles away from my home in Columbus. Each day, I cheerfully drove the highway out to that school, singing songs of Zion and conversing with the Lord, about His goodness in my life, both to and from school. My first year teaching there had gone well. I had fallen in love with my students and in turn, they had fallen in love with me! I had disciplined some of them at times, but I felt that I was having to do things that had their own parents already done, I would not have to be doing while they were in my classroom! That year went well and I had anxiously looked forward to the next school year!

Upon entering my last school system, I had been eager to get started, teaching the students I was anxious to get to know. Unfortunately, a few weeks into the school year, I had to be hospitalized and have brain surgery so that my doctors could determine *"what in the name of medicine"* was causing the seizures which had began to occur in my head! I was out of school for a couple of months and then Derrick and I journeyed to Atlanta so that I could be seen by the physician at Emory. At the end of my second visit, the doctor told us that the lesions that had appeared on my brain had *"dissipated!"* I was encouraged to return to my teaching duties at that school. The kind physician told me that I could go back to teaching the students I had just begun to know, but he warned me that I was to *"take it easy"* at school every day. I could still teach English literature, but I was told that I needed to refrain from getting involved in other activities, like Drama Club, Pep Squad, or anything like the things that I had been used to doing, until the seizures in my head stopped occurring. I told him that I would just *"teach"* my students, as I had been taught to do!

So, Derrick and I returned to my school to speak with my principal about my returning to my position there.

When we walked into the school building that morning, I was greeted by several students I had already come to know since I had begun teaching there. At once, I was put at ease by the kind faces and warm smiles that met me in the front office. Derrick and I were told that the principal would see us just as soon as the first bell had rung, and he would come to the office to get us, so we sat down in the beautiful chairs there and smiled at the faces that greeted us as we awaited him. When the principal, Mr. Womack, accompanied by one of the assistant principals, Mrs. Cope arrived in the front office, Derrick and I shook hands with each of them. Mr. Womack then led us down the hall to his office so that we could *"talk"* about my returning to school.

In Mr. Womack's front office, his secretary greeted us with the warm smile I had already come to know since my arrival at the school just a few months earlier.

"Good morning," Mrs. Kelly said.

"Good morning," I replied.

"Come on in here, Mr. and Mrs. Bryant," Mr. Womack said, as he led us into his office.

He sat down behind his desk and Mrs. Cope, Derrick and I sat down in chairs in front of him. Somehow, they seemed to have been put there just for us to sit in.

"Now, what can I do for you?" Mr. Womack asked, a bright smile upon his face.

It was a strange question, I thought, and I knew the expression that crossed my face said so. *"I am ready to return to school,"* I told him.

An even stranger expression rose upon his face.

"We went to the doctor yesterday, at Emory in Atlanta," Derrick interjected. *"He said that Denise could return to her classroom."*

At that, Mr. Womack sat forward in his chair. *"I don't understand,"* he said.

"What do you mean?" I asked.

"I thought that since you had begun having brain seizures, you wouldn't be returning to the classroom," his voice began to rise. *"Isn't that what you said?"*

"No, I didn't say that," I told him. Obviously, he didn't know that the seizures had begun *before* I even came to teach at the school months earlier. *"I said that I would follow the doctors' orders in this situation. Derrick and I were ready to do whatever he told us to do. We saw him in Atlanta yesterday, and he told me that it was perfectly alright for me to return to my classroom."*

"He just told us that she should take it easy," Derrick interjected.

"He didn't tell me to stop teaching," I said.

"But, I thought you wouldn't be returning to your classroom," Mr. Womack said, somewhat smugly.

"We weren't sure whether I could do that or not," I said. *"We needed to see what the doctor had to say after my surgery, so we waited for him to tell us."*

Again, Derrick spoke up and said *"He just told her that she should take it easy."*

"Oh," Mr. Womack said, bewilderment having now crossed his face. He sat back in his seat and seemed to take a deep breath. Then he said something that took me completely by surprise! *"Why don't you just substitute teach?"* he asked.

"Substitute teach?" I asked. At first, I was shocked at his suggestion! I knew I had begun to experience seizures months before I came to teach at that school! I realized that I had had to be put on *Leave of Absence* in order to undergo a brain surgery, so that the doctors could determine why the seizures had ever occurred! I knew that Derrick and I had not been sure whether or not I would be able to return to school to teach after my brain had healed! I also had been made aware, although he didn't know that I had any knowledge of it, that Mr. Womack had a *"friend"* that he intended to step in and fill the position that would become vacant as a result of my sickness! Obviously, my returning to the classroom had not been part of *his* plan!

"No," I told him, adamantly. *"I had no intention of becoming a substitute when I went to college and earned a degree to teach Language Arts! Therefore, I will not, under any circumstances, be a substitute teacher!"*

Derrick could feel the heat that had begun to rise up my arm as I sat next to him. He touched it, as if to calm the anger that had begun to make its way up to the top of my shoulders.

"Well," Mr. Womack said, *"I will have to talk to the superintendent about it, and then I will get back with you."*

"You do that!" I said, immediately rising to my feet. *"And just let me know when I can return to my classroom and my students!"* With that, I turned away from him and walked straight out of his office. I left Mr. Womack, the Assistant Principal and my husband in the office and walked out of the school building!

"Mr. Womack," Derrick said, somewhat apologetically, *"Denise is just a little upset. We don't know what happened, but we do know that she doesn't intend to stop teaching. Please just call us and let us know what to we should do."* Then, he rushed out of the office and found me standing on my side of

the car, waiting patiently for him. *"Are you alright?"* he asked me, unlocking his side of the car.

"I'm fine," I lied. *"Let's just go home."*

For a moment, Derrick looked at me, not sure about what he should say to calm me down. After a brief pause, he took a deep breath and opened the car door. All the way from the school to our home, I was silent. Thoughts about what had just occurred in Mr. Womack's office ran rampant through my head! I could not understand why he would even suggest that I should become a substitute teacher! I could hardly believe that he thought I was incapable of returning to my classroom, to my students! I also could not understand why the Assistant Principal, Mrs. Cope had sat silently by, with her head lowered, while Mr. Womack suggested that I become a substitute teacher, instead of return to my classroom to do what I had spent many hours early in the morning and late at night studying for, taken many exams to prepare for, earn a Bachelor of Science Degree to do and then hired to do—teach! She had known of me before I came to teach at the school where she worked, and her niece had been a friend of mine who had graduated from high school with me years earlier,

Later that evening, after the sun had gone down, my telephone rang. With a very official tone of voice, Mr. Womack told me that I could return to my classroom the next day.

"Thank you," I said, and then, without any other words I could find to say to him, I hung up the phone.

When I returned to school, the first school semester was coming to an end. I felt like I hardly even knew the faces that greeted me each class period, but I was glad to be back with them, and they seemed to be glad to see me. They really made me feel welcome back, and the remainder of that semester ran successfully.

In my second year at that school, things changed. In the new school year, I didn't know it, but God had other plans for me. I had written about my being attacked by a male student in the first semester of my second school year of teaching in my first book. I had written about my encounter with *"David,"* and I had forgiven him for attacking me, because I realized that he had not been given the teaching from his own parents that my children were being given from Derrick and I. David, too, was a piece of fruit that had fallen from its tree, but had never been picked up, cleaned off and put in its proper place! I was no longer angry and upset with him for the bruises he had placed on my back when he threw me up against the wall outside of our classroom. The pain I had experienced when he cursed me, called me names, battered me in front of his classmates and then pushed me out into the hallway, had somehow subsided.

My experience in that school system caused me to leave the students I had come to know and love, and begin teaching at a high school much closer to home. Although he was never convicted of the brutal attack he had committed against me, a while ago, I heard that David was put in prison, given ten years for having assaulted someone else and taking part in their murder.

"Dearly beloved, avenge not yourselves, but rather give place unto wrath: for it is written, Vengeance is mine; I will repay, saith the Lord."

Romans 12:19

ELEVEN

DICTIONARIES DEFINES *FAMILY* as a group of persons, generally consisting of parents and their children, who form a household or who are connected by a bloodline. Family is also a class or group of related things. That would make the body of born again, baptized believers a family! They all belong to the household of faith! They are bound together by the love of God! It also goes on to say that a friend is one who cherishes regard for another person; an intimate and trustworthy companion. He is one who regards another with favor or brotherly affection. Friends are bound together by love, kindness, and affection. In our modern society today, families are broken up and real friends are very hard to come by.

I know that Webster gives us good definitions for families and friends, but I love the way the Bible talks about them. In the days described in the Old Testament, families were ordained by God. Unlike today, fathers were the heads of their households. Mothers were virtuous women who were honored and respected. Children were obedient because to do so would entitle them to God's promise of long life, upon the land He had so graciously given to them. Oh, to be part of a real family was a wonderful thing! God ordained families with a purpose and each devoted their lives to fulfilling that purpose. Because of God's promise, Abraham knew that he would be the father of many nations. His family would be great and plentiful! He was obedient to God because he knew that obedience was better than sacrifice! He proved that obedience by his willingness to make the ultimate sacrifice of his only son because he believed that his faith in God would see him through the ordeal!

What are families doing in the world today? In my speaking across the country, I talked about the breakdown and dysfunction of the family in today's society. If only, we had more fathers like Abraham! If only we had more men, heading their households, who are willing to commit their lives, their families, and their children to the Lord! If we had men and women who are willing to commit their lives to Lord and live righteously before their own children—then we would have children who are raised up in the fear and admonition of the Lord! We would have children who love God and as a result, love, honor and obey their parents! I believe that's what God intended when he put the first family in the Garden of Eden!

Several years ago, there was some talk about holding parents responsible for the crimes their own children commit. People almost lost their minds over the thought of being held accountable for their own **out-of-control** children who carried and used weapons, used and sold drugs, and participated in criminal activities! But do you know what the Holy Spirit showed me about that? The Scriptures say that God is going to hold parents accountable for those children's actions! After all, Ephesians 4:4 says *"And ye fathers, provoke not your children to wrath: but bring them up in the nurture and admonition of the Lord."* Well, if children are brought up by their parents as God instructed them to, they wouldn't do some of the horrible things that some children are doing today! If we raise our children the way we should, the Bible says that when they are old, they will not depart from the way they were brought up! Even if they should go astray, they will come back to the way they were brought up! God says that we are responsible to do just that! You see, families are important to Him—He created them!

Friends are just as important to Him as well! John 15:13 tells us that *"Greater love hath no man that this, that a man lay down his life for his friends."* Jesus must have thought much of friendship! He made the ultimate sacrifice when he chose to come down from Heaven and dwell among men, teaching them the way God intended for them to behave so that they might have life more abundantly! He endured the agony of the cross in order that we might have life everlasting! God gave to us, saints and sinners alike, a gift which no matter what we did right, we could never do well enough to merit . . . His only Son to die—not for anything that He had done, but for the sins of the whole world! In His life, death and resurrection, Jesus taught us what real friendship was actually about!

We are commanded that we are to *"love the Lord thy God with all thy heart, and with all thy soul, and with all thy mind. The second commandment is like unto it, Thou shalt love thy neighbor as thyself."* Well, who is your neighbor? A neighbor is that someone who lives near you or one who is near by chance. He might be a family member. He may even be a friend! God commands that we have love for one another, for our family members and our friends! Many churches observe *"Family and Friends Day,"* but I don't think that the worshipers attending those services really believe that those occasions should remind us of what Christ expects of us! They are days for us to begin again, recommitting our lives to God and to His Word! Before going to the cross, Jesus gave us a new commandment: *"That ye love one another, as I have loved you. By this shall all men know that you are my disciples, if ye have love one for another."* So *"family"* is an institution ordained by God and friends are those of the *"Household of Faith!"* God expects us to abide by that commandment. He has told us to *"see that ye love one another for ye have been called unto liberty; only used by liberty for an occasion to the flesh, but by love, serve one another. Let us not be desirous of vain glory, provoking one another, envying one another. But, Bear ye one another's burdens, and so fulfill the law of Christ."*

Each and every day of my life, my faith has been on trial! As far back as I can remember, from the age of eight, watching my mother and my grandmother being put to death at the hand of my father, and then my being sexually molested in the home of my caregivers, my faith was being put on trial! Even up to that point, I was being prepared to share God's Word with men and women who would come before me. Often, I have recalled the test that Abraham passed as it is revealed in Genesis, Chapter 22. Verse 1 says that it came to pass after these things, that God did tempt Abraham, and said unto him, *"Abraham, and he said, Behold here I am. And God said, Take now thy son, thine only son Isaac, whom thou lovest, and get thee into the land of Moriah; and offer Him there for a burnt offering upon one of the mountains which I will tell thee of."* What did Abraham do? How did he respond to the challenge put before him by God?

Verse 3 doesn't tell us that Abraham discussed the plan with his wife Sarah, but it does tell us that he *"rose up early in the morning, and saddled his ass, and took two of his young men with him, and Isaac his son, and clave the wood for the burnt offering, and rose up, and went unto the place of which God had told him."* As he was about to do what God had required him to do, offer his son, Isaac, as his burnt offering, God told Abraham to stop and take Isaac down from the altar! God had provided him a ram in the bush! I believe that because of that experience, Abraham witnessed the awesomeness of God!

The Canaanite woman, who was not described as one of the chosen of God's people, was too on trial. Matthew 15:21-28 tells the story about Jesus going *"out of His way" after admonishing the disciples to shake the dust off of their feet because the people would not listen to them. He told them to "let the people alone."* He departed out of the city into the coasts of Tyre and Sidon; not to those cities which were included in any share of His works, nor into any part of the land of Israel, which was in that direction. He went another way because His mercy was in store for the Canaanite woman, a Gentile!

The woman of Canaan *"cried out"* to Christ when He arrived. She began to relate her misery to Him. Her daughter was grievously vexed with a devil. She was bewitched—possessed! She was bewitched like the children who went around calling themselves the *"Trenchcoat Mafia"* over in Littleton, Colorado some years ago. Possessed like the children back in Atlanta, Georgia a few years ago in an area school who pulled out semi-automatic weapons on their classmates—or a couple of years ago—like one of my former students, who walked into a grocery store with an automatic weapon, demanding money, that somebody's mother and father had worked hard to earn so that they could feed their own children. Satan stood by and watched this boy and his friend attempt to hold up a grocery store. He watched this young man be shot and fall to the ground. Then he probably laughed himself silly as that boy's mother put her own firstborn son's body into the ground! Like many other youths, he was bewitched by drugs and alcohol like some children in your community! Possessed by the spirit of infirmity, abuse, premarital sex and teenage pregnancy, like the children in both yours and my communities! This Canaanite woman's daughter indeed had a problem. Her mother wasn't very different from you and I—but she didn't take her daughter to a therapist or a psychologist. She came to Jesus to ask Him for healing in her daughter's behalf. The girl needed healing at that very moment!

This woman asked Jesus for mercy, acknowledging Him as the *"Messiah."* Although she was a Gentile, she was counting on the promise that had been made to the fathers of the Jews. She did not ask for merit! She did not ask Jesus to do her a favor! She didn't ask for money! She didn't ask Him to help her get her rent or her other bills paid! She didn't need Him to find her a boyfriend or a husband! She asked for **mercy!** She brought her daughter's situation to Christ's attention! That's what we all need to do, isn't it? I don't know about you, but I need Christ's attention each and every day of my life!

What did Christ do? How did He respond? He turned His back on her! Isn't that something? He turned His back on this woman who had come to Him, begging for mercy! Some think that Christ turned His back on the woman so that He wouldn't offend the Jews. After all, He had come for them, the chosen people of God. He had already told His disciples not to go the way of the Gentiles, according to Matthew 10:5. I believe that Christ knew the strength of the woman's faith, and by ignoring her request, He actually put her faith on trial!

Personally, I have learned a lot from the Gentile woman. She was on her way to her testimony. I have to reiterate that you cannot have a testimony without a test! And I have also learned that you cannot have a message without having gone through some mess! That is what the message is—it is *"aged mess!"* That is exactly what it is, and I have thanked God numerous times for my aged mess and I have also thanked Him for my tests! Because when it is all over, I'm going to sure enough have an *awesome* testimony! And when He brings this mess to an end, look out! I believe that my message is going to be something *extraordinary!* So, in taking a look at the Canaanite woman's test, it is clearly possible to see her testimony!

First of all, Jesus turned a deaf ear to her. Of course He had heard her, but He had chosen to ignore her. Remember that He was always open to the needs and wants of people. He was attentive to the cries of the poor and always ready to give an answer of peace to those who suffered. But to this poor Gentile woman, He turned His back! Now how would you have reacted to that? Some people, when God doesn't answer their prayer, have the nerve to get angry with Him! Some people get downright indignant with the Lord! Imagine getting *"ticked off"* with the one in whom we move, breathe, and have our being? Christ did not respond to the woman, but He knew what He was doing. Therefore, He possibly did not answer her so that she would be more earnest and more sincere in her prayer.

God doesn't always give us an immediate answer. Sometimes, He wants us to prove and improve our faith. The result is that usually after His appearance, it becomes more glorious to Him and more welcome to us! Even in the end of our trials, after we have been through the storm, God is still glorified! I have learned that sometimes, we have to *prove* our faith in order to *improve* our faith!

Secondly, the disciples spoke a good word for her and spoke further discouragement by rationalizing his refusal to her. So, they told her to *"go away."* They wanted her to go away so that she wouldn't have further discouragement and ridicule. They did not want her request to be further refused. *"So, please send her away,"* they said, *"for she crieth after us."*

Jesus told the disciples that He was not sent for anyone **but** the Jews, the *"lost sheep"* of the house of Israel. The Canaanite woman **was** a lost sheep, and she **was** in need of His care and attention, but she was a *lost sheep* from the *wrong pasture!* Some of us are still in the wrong pasture today! But, she was a lost sheep, nonetheless. Romans 15:8 told us that Christ was a Minister of circumcision, and although He was intended to be a light to the Gentiles, the fullness of that time had not yet come! He had not gone to the cross yet! The veil had not yet been torn! It would take Jesus' own crucifixion in order for that to take place! He would have to bleed and die on the cross for that to happen! In the meantime, Christ's personal ministry was to be the glory of His people—the children of Israel! I have often thought about the crucifixion of Christ that He went to the cross willingly, that He didn't go because somebody made Him go, but because that was what He had born on earth to do! The fact of the matter is that if He had not gone to the cross, we would not have a direct line to Him today! If He had not gone to the cross, we would not be able to see God for ourselves! We would still be talking to the high priest who went into the *"Holy of Holies"* with bells on—just in case—and a rope around his waist—just in case he didn't come out of there! We could not even go to the Lord ourselves! Some religions are still hung up about that! Some think you have to go to somebody and *"confess."* The Bible tells me that confession is made unto salvation through Christ Jesus! So we don't have to tell anybody anything but the Lord! So the Gentiles, as a result of Christ's crucifixion, became privileged to the love and the mercy of God!

The woman continued her plea for mercy and Jesus insisted that it was inappropriate, this *"thing"* that she wanted Him to do, to heal her daughter. He told her, *"It is not meet to take the bread that belongs to the children of the house of Israel and cast it to the dogs!"* Well, who were the dogs? He was calling the woman a *"dog?"* Do you know how we would have acted? Being referred to as a *"dog?"* That might have driven her to despair, but she possessed extraordinary faith and her faith was on trial! Remember that Christ had preached to the Samaritans and salvation had been reserved for the Jews, but the Gentiles were despised and were even referred to as *"dogs!"*

That seemed to cut her off from all hope and might have driven her into despair, **BUT** this woman had very extraordinary faith! Remember that Christ preached to the Samaritans, but salvation was reserved for the Jews! The Gentiles were despised by the Jews, even called dogs by comparison with the house of Israel, who were dignified and privileged! Christ Himself seemed to allow it . . . for the moment. But thank God, the tables turned, not only for the Canaanite woman, but also for you and me!

There is a lesson about humility in the story about the woman's faith being put on trial. I hope you get the message here! Be reminded that you cannot build a kingdom without faith! Those whom Christ intends most significantly to honor, He first humbles and lays low in a sense of their own meanness and worthlessness. We have to first see ourselves as unworthy, deserving the least of all of God's mercies, before we are fit to be dignified and privileged of them. In other words, we must learn to first *die* to ourselves in order to be blessed and used by God!

That is what is most likely wrong with so many of us today! We need to die to ourselves! That pride that keeps on rearing its ugly head needs to die each and every day so that God can respond to us! That sin of familiarity needs to die in our homes so that we can find or recapture the thrill that has been long gone! We need to stop thinking that we are *"all that and a bag of chips!"* so that we can really be the men and woman that God has created us to be! Like that Canaanite woman, we must not be so easily offended when we are not highly esteemed! There were times that I had to tell some of my students, whose lives I have had the opportunity to touch, that they needed **to** *"get over themselves."* Most of us need to get over ourselves!

We need to exercise our faith because you cannot build a kingdom without it! Christ rejoices when, through our greatest trials, we exercise great faith! When we keep the faith, through the storm and rain, through sickness and pain, through hard trials, even through the fire, it is then that we come forth, shining like pure gold! I have had to remind myself of that several times while writing this book that *"I may be going through the fire right now, but I shall come forth, as pure gold!"*

What then was the children's bread that Jesus was talking about? That refers to the special ordinances, church privileges, spiritual dignities, school honors, even parental honors like the ones that we heap upon our children for making the Honor Roll . . . the blessings of God! Common charity must be extended to all, but God's blessings are expressly intended for the household of faith! The Word of God itself is beyond the understanding of those who are outside of the household of faith? When you have a moment, ask yourself this question: *"Am I in the house?"*

Here is the strength of the woman's faith. It is the result of her faith being put on trial! Even after being called a *"dog."* A proud heart could not have withstood it! *"Who does He think that He is calling a dog? . . . I'll have you know that I am the president of the choir? . . . Why, I'm the chairman of the Deacon's Board! . . . I don't know whether you know this or not, but I am the Sunday School Superintendent! . . . Or . . . I was elected Class President at my high school this year! . . . Perhaps . . . As a matter of fact, I have been a member of this church since the first brick was laid . . . Or . . . I was Valedictorian when I graduated from high school! . . . And you have the nerve to call me a dog?"*

Now the Canaanite woman could have reminded Christ that she was a woman in misery about her daughter's condition, but she didn't. Instead, she exemplified a humble, believing soul that truly loved Christ and broke through His discouragement! She continued to pray for an answer! She continued to stand on the Word of God! She was talking to Jesus and the Bible tells us that He *is* the Word that was made flesh and sent to dwell among us! Sometimes, when the answers of our prayers are deferred, detailed, delayed—or whatever *"D"* you prefer to use there, God is teaching us to pray more and to pray better! Even Christ, in His agony, before the night he was betrayed, prayed more earnestly! Now if Christ did that, then who are we not to do so?

The Canaanite woman told Jesus that whether she was an Israelite or not, she came to the Son of David for mercy and she would not let Him go, until He blessed her! Her faith was on trial, yet she maintained her belief that although Christ had not come for her people, she believed that He could help her and He would show her mercy! She prayed, *"Lord, help me!"* Just saying that would help us overcome many of the discouragements which sometimes bear us down or overwhelm us! She took a stand on the **Word of God** and asked that Christ give her what she came there for—healing of her daughter!

After Christ referred to this woman as a dog, she continued to request His blessing as a result of her faith. She could not object to what He has said to her, so she acknowledged it and made the best of it. *"You are telling the truth Lord,"* she said. *"But do not the dogs eat the crumbs from under their masters' tables?"* She confessed that she could not deny that she is unworthy of the children's bread, however, she is willing to settle for the crumbs from under the table!

The woman demonstrated her faith in a mighty way! There was no unbelief in her! Unbelief mistakes recruits for enemies, and draws dismal conclusions, even from comfortable premises, but faith can find *encouragement* in discouragement! The woman had humility, which made her glad to even get crumbs! Those who are conscious of themselves and the fact that they deserve nothing are thankful for the little things! The least of Christ's blessings is precious to a believer, even the very crumbs of the **Bread of Life!** That woman had faith, which encouraged her to accept the crumbs! Even the prodigal son, in coming to himself, realized that his father had enough bread in his house to spare some crumbs for him! That's why he **RAN** back home! He confessed his unworthiness and was willing to settle for being a servant! He was willing to settle for crumbs!

After the woman's extraordinary display of faith, Christ turned things around for her. He commended the woman by saying, *"O woman, great is thy faith."* Because of it, He healed her daughter! How many of us need something from the Lord? The Bible tells us that the Canaanite woman's daughter was healed from that very hour and from that moment was never vexed by the devil again!

At times, I have found myself questioning my own faith, but when I think about this woman's attitude, I feel a bit silly! In my lifetime, God has done so much for me, that I can have no shadow of a doubt in Him! I have no choice but to stand on the Word of God! I have heard people say things like *"I can't do anything with my son or my daughter,"* or *"I've done all I can to save my marriage, but I have not been able to make it work!"* Others have said *"I can't seem to keep a job,"* *"Why are people always picking on me?"* or *"When are we going to get out of debt?"* or even *"Why doesn't the pastor recognize me for the works I've done in the church? After all, my great granddaddy laid that first brick!"* But notice the pronouns at work in those phrases: *"I," "me," "my,"* and *"we."* Do you know what's wrong with them? They all leave God out! Proverbs 3:4 tells us to *"trust in the Lord with all our hearts and lean not to our own understanding."* We have **NO** choice other than to acknowledge Him in all our ways, and if we will do that, we have the promise that He will direct our paths! Now, you don't have to take my word for it! It's the **Word of God!**

The battles we face every day in our homes, in our schools, on our jobs, in our churches—they are not ours! They belong to the Lord! We need to stop trying to fight God's battles because He needs **NO** help from us! Roman's 8:37 is our reassurance. It says that *"In all these things, we are more than conquerors through Him that loves us!"* That says that because of our faith in Him, we are **MORE** than conquerors!

People must get this message and keep it in their hearts, today, tomorrow, and for the rest of their lives, that because they love the Lord, they must believe that whatever comes their way, the ups and downs, the good and the not-so-good, the positives and the negatives, the sunshine, the wind and the rain, the sickness and the pain, whatever the devil throws at them will all work together for good, for those who love the Lord and keep His Word! And I do love Him!

In 1958, I realize that God had brought me into this world and, in 1970, He saved me, despite Satan's numerous attempts to destroy me so that I could not do something very special for Him! On numerous occasions, I have exhorted others to go on with determination, ignoring Satan's attempts to convince them that they couldn't make it! He has been a liar from the very beginning, and he is still a liar and the truth has never been in him, is not in him today, nor will it ever be! Christian men and women must constantly demonstrate their faith in God and ultimately expect His mercy in their lives! We have to start confessing *"I don't care if it's just crumbs, Lord. Just throw me a few crumbs!"* God knows we all have problems and we all have issues! We just have to come to Him with our faith and stop running to Him with our problems, because we cannot build His kingdom without faith! Christ has already told us that *we* are overcomers and He proved that it was possible when He overcame the world! We are *more* than conqueror because we can stand on the Word of God! Even in the midst of the greatest trial you have ever endured—the greatest test of your faith, you must stand! And having done all to stand, don't give up, *keep on standing!* Know that you are able to endure the storm by holding onto Him who is able to calm the waters! Know that you are able to withstand the tempest by the one who speaks *"Peace"* to your very soul! We must be bold, be strong, and know that the Lord, our God is with us! Amen!

TWELVE

SOME OF THE painful experiences that seem to constantly cross our paths in our lifetimes sometimes seem nearly unbearable! Even when we spend each day trying to do the things that we feel God has ordained us to do, trials seem to find their way into our paths! At times, we find ourselves in situations in which we know we have done nothing to reside! Satan causes others to do things to us that they would not ordinarily do. The *"doers"* don't even know what they are doing, why they are doing it, or to whose lives they are bringing tears, anguish and frustration into. Many have done nothing to bring the trials and tribulations they have to endure. They have been good and faithful servants of God! Even though the children of some were not living as righteously as their parents, mothers and father have prayed for them each and every day.

For many years, I had gone across the country, sharing with others just how good God had been to me in my own life. Many times, I had testified that He was more than able to deliver them from their own trials and tribulations because He had delivered me out of my own! I had not been just only *"talking"* about how He was able to bring His children out of any and every negative situation they had found themselves in. I was able to *show* others because I, myself, was living proof! God had shown His awesome power in the life that I had been living since my childhood! I had been openly sharing with everyone, children and adults, the old and the young, men and women alike, the goodness that God had shown me in my own life!

One Wednesday in October 2002, I asked my students to ***"Please be quiet!"*** as I attempted to teach a lesson on Walt Whitman poetry. One student turned around and continued to talk to a classmate who was seated behind her. I repeated my request that the class come to order. The student, Krystle, would not turn around, but kept on talking, so I asked that she remain after class for a few moments so that I could talk with her. When I said that, she stopped talking to her classmate. When the final bell rang, Krystle hurried out of the classroom, not allowing me the opportunity to speak to her at all! As a result, I went to my desk, sat down, and filled out a Detention Notice that I intended to give to her when she came to class the next day. I knew that if she had to serve detention, she would ***have*** to stay after school and talk with me—or her parents would become involved! That would be fine with me because I really wanted to talk with them, and perhaps we could get their daughter some help that she obviously needed!

On the next day, the members of the class were reading aloud the poems that they had written themselves. After Krystle had read her poem aloud to the class, she walked over to my desk to turn hers in. When she approached the desk where I was sitting, I spoke to her quietly and told her that because she had not done as I had asked her to stay after class yesterday, so that I could talk to her, she had been given Detention. I told her that I wanted her to let her parents know about it, and she should make arrangements for getting home from school on the following Tuesday. When I told her that, she said nothing, but simply took the Detention notice out of my hand and walked away from my desk.

Towards the end of the class period, the students were completing some surveys that I had asked them to fill out and give to me before leaving class that day. Just before the bell rang, I asked the students to pick up any books that had been left lying on the floor around their desks and put them underneath. Aloud, Krystle said that she had not put the two books that were lying on the floor underneath her desk, so she was **not** going to pick them up! I told her that it was alright that she had not put them there, but I asked her to ***"Please pick them up anyway."*** She bent over and started picking the books up, but fussed about having to do it. As usual, the other students hurried out of class. After putting the books underneath the desk, Krystle hurried out of the classroom, swearing about having been ***picked on***. Obviously, she had not heard me ask ***all*** of the students to pick up the books and put them underneath their desks before leaving the classroom.

As soon as she was out of the doorway, she began cursing loudly! I followed Krystle out of the classroom to stop her. She swore violently as she hurried down the hall. I followed her, hoping that I would be able to calm her down and keep her from making a scene all the way down the hallway. Several times, I called her name, but she kept going. When she reached Missy Woodard's classroom, I had caught up with her. I pushed her into the classroom because it was the only way I could stop her and attempt to get her to stop cursing! Immediately, she turned on me and yelled that I was *"just picking on her."* I had wanted her to go on out of the building, calmly and quietly, because her loud cursing would bring a lot of attention to her and the entire situation! I knew that someone—possibly the principal—would be at the end of the hall! If she continued to curse the way she was doing, she would probably be suspended, or worse!

I asked Krystle why in the world she was carrying on the way she was. Again, she told me that I just didn't like her! She cursed both Missy and I, who had also begun trying to calm her down. I didn't understand why she thought that I didn't like her, because I had never said that to her or any of my other students before! She continued to curse me. Missy intervened and tried to calm her down. Krystle seemed to get even louder and louder, angrier and angrier! While Missy stood between us, she leapt at me, hitting me several times! Missy moved to one side and turned to look at her. I put my hands up and then grabbed both of Krystle's hands at the wrists. I told her that I was *not* going to let her fight me! She began to cry, and then she sat down on top of a nearby desk. I asked her why she was behaving the way she was. I had never given Krystle any indication that I did not like her or any other student since I became a teacher! She had been a challenge, having to be asked to stop talking constantly, but I had *never* indicated that I disliked her! Missy told me to go on out of the room and calm down because I had obviously become extremely upset about the entire situation!

I told her that I would, but first, Krystle *had* to calm down!

Missy told me that she would take care of everything, and I should just leave the room. I went into the hallway and two other teachers were standing just outside of Missy's room. Neither of them said anything to me. Aloud, I said that I did not know what in the world was going on, unable to understand Krystle's behavior towards me! The Assistant Principal came down to the room, quickly walked past us, and went inside the classroom. Soon, he opened the door and instructed me to go down to my classroom and write down what had happened. I turned and walked down the hall to my classroom. I was bewildered that something of that nature, being attacked by a student for the *second* time, had happed to me again in my teaching career!

Shortly, the principal, Mr. Womack, came down to my room, walked inside and asked me what had happened. I began to tell him the story. Several times, he stopped me in mid-sentence and asked me the strangest questions! He acted as if I was confused. It seemed that he was the confused one! He told me that he was just trying to get a clear understanding. I repeated that I was clear headed, and what I was trying to tell him was the truth! Again, I told him what had happened in Mrs. Woodard's room. I *never* told him that my student, Krystle, had actually attacked me because I *did not* want her to get into any worse trouble that I thought she would be in once Missy told her side of the story. Shortly afterwards, Mr. Womack gave me his cell phone and told me that I should call my husband and tell him that I had not gotten home because I was being temporarily detained at the school. Then he left me alone in my classroom.

Shortly afterwards, I finished typing the report about what had transpired, got off of my computer, got my things together, and I left the room. Hurriedly, I walked up to Mr. Womack's office. I knew that two of my younger sons would be at home wondering *"what in the world"* was keeping me from getting there! When I got to the end of the hallway and reached Mr. Womack's office, I recognized Missy sitting in a chair near the door. I could see a strange frozen expression on her face. Someone else was seated in another chair, but I could not really see them. I assumed that it was Krystle. When Mr. Womack saw me at the doorway, he leapt out of his chair and began screaming that he had told me that he would get back with me *after* he had finished what he was doing in his room! He yelled that he had told me that I was supposed to wait for him in my room until he came back to get me. A puzzled expression crossed my face because I knew that he had not said anything like that to me! I didn't understand what in the world was going on! As he walked briskly towards me, I told him that I would wait for him, but I asked him why in the world he was yelling, and why he was using that tone of voice speaking to me!

Briskly, he guided me out of his office and led me down the hallway, towards my classroom. As we walked down the hall, with a calmer voice, he told me that he just wanted me to wait so that he could talk to me *after* he had finished talking to those persons who were in his office. We went to my classroom and he asked me if I had gotten in touch with my husband. I told him that I had called but Derrick had gotten home yet. He told me to keep trying to reach him. Then, he said that he would come and get me when he was finished with the people who were in his office.

When I reentered my classroom, I put my things down and sat down behind my desk. I was a bit overwhelmed, and I did not understand what was going on, but I had the feeling that I would know very soon! After a while, I walked up to the Teacher's Lounge to make some copies of some work that my students would need in the upcoming week. It took me about twenty minutes to use an entire ream of paper. When I finished, I collected all of my things, turned off the copier and the lights, and opened the door. I was surprised to see Mr. Womack and Missy coming down the hall together, heading to her room. She did not even look at me. Instead, she looked down at the floor in front of her. I shook my head, wondering what in God's name was going on! I didn't know what, but I knew that *something* was happening! When I saw the two of them go into Missy's room, my puzzled expression and I turned and walked down the hall towards my classroom.

Shortly, Mr. Womack came back to my room and asked me if I had called my husband. I told him that I had called home, but he had not gotten there yet. He told me to keep trying, and he left his cell phone with me once more. After he left, I called my house, but Derrick had still not gotten there. A few minutes later, Mr. Womack returned to my classroom and the Superintendent, Dr. Alice Foster, was with him. She brought with her a letter, putting me on Administrative Leave until *"everything"* was straightened out. I was totally confused because I didn't understand why I needed to be on leave of absence for any reason! Dr. Foster would not answer any of the questions that I asked her. She told me to just take the letter and wait until *"everything"* had been straightened out. Somewhat frustrated, I finally said, *"Alright,"* and took the letter out of her hand. She and Mr. Womack turned and quickly left my classroom.

About a minute later, Mr. Womack returned to my room and asked me if I was ready to go. I told him that I guessed I was, so I quickly got my things together. As we walked down the hall together, I asked him how things had been going for him and his daughters since his wife had passed away just a few months earlier.

He seemed to be surprised at my question. After a moment, he told me that it had been difficult for him and his daughters, but they were doing fine. I told him that anytime he needed me to talk to his girls, he should just let me know, and I would be happy to do so. I had been counseling young ladies across the country for some years now, I told him. He said that he appreciated my willingness to help him and his daughters out, and he would let me know if he needed me. As we approached his office, Mr. Womack asked me if I would just step into his office for a moment because some people inside wanted to talk to me.

I simply said, *"Okay,"* and walked inside the office.

Two plain clothes police officers and a lady from the Department of Family and Children's Services office were waiting to talk to me.

"What is going on?" I asked. I turned around so that I could ask Mr. Womack, but to my surprise, he had somehow disappeared!

I turned back to face the police officers. One of them told me that he needed to read me my rights!

"What!?" I exclaimed.

The officer repeated the statement.

"Okay," I said. *"But FIRST, you need to tell me WHY you need to read me my rights?"*

Just then, Derrick entered the room. *"What's going on in here?"* he asked.

The policemen turned to him asked if he was my husband, and he said *"Yes."* Quickly, both officers took him out of the office so that they could explain to him what was about to happen to me!

When they left me and the woman who had not said anything up to that point, she decided to ask me if I had ever hit a student before.

"No!" I said, adamantly. *"Is THAT what this is about?"* I asked her. *"I have NEVER hit a student in my life!"*

She simply nodded her head and began writing on the pad she had in her lap. Moments later, the policemen came back inside of the principal's office with Derrick. When he entered the room, he told me to *"say nothing."*

"I will do that," I said, *"but I just want to know what in the world is going on!"*

Again, Derrick told me not to say anything. I simply sighed and nodded my head. The policemen reiterated my rights to me. They asked me if I understood.

"Yes, of course," I said. Still, I was overwhelmed and could hardly believe what was happening to me!

One of the policemen said that he would take me to the police station.

Realizing that I was being arrested for *"something"* I had no idea about, I was in a state of shock! Both officers accompanied me out of the school to a squad car that had been parked at the curb. My husband and his brother, whom I had not even known was there, followed us outside of the school. The officer told me that he wasn't going to handcuff me. That was a relief! He told me that I just needed to get into the car, so I did.

At the police station, I was booked and charged with **"battery."** I didn't really understand why, because I knew that I had never *"battered"* anyone! Inside of the jail cell, I began to talk aloud to the Lord. I knew that sometimes, He allowed us to land in situations that we are unfamiliar with. That was what was happening to me! God knew that I had done nothing to be arrested for! I was sure of that! He also knew that some lies had been told and were being spread about me! I knew that He was aware of what was going on. I also believed that God knew that I was innocent of the charges that were being brought against me! He also knew who was actually responsible for the awful situation in which I had been placed. But I believed that He was going to see that the truth would eventually be told!

I remembered having read about the time that the Apostles were put in prison, having been punished for preaching the Gospel of Jesus Christ, but they were confident that God knew *who* and *where* they were—disciples, falsely accused and put in prison! Christ knew that they had been arrested and jailed after preaching to a multitude of people out of surrounding cities. Among them were sick folks and some who were *"vexed"* with unclean spirits, but they had been able to speak *The Word and* heal many! Even after having been jailed, the Apostles were freed when the angel of the Lord **came *"one night, opened the prison doors and brought them forth."*** Although I had tried diligently to teach my students each day, none of those days had passed without Christ's presence! In fact, in my entire teaching career in the public school systems, I had *never* been able to leave Him out of my car, the parking lot, or my classrooms! English Literature actually *began* with Him, so how could He be left out of it?

When Derrick picked me up from the Police Station, I didn't say very much. I knew he was worried, because that was a state that he had never seen me in, but I was so outdone that I did not even know what to say or how to say it! I just wanted to get home to see about my sons and let them *see* that their mother was alright! Quietly, I prayed that their lives had not been completely torn asunder in the past three hours! Somehow, I knew that the news had already been aired that I had been arrested and charged with assaulting one of my students! I just wanted to get home, take my boys into my arms, and assure them that the God that we had been worshiping all of our lives was *still* in complete control, and He would take care of the whole situation!

When we got home, I did just that! My sons were confused, unable to understand why anyone would accuse their mother of anything like the charges that were being brought up against her! I assured them that I didn't want them to worry because God had already taken care of it! I told them that I had talked to Him about it when I was placed behind prison bars. I had surrendered the entire situation to Him that day, because I had surrendered my life to Him a long time ago! I knew that God was aware of what was happening, and I believed that He knew who was responsible. Ultimately, I knew that He would take care of it because I knew that He would never forsake me!

"We are troubled on every side, yet not distressed; we are perplexed,
but not in despair; Persecuted, but not forsaken;
cast down, but not destroyed;"

2 Corinthians 4:8-9

On Monday, Derrick, our attorney, and I met with the Superintendent, Dr. Foster, and the school's attorney. As Derrick and I sat in her office, Dr. Foster told us that because I had been accused of battery, concerning the student, they were going to fire me as a teacher in that School District, and they would seek that my license to teach in the State of Georgia be revoked as a result! I was appalled, knowing that I had done nothing to deserve that!

A few days later, the local newspaper contained the Sheriff's statement: *"The student was not injured or hurt in the incident. I know that for a fact because the student went out to eat supper after leaving the hospital that evening."* He also stated that *"The teacher has no past criminal history and certainly no history involving battery."*

I had written about the night that I speechlessly watched my father shoot and wound my little brother Michael and our grandfather, and then shoot and kill my grandmother, my mother and himself! In the line of fire, I had not received a single scratch from the bullets being rendered by my father, Tony, or my grandfather, Linwood Martin, as they shot across the room at each other in the shotgun house on Baldwin Street! I had done nothing to bring about the night of horror! How could I not relate to Job? He had done nothing to bring upon himself the tragedies that he had been forced to endure!

In my own reading, I had already gotten the impression that Job was a prayerful man! I don't know if he was praying at the same time that his sons were having a good time, feasting in their houses and sending for their three sisters to eat and drink with them. But I read that after the partying was over, Job sent for his children and prayed over and for them. He got up early the next morning and offered burnt offerings according to the number of them all, *"for Job said, It may be that my sons have sinned, and cursed God in their hearts."*

While they were probably just about to suffer some tremendous hangovers, Job was already on his knees, praying for them, continually!

Shortly after that, God's angels came to present themselves before the Lord. They had company though—Satan also came among them and although He knew his reason for being there, the Lord asked him why he had come. Satan had already rebuked God and shown himself to be against Him. I don't know if Satan knew this, but God already knew why he had come along with the others! God knows everything we are about to do before we even do it, doesn't He? Of course, He does! He asked Satan why he had come, not because He didn't already know why, but so that he could *admit* his reason for coming! Satan replied, *"From going to and fro in the earth, and from walking up and down in it."*

He had not even answered the question, so God brought up the subject for him. *"Satan, hast thou considered my servant Job, that there isn't one like him in the earth, a perfect and an upright man, one that feareth God, and escheweth evil?"* Those very words came to me when I was arrested and placed behind bars, having been accused of committing a crime that I had never even *remotely* considered doing! I realized that Satan had already seen Job, going about his daily tasks, taking care of his wife, having worked hard enough to take care of the sheep, camel and oxen that had been provided for him! He had probably even seen Job on his knees daily, thanking Him for the blessings that He had brought upon his life! Of course, He had observed Job's sons and daughters doing their own things—partying it up daily, from dusk until dawn! No doubt, He also had heard Job praying, asking God to forgive them for the sins they willingly committed! Most likely, he already knew that Job's wife would, at the end of his and her own rope, advise her husband to just curse God and die! The one stipulation that God made upon Satan's actions was that he *"Behold, all that he hath is thy power; only upon himself put not forth thine hand."* So . . . the Devil, as he usually does upon the lives the children of God, **got busy** doing as much as he could possibly do to break Job down!

Chapter Two tells us that Satan left God's presence and *"smote Job with sore boils from the sole of his feet unto his crown."* As Job suffered from the unexplainable attack upon his body, he sat down among the ashes. It seemed that I myself could understand how he must have felt. What could he have done to bring such misery upon himself? It had been a year since I had begun to ask myself the same question! It had been just a few months earlier that I had begun to suffer brain seizures that resulted in the surgery so that the doctors could determine why they had began. And after trying to recover from that, I would be falsely accused of attacking a student that I had had every intention of at least *trying to* help! And here I was, for the first time in my life, placed behind prison bars!

Experiencing the coldness of that cell, I didn't even try to meditate or pray silently, because I wanted nothing to prevent the Lord from hearing every word that came out of my mouth! *"You know me!"* I yelled. *"You know that I would never do anything like what that they are accusing me of!"* Tears began to make their way down my cheeks. *"I have devoted my life to helping others overcome the tragedies and trials they have faced in their own lives, and now something like this is happening to me?"* I knew that my voice was rising and others would be able to hear me, but I didn't even care! I wanted to make certain that God heard every word that proceeded beyond my trembling lips! *"I know that you were right there!"* I told Him. *"You know that I have never hit any one of my students! You know that I would never even consider doing anything like that! You were right there and I know that You saw what happened! So what is THIS about? Why am I behind prison bars?"* I asked Him, but I didn't expect to get an answer back from Him right then!

Just the thought of what Job had undergone and his attitude about the entire situation made me take a sincere look at what I, myself, was having to go through in a whole new way! Right then, I decided that I had undergone much less than Job had undergone in his lifetime, and if he could keep his faith in God in tact in the midst of his trials and tribulations, who was I *not* to hold onto my own? *"Lord,"* I said aloud, with a calmer tone of voice, behind those jail bars, *"Please just take care of my family. Take care of Derrick and our sons! I know that you are the author and the finisher of my faith, so please just give me the strength to hold on and wait for my change to come!"*

Months prior to that episode were full of much sadness and truly unexpected turmoil. Several times I had to be hospitalized, suffering with the grand mal seizures which left me in an unconscious state each time they occurred. The last time that I had one, it was witnessed by my three sons for the first time! We had been at Peachtree Mall—just browsing though, not shopping. We had spent about thirty minutes talking with some students I had taught a couple of years earlier. I had not seen them in a while, and the reunion was an uplifting one! After hashing over some of the most exciting things that had happened in their lives since we had last seen each other, I told the students and my sons that we would have to go so that we could get on home. As we were about to walk back through the shopping center, to the end where my car was parked, the Grand Mal seizures (the ones that I had not been having in a whole year) began to occur! My oldest son, Tjai, had to get his brothers and I out of the shopping center, through the crowded parking lot, and into our car, so that he could get us over to the Fire Station and find his dad. Neither of my two younger sons, Chris and Little Derrick, really knew what in the world was happening because they had never witnessed anything like that before! It really scared them to see the seizures take complete control of their mom, for the first time!

Urgently, Tjai drove down Highway 185, towards the Fire Station where his dad worked. Derrick had left home early that morning on his way to work, so Tjai thought that he would find him there. In a matter of moments, we arrived at the station. Tjai told Chris and Little Derrick to sit tight and keep their eyes on their mom, so that he could find their dad as he hopped out of the car. As it turned out, Derrick had left the station, heading for the shopping center, looking for us! Tjai rushed out of the station, hopped into the car, and headed home because he didn't know what else to do!

Shortly after we had arrived at the house, Derrick appeared and drove up the driveway. Later, he said that he had been at the mall looking for us. When he couldn't find us anywhere in the mall, he had left and headed home. After he pulled into the driveway and got out of his truck, he saw the paramedics and realized that I was probably having some of the same Grand Mal seizures that I had not been experiencing for an entire year! By the end of the day, I was placed in the Intensive Care Unit of St Francis Hospital. Since I had been there several times before, the nurses seemed to be familiar with me, whether I remembered them or not.

After I had been released from the hospital and my life began to calm down, I started my daily ritual of reading some Scriptures before getting busy doing the *"whatever"* my husband had encouraged me to do. I had become *"disabled,"* no longer having to go to a job every day. Randomly, I opened my Bible to Luke, Chapter 11. I decided that I would read the chapter entirely. When I got to the end, six words jumped out at me from verse 46: *"Woe unto you also, ye lawyers!"* Lawyers? The Chapter was mainly about them. I had read that Chapter and those verses before, but I didn't remember anything being said about *"lawyers."* You know, sometimes we read the lines found in various Books in the Bible several times and somehow, we find something different each time we read them. *"Lawyers,"* I said aloud, remembering the attorney who waited for Derrick and I to come out of the Probation Officer's room. I had been sentenced to one year of probation for committing the crime of brutality that I had never even ***thought*** about committing, accused of attacking the young lady who had actually attacked me! The Assistant District Attorney who had stood sternly in a courtroom, before the judge, me, my husband, our pastor, our attorney, and a courtroom full of other people was now apologizing to me for having accused me of the crime that even *he* actually knew that I had not committed!

"*Then why did you—*" I began, a puzzled expression having crossed my face.

"*Denise,*" Derrick interrupted. "*Don't even bother to ask him. It's all over. Let's just get out of here and get on with our lives.*"

"*Woe unto you, lawyers! for ye have taken away the key of knowledge: ye entered not in yourselves, and them that were entering in ye hindered.*"

Luke 11:52

In a way, I could understand what my husband was saying. What I didn't understand was how the attorney, with the apologetic expression that had found its way upon his face, could have stood before everyone in the crowded courtroom and accuse me of committing a crime that even **he** knew that I had not committed! How he could do that, I realized that it would take me some time to understand! I held Derrick's hand and walked away from that attorney, out of the courthouse building, and away from the entire experience, thanking God for having given me the strength I needed to get through it!

I would always remember the way I had felt when, in the crowded courtroom, the attorney had read aloud, quoting lines that I had written in my first work, *Opening the Door,* about the anger that had filled me, after being attacked in a classroom, during my second year of teaching. After school, in the Annex of the building that was being vacated, a friend of that student had approached me with a threat. Aloud, the attorney had read the lines I had written in *Opening the Door* in the courtroom: "*If you want me, I'm standing right here! Just come over here and get me!*" I had challenged him. "*Come on! Do it! Do it so that I can stomp your a—into the ground!*" Somehow, the attorney had forgotten to read the lines before that—the ones that talked about my being attacked in my classroom just two weeks prior to that day! He didn't talk about the fact that the first student had physically attacked me two weeks before. That is what had driven me to that point! His purpose for reading that part of the story aloud, in the crowded courtroom, was to convince the judge that I was indeed a violent person, capable of having actually attacked the young lady who was in the courtroom, standing nearby, with visible tears streaming down her face!

And here the judge was . . . apologizing for having had to take me through the anguish of being accused of attacking the student, when even he knew all along that the charges that had been made against me were false! At the end of the trial, my husband quickly ushered me out of the courthouse. As we walked to our car, he assured me that everything was going to be alright because God knew what had happened. *"Don't even worry about it,"* Derrick said, as he ushered me into our Expedition. He could not help but see the tears that had begun to trickle down my cheeks, as he started the car. *"God knows the truth of the whole matter,"* he said. *"And even more important than that, God knows you!"*

Upon hearing him say that, I swallowed the lump that had made its way into my throat. I knew that God was expecting me to forgive everyone that had brought such sadness into my life! Of course, I had a choice whether or not I would do that, and that choice was really mine! As a Christian, I knew that I had to forgive all of those who had brought such sadness and turmoil into the lives of my husband, our children and I!

As we drove away from the courthouse, I remembered something I had read just a few days ago. Luke 11:46 said *"for ye lade men with burdens grievous to be borne, and ye yourselves touch not the burdens with one of your fingers."* Verse 47 contained a warning: *"Woe unto you! for ye build the sepulchers of the prophets, and your fathers killed them."* I had continued to read on down the page. When I reached verse 52, the words caused me to quiver! *"Woe unto you, lawyers! For ye have taken away the key of knowledge: ye entered not in yourselves, and them that were entering in ye hindered."* As we approached our street, I could not help but think of the lawyer who had tried me, in a courtroom full of people, some of whom had been my students, the judge, my pastor, my husband and I, and accuse me of lies that even *he* knew had been falsely brought against me!

THIRTEEN

WOMEN AND MEN of God have been commissioned by God to *"go ye therefore, and teach all nations, baptizing them in the name of the Father and of the Son, and of the Holy Ghost."* In 2010, we must admit that many Christians have fallen short of that assignment. I'm not referring to anybody besides myself because I haven't done as much as I could do to fulfill that commission myself. However, I make no excuses for my shortcomings. I have figured me out—and I've figured some other folks I know out, too!

The word commission means duty or responsibility. It means obligation. In the life of a Christian, it means assignment. Christians are on assignment from and by God! I am on an assignment. It is the purpose for which I was saved! I pray that you feel the same way I do! Jesus didn't save us so that we could just shout and get happy! I hope you don't think that God saved you and I so that we could *"look"* holy! My prayers are that you don't really believe that we were redeemed so that we could just look good when we sit up in church and say *"Hallelujah! Thank you Jesus!"* God saved each one of us so that we could be someone else's reward! Allow me to interject here that it wasn't just for you and me! Jesus came to save us so that we could be someone else's reward! Once people get that message, they will really begin to be about our Father's business!

We have all been given the commission to teach! As an educator, this responsibility was very familiar territory for me. I became a teacher in the secular world out of my desire to fulfill my spiritual obligation to God! Like many others, I felt I was *"called to teach."* Well, guess what? Educators in the secular world are not the only people who have been called to the ministry of **teaching!** Men and women, the young and the old, those who have become members of the Body of Christ have been commissioned to go into *"their world"* and spread the good news of the Gospel of Jesus Christ! I say *"their world"* because wherever it is that you do what you do, that is your world!

A little while back, I was speaking at a church in Chattanooga, Tennessee, delivering the morning message in commemoration of a woman's day celebration. In the weeks prior to the program, I had been studying the scripture found in Matthew 28 that had been given to me. What would I say to this group of men and women in the traditional Baptist church in which I had been asked to speak? In the past months, I had been received, albeit reluctantly at times, in several Baptist church pulpits by ministers who were not quite sure that they would be able to relax and allow God to use me—a woman—behind their sacred desks. Again, I found myself treading on hallowed ground that had been, in the recent past, tread upon predominantly by males.

I began to study the scriptures and in my mind, turn over and over the theme that had been chosen for the occasion. I wanted to say something to stir up Christian men and women to recommit themselves to the great commission that they had been given by the Master Himself! I felt that it was important to admonish them to, as my former past pastors would say, make Christ's *last* commandment to the church their *first* priority. I pondered and prayed over the story that preceded those words. I tried to put myself in Mary Magdalene's sandals, as she approached the sepulcher that third day after Jesus' crucifixion. I could imagine the anxiety that she and her companion, the other Mary, must have felt upon finding that the body of their Lord and Savior indeed was not there! How shocking it must have been to hear the words *"He is not here for He has risen as He said"* from the celestial body they had met at Jesus' empty tomb. The story was an astounding one then, and still is today! At once, the Scriptures say, they went away from the sepulcher with **"joy"** and **"fear"** in their hearts! They had heard and immediately believed that Jesus, the Son of God, had indeed been resurrected in the three days as He had said that He would be!

On their way to tell the good news, the women met the risen Christ Himself! It was true, He had indeed arisen! *"Go,"* He instructed the women, *"to the disciples and tell them that I will meet them in Galilee."* Without question, the Bible says, the women went to take the word they had been given to the apostles. It had never occurred to me before, but I realized that upon receiving those instructions from Christ, those women became the apostles' apostles! I got pretty excited about that! After all, the word *"apostle"* simply means *"one who is sent."* The two Marys were sent by Christ to tell the good news of His resurrection! They were women, and Christ trusted them enough to deliver the message to His disciples!

Ah! I was duly inspired! I read further in that twenty-eighth chapter of Matthew and discovered that those women met with the disciples and relayed the message that they had been given by Christ himself! According to the Scriptures, the disciples went to Galilee to meet the risen Savior and upon his appearance, they fell down and worshiped Him; however, some doubted—just like people do in our world today! I thought about the fact that although the women had no problem in readily believing that Jesus had risen, some of the apostles who had walked, talked, slept and ate with Him, had room for doubt! It is no wonder that some people in our world today continue to doubt!

In spite of the doubt that existed in the apostles' hearts and even amidst the strains of doubt that still exists in our society today, in our churches, our homes, our families, our entire world, Christ gave us a commission and that assignment is still very clear! We are expected to *go* into *all* the world and teach *all* nations, baptizing them in the name of the Father and of the Son and of the Holy Ghost! And what are we to teach them? We have been commissioned to teach them to observe **all** things, whatsoever Jesus commanded us—the very Word of God!

In 1965, the government made a terrible mistake—a mistake that generations have seen manifested in the twenty-first century—prayer was taken out of the school system! In a strategic ploy of Satan, prayer was taken out of public school systems all over the country and many have realized that it was indeed a mistake! However, I believe the situation is not hopeless! No, it's not hopeless. God is *still* on the throne! He is still in charge! He sits high and looks low over our entire world, our country, our states, our cities, our schools, our homes, our families, our very lives! And just when it seems that our society is about to sink even lower, God shows up and reaches down, wherever we are, no matter how low we are, to pick us up!

There is very much power in prayer! It invites God to be active in our lives. Traditions make the words of God ineffectual—of no effect. Prayers by recitation are not communication with God. We must tell our children to pray because that allows them to *talk* to God! Faith in and acting on God's Word *does* change things! Apart from God, prayer will change *nothing*. God hears us when we pray in line with our faith in His Word. God will not violate His word either! I have learned that God will not take our will away from us. He allows us to do whatever we choose to do.

Many times I have seen worshipers go to the altar and bow their heads down in prayer. Before they begin their conversation with the Lord, they put down the baggage that they have been carrying for a long time! I can relate to that because I have done the same thing myself! We kneel and pray, asking God for His help so that we can overcome the issues in our own lives. We ask Him to have His way, and we believe that our prayer gives Him our permission to go ahead in our own lives! But many worshipers put down the baggage they have been carrying around in their lives and pray and then, when they come to their feet, they pick up the baggage and carry it back to their seats—and back into their lives! I believe that God must shake His head, disappointed that we have still *not* given that baggage to Him!

The answer for this time requires an adamant return to the basics! We've got to go back to the old landmark! We've got to go back to the old time way! Now there are some who don't know what that means, so let me break it down for you. You see, when I was growing up, we didn't have any problem showing respect for other people, because at home, we were taught to be respectful . . . *or ELSE!* When we went to school, we would never have dreamed of talking back to the teacher, because before we could even get home, our parents would already know what we had done! On our way home, *"Mrs. Bee"* would be sitting on her front porch, and she would chastise us for acting up at school, and she would also remind us that we know better than to act like that! And if she felt like it, she would ease on down off that front porch and warm up our behinds for Mama or Grandmama, who would be at home, waiting for us, when we got there! Now, you know what was waiting for us at home when we got there? Things were done the *"Old Time"* way! The *"Old Time"* way was a time when mothers and fathers *used* to sit down and teach us how to bless the food, and to ask God to bless those who were less fortunate than we were. We didn't have very much, but we were thankful for what we had! We were taught to be grateful! Mothers *used* to teach their daughters how to clean up and cook—not microwave! Fathers *used* to teach their sons how to be men, and how they should take care of the families that they were going to have in their futures! It was a time when premarital sex and promiscuity were not popular! Families *used* to pray together and stay together!

In God's divine order, men were created to lead and be heads of their families. I'm not trying to say that it's time for women to take care of their own families or take over and be the head of their households, or anything like that! I do understand the need to encourage and stir up women in this new millennium however! In my previous high school English classes, I taught proverbs. Many times, I shared a very potent proverb with my students that said *"If you educate a man, you teach him: but when you educate a woman, you educate a nation."* Several times, I got some flak from some of the young men in my classes because they thought the proverb was a *"sexist"* one. However, after we discussed it, they would all agree! I agreed with my students that a woman *is* a child's first teacher. The child she brings into the world receives the benefit of her knowledge and wisdom. She passes that knowledge on to her children, who in turn, pass it on to their own children!

Women are born nurturers who are born to teach! It is a God-given instinct! As nurturers, we are expected to teach! Some people can't handle that because they think that women are to sit at home, be sweet and beautiful, cook and clean, and most of all, be **QUIET!** As a matter of fact, some have taken the passage of Scripture that women are to keep silent and many ministers, teachers or speakers have gone wild with it!

I was speaking at a women's program some time ago and I quoted I Timothy 2:8-11 which says that *"I will therefore that men pray everywhere, lifting up holy hands, without wrath and doubting. In like manner also, that women adorn themselves in modest apparel, with shamefacedness and sobriety; not with broided hair, or gold, or pearls, or costly array; But (which becometh women professing godliness) with good works. Let the woman learn in silence with all subjection."* I asked the congregation to look up from their Bibles, and then at me, because I wanted to make sure that they heard *exactly* what I needed to tell them. When the worshippers' eyes were focused on me, I said, *"I was NOT there!"* I, nor any woman that I know, was among the women that Timothy referred to! At the time, Timothy had been led by Paul, as to how to direct his charge as an evangelist at Ephesus! He had been sent there to calm the people down and somehow get the church in order! A lot of today's preachers/ministers/ evangelists need to go back and read *The Book* so that they can get their messages straight!

Many women are teachers of Sunday School classes, elementary and high schools, colleges, etc. In most churches, there are usually more women in the pews than men! In colleges, there are more female teachers conducting education classes day-by-day than men! Obviously, many people are misunderstanding *The Word!* Everybody should pray and ask God for some clarity, and *then* go back and read it for themselves! Proverbs 4:7 states that *"wisdom is the principal thing; therefore, get wisdom; and with all thy getting, get understanding!"* So, before we go erecting a monument on a particular verse of Scripture, while we proceed to break every other commandment that God gave to Moses on Mount Sinai, we need to pray and ask the Lord for wisdom so that we can get a clear understanding of *His Word!*

In the Old Testament, Joel 2:28 says *"And it shall come to pass afterward, that I will pour out my spirit upon all flesh; and your sons and your daughters shall prophesy, your old men shall dream dreams, your young men shall see visions."* The New Testament tells us in Acts 2:12 that *"it shall come to pass in the last days, said God, I will pour out my Spirit upon all flesh; and your sons and your daughters shall prophesy, and your young men shall see visions, and your old men shall dream dreams."* God said it and I believe it! Women and men of God have been commissioned to *"Go ye therefore, and teach all nations, baptizing them in the name of the Father and of the Son, and of the Holy Ghost!"* It is sad to say that many Christians have fallen short of that assignment!

It seems that we have not fully accepted our assignment because we have too many issues! We've got too many problems! When I began writing **Peace, In the Midst of the Storm,** I openly shared with readers that most people have **too many** secrets! **Too many** things happened to them when they were children! As adults, they've undergone **too many** failed relationships—**too many** failed marriages! There are **too many** skeletons in most of our closets! We have carried **too much** baggage from pillars to posts! And the devil is **so glad!** He loves it when we are unable to do what God has called us to do! The Grand Mal seizures that I had begun to suffer got me out of the classroom where so many young people needed the help that God had given me pass on to them! I already knew that the devil was *"peacock—proud"* when I was so bent over that I could in nowise lift myself up! Oh yes! Satan rejoices in our failures and our shortcomings! He is thrilled when we are so filled with the guilt of our past mistakes that we can't witness to anyone about the goodness of the Lord!

When those planes crashed into the twin towers up in New York and so many lives were lost, many families were broken up, and many believers turned away from God, the devil rejoiced! When our children go out and get involved with drugs, alcohol and crime because either we have not done all we could have done to teach them about Jesus, or they become prodigals, leaving home and taking steps in the *"wrong"* direction, he most likely stands up and applauds! When we fail to serve God because we are too caught up in failed relationships or failed marriages, Satan laughs! He mocks us! How long are we going to allow that evil one to make fun of us and our God?

I truly believe that God has commissioned Christian men and women to go into the entire world and preach the gospel of peace to all nations. I believe that He is expecting us to teach all men, women, boys and girls to live after the examples that Christ came to earth to show us how God wants us to live! Yet we have children in schools all over the country who turn semi-auto automatic weapons upon their innocent classmates instead of turning their lives over to Him! Please don't think it's just a coincidence that the current tragedies befalling our times are taking place with children in and around institutes of learning! You can hardly turn on the daily news without hearing some horrible news that is relative to our children! True believers of the Gospel of Jesus Christ are cast aside or asunder—just so Satan can find any possible way to lead the children of God away from Him!

I, myself, had to resign from my teaching position as a result of Satan having his way in the lives of so many others in the school district where I taught! Numerous Grand Mal seizures I had already experienced began to occur more frequently as a result of it! Then, if that wasn't enough, Satan had his way in the lives of others who rose up against me, abused me and lied ultimately, influence those who had me placed behind prison bars, accused of crimes that I have never dreamed of committing!

Derrick told me something that stayed in my mind during the many days that I spent at home, alone, while he was at work and our children were at school. He reminded me that God had **never** called me to go backwards! The things that had occurred in my life in the past, although traumatic at times, had **already** happened—in the past! God had never called me to go backwards, my husband reminded me enough times to dry my eyes up and stop the warm, salty tears from falling. God wants us to be successful, he reminded me! I confessed that, inside, I already knew that! I had ministered to people across the country and told them that same thing! Here I was having to be reminded of the things that I had said to others! There is no defeat in the lives of those who follow Him! There are times when we might be taken off course or slowed down a bit, but never defeated! *There is victory is Jesus!*

The most common problem in pursuing your destiny is having a *"broken focus."* God chose us—we didn't choose Him! He never threw us away either! He put a new spirit inside of us, and as long as we are in our vessels, there is always room for improvement! *God is a God of progress!* The work He began in us, before we were pulled out of our mothers' wombs, if we obey Him in our lifetimes, He will complete!

Jesus sat and ate with the sinners or the *"low life"* folk. The *"so-called"* religious, self-righteous murmured about Him because of it, but God will go the farthest extent to get you back to where you need to be, if you will only submit to Him! The Pharisees thought that Jesus couldn't possibly be the promised Messiah because they thought that the god they believed in was one who hated the lowly and loved the righteous! Jesus spoke an uncommon parable in Luke 15 and made it personal and clear enough for them to understand. He told them that they were all going to be responsible for the lesson that He was about to teach them. The message of this parable is about this same thing.

Sheep were valuable to them in that day, but it really didn't have anything to do with the shepherd's stock. It had everything to do with God's attitude towards a lost soul! It was about the one that was lost and had gone astray, left home or the ministry to go somewhere else, etc. God then, and still continues to put a great price on the life of one of His children who is lost! As long as you seek God's face for a loved one, He will continue to draw them. Our names were written in the Book of Life at our birth! It is not removed until a child reaches the age of accountability and denies God for himself—or herself! Their names are not put back into the Book until they turn from their wicked ways and back to Him!

Luke 15:7 tells us that Jesus said, *"I say unto you, that likewise joy shall be in heaven over one sinner that repents, more than over ninety and nine just persons, which need no repentance."* It's in the Book! God's attitude towards the lost should be *believers'* attitudes towards them! We are the light of the world, *in* the world, but *not* of it, and that light is supposed to shine in darkness! We are separate, not segregated, by virtue of the fact of whose we are! The world needs to see our light so that they can make the transition from their own darkness into it! We *must* have *The Word* in our mouths in order to point the way to righteousness. Prejudice is the product of a lazy mind! We accept what people say about others and don't take the time to find out for ourselves! You don't have to tell the lost that they are lost and going to Hell! I believe that they already know it! They are doing the best they can, living the worst they can! Sinners won't just voluntarily come to the light. Jesus demonstrated that they *must* be *led* to it!

The parable of the prodigal son has been grossly misunderstood because the emphasis seems to be focused on the son. However, I really believe that Jesus is talking about the father, who is mentioned twelve times in the passage. The parable is about the father's attitude when his lost son returns home. The son wants his inheritance early. Most of us are prodigals, are we? We finally woke up one day between the ages of twelve and eighteen and wanted *this* thing *now!* Thinking we could do better on our own, we directly rebelled against our parents *and* against God! Most of us actually went out on our own. At the time, we didn't realize that we could not separate ourselves from the source and still be sustained! Unfortunately, some folks had to get down to the very bottom before they woke up! Sooner or later, time has run out for many! That is when God got most of our attentions! The son was a covenant son who belonged to his father's household. He had to go out and eat with the pigs—that was even *below* the bottom! He couldn't even have sank any lower than he did! Fortunately, one day, he woke up! He decided to get up out of the mess he had been lying in, go back home and request a servant's position. He didn't even know it, but his father had been looking for him every day! Each day, he had been standing at the gate and watching, hoping to see his son turn the corner. When the son finally returned and was heartily accepted by his father, the man put shoes on his son's feet, a robe on his back and a ring on his finger, and the Bible says that he killed a fatted calf to prepare a feast for his son! The man had to have been waiting for his son to come home! I believe that God has been waiting on many of His children to come home, and He has given each of us times to get up and come back to Him, our Creator!

The happiest people on the face of the earth ought to be Christians! God said that He would never leave or forsake us! That should give every believer confidence and make them happy! Psalms says *"Blessed (Happy) is the man that walketh (lives by) not on the counsel (advice) of the ungodly, nor standeth in the way of sinners, nor sitteth in the seat of the scornful (those who leave God out or oppose Him in their daily lives). But his delight is in the law of the Lord; and in his law doth he meditate (go over and over again) day and night. And he shall be like a tree planted by the rivers of the water, that bringeth forth his fruit in his season; his leaf also does not wither; and whatsoever he doeth shall prosper."* Someone who meditates or continually goes over the *Word* will be able to endure the storms of life—like the evergreen trees that stand firm, regardless of the weather! Now, that doesn't pertain to *"part-time"* Christians, those who attend services on Sunday and/or Wednesday, or those who join, but don't do anything in the ministry. Meditation means continuous practice, or doing something over and over again! The promise of prosperity is given to the *"working"* Christian, according to Psalms 1:3, to the one who is like that *"tree planted by the rivers of water, that brings forth his fruit in his season."* If all you do is seek ye first the kingdom and not do anything on our way there, those *"all other things"* will *not* be added unto or given to you!

Ecclesiastes 2:24 says that *"There is nothing better for a man, than that he should eat and drink, and that he should make his soul enjoy his labor."* That simply says that we are to live our lives to its fullest because it is given to us from the hand of God! I once heard a minister say that if you don't enjoy your job, your labor, or your life, you should change it! We are supposed to look for *"tens"* to associate with and at least, move in that direction ourselves! Those whom you closely associate with, your mannerisms will become like theirs.

If you stay around the *"same folk,"* you will become just like the *"same folk!"* That's the truth! We must set our sights a little higher. After all, God is able to do exceedingly and abundantly more than you or I can even ask or think!

I remember talking to some women at a retreat once where I shared with them something that I had once told others. I told them to remember that God made had Adam and put him in the Garden—*first!* Then, I said, *"He gave him three things: a place to stay, He gave him a job to do, to take care of the garden and the animals that God had put there, and then, He gave Adam one commandment which referred to one of the trees in the garden, to keep: "Do not eat,"* I said. *"It was not until God had given Adam those three things did He put him to sleep and a woman in his life. So if ladies are looking for a man, even in our times, they must make sure that he has a place to stay, a job to do, and a commandment on his heart! Amen!"* The ladies in the room almost exploded! A place to stay, a job to do, and a commandment on his heart! *"They were not to get somebody to just come and move into their house with them,"* I told them. *"And even if they did get married, and they find that the woman's house is better for the newlyweds to move in together, he should first come with a residence of his own! If he sees you over the counter at Burger King where he is working, and sees you driving a Lexus, living in your own house, of course he's going to say the "right thing!" He's not crazy! Look at what you have to offer! I'm not saying that we are supposed to be materialistic, but God elevated you to the level where you are for a purpose! You need a man that can meet you where you are! You don't just need ANYBODY,"* I told them as I raised my hand. *"You're up here, and he's down there—waving at you! Winking!"* The ladies laughed. *"You should just wave back and say, 'Hey honey, how are you doing? That's good. You take care!' God wants you to have somebody who can enhance you!"* I told the ladies.

> *"And the LORD God took the man, and put him into the garden of Eden to dress it and to keep it. And the LORD God commanded the man, saying, Of every tree of the garden thou mayest freely eat: But of the tree of the knowledge of good and evil, thou shalt not eat of it: for in the day that thou eatest thereof thou shalt surely die."*

> **Genesis 2:15-17**

1 Timothy 4:4 says that we are to keep the pleasures of life in their proper perspective. We are to keep our focus on the Creator—*NOT* the creation! We are supposed to make sure that God is always *first* in our lives and believe

that we can give up whatever He has given to us at any time! Even if that something has been taken away, God can give it to us again! *(1 Timothy 6:17)* God gives us all things richly to enjoy, but remember that you cannot enjoy what you cannot afford! While we live, we are to use the things that God gives us and enjoy doing so because, for one thing, they won't last, and secondly, we can't take them to the grave with us! All that we have is vanity that is empty, passing and of no eternal value. So just remember, while you live, you may use it and also enjoy it, because it just won't last forever and you definitely can't take it with you! Money can make you happy for a moment, but it can't bring you joy! Happiness is temporary, but joy is eternal! The real substance of life is found in the Word of God!

God is calling us to be detailed and distinguished! At times, we blend too much with the *"world!"* We may desire what others have instead of encourage them to desire what we have! God does not want us to just barely get by when He is able to do exceedingly above and beyond our desires! Christians must not worry about everyone else! We *should* be different! We have to be *marked* for the Holy Ghost! We have to think differently. Traditions have made the Word of God of no effect in the world today! You don't have to take my word for it! Just turn on the television set and view CNN at any time of the day! You must realize that God created us to be like Him! However, there is a price to pay to be exceptional! The anointing is costly, and it also attracts the devil! When you discover your distinctness and the vision that God has put within you, you will discover your enemy—or rather, he will discover you and set out to *destroy* the anointing that God has placed within you!

A short time ago, I discovered that for a very long time, God had been waiting on me! He has most likely been waiting on you, too! Some people have gone to the grave, never having answered the call upon their lives. Some have been too busy, doing what they thought they were brought into existence to do, to stop, look, and listen for direction so that they could find out what they were actually created to do! Once, I got the message that in order to discover my distinction, to determine my own destiny, and acknowledge the vision that God had for my life, I had to take a few steps *away* from the world, and step *toward* a closer relationship with Him! God's true believers must *first* get away from those who are more critical than encouraging! They have to move away from those who belittle or embarrass them. Avoid those who stifle their abilities and their anointing! *THEN,* believers are to walk with those who build them up and those who may even get excited about their potential! We are to *walk with those who remind us of the talents and abilities that God has so richly blessed us with!*

It has taken quite a lot time in my own life, fifty-one years exactly, to get to the place that I am today. Having so much time alone and so much time to spend with the Lord each day, to desire to discover my own destiny has become somewhat overwhelming! I hope that whoever is reading this book realizes that it is time to shake off any idea, thing, or person that will keep them from their destiny as well! Will God find you in a state of faithfulness and obedience when He calls you home?

"His lord said unto him, Well done, thou good and faithful servant: thou hast been faithful over a few things, I will make thee ruler Over many things: enter thou into the joy of thy lord."

Matthew 25:21

One evening, during the **Healing Hearts Ministry**, I encouraged the men and women seated before me to see *themselves* in the lives that had been written about, talked about, and shared with people all over the world! I told them that if they could hear about, read about, or even talk to others who had experienced problems in situations that they themselves had been in, they would be able to earnestly *believe* that the troubles in their own lives would *not* last always!

One evening, I told the men and women that it was time for their lives to be healed! Eyes widened when I said that traditions of mankind had made the commandments of God of *no effect* in several lives—even some of those who were present at the meeting! Since some possibly had difficulty believing what I said, I asked them to pick up their Bibles and turn to Matthew 15, Verse 6. *"But in vain they do worship me, teaching for doctrines the commandments of men,"* the Scriptures said. Even today, I told them, *"God's people seem to get closer to Him with their mouths and honor Him with their lips, but their hearts are far away from Him! Just watch the news! Okay! Okay! Just hang around others on the job, in the beauty or barber shops, or in the break rooms of the places where they work!"* Many heads nodded in agreement. *"Better yet,"* I said, *"go to church and remain on the grounds after the worship service is dismissed!"*

Many of God's people are still drawing nigh unto Him with their mouths and honoring Him with their lips, but their hearts continue to be far away from Him! Actually, the world is *filled* with broken hearts! I don't think a lot of ministers realize that broken hearts make it challenging to worship the Lord! Issues of life tend to keep us from surrendering our hearts to God, and most of life's issues are *not* being addressed in the local churches! Well, even the disciples didn't want to deal with the Canaanite woman's problem, did they? She was bringing her problems to the place where actual worship and teaching of the Gospel was being held. They tried to get her to go away, but it was Christ who heard her and recognized her need!

Out of our mouths proceed the issues of our hearts! That is probably why someone said, many, many years ago, that we should *think* before we *speak*! The words that come out of the mouth can defile the listener. We don't always speak things that are not as though *they* are; we speak of the pain and anguish that has become a part of who *we* are! We are hurt, and as a result, we hurt others! Don't you know that hurt people are the ones that *hurt people?* Remember the story that was told in Matthew 15:22, about the Canaanite woman who got in line for her own deliverance? She had traveled a long way from her home to where she knew that Jesus would be. When she saw Him, she cried out to him and said, *"Have mercy on me, O Lord, thou Son of David; my daughter is grievously vexed with a devil."* Most people could fill in the term—*"devil"*—with their own problems! In Verses 23 through 27, the woman is forced to *demand* her daughter's deliverance. Soon afterwards, as a result of the woman's *"show"* of faith, her daughter was made whole! Right after that, many others were healed and delivered from *their* infirmities as well!

What is extremely sad is that many people, the young and the old, men and women, adults and children, husbands and wives, sisters and brothers, nieces and nephews, and well . . . *most* people on earth today are *not* asking the Lord for His assistance! They are trying, although unsuccessfully, to take care of their problems themselves! Some are even going to their physicians: mental or physical—for the help that they *think* they need! Others are trying to *fix* their problems themselves, thinking that they can handle them on their own. Many are attending church services regularly, taking their problems to the altar, praying about them, and then afterwards, picking that same old *baggage* up and carrying it back to their seats and later on, to their homes! It has not yet occurred to most that they carried the problems to the altar, but failed to leave them there! Oh, then there are those who have found something other than worship, even though temporary, to *fix* their problems—drugs, alcohol, friends or foe for example.

There IS an answer! Going to church is a step in the right direction, but if you simply go and attend worship services, taking your *baggage* with you, putting it down next to your seat during service, and then picking it up and taking it back home afterwards, you still haven't gotten rid of your problem! Even today, Pastors and Evangelists continue to stand in pulpits, behind sacred desks, and emphatically expound upon their versions of the Word of God, **BUT** most of the listeners, those who brought their own *baggage* to the worship service with them, are just picking it up and taking it back to their residences afterwards! Some are even carrying it to psychologists, hoping to get some relief from the things that have stifled them for most of their lives. After the visits have ended, and the fees have been paid, they realize that the *baggage* has continued to keep its place! However, I must reiterate that *there IS an answer!*

II Timothy 3:1-17 says *"This know also, that in the last days perilous times shall come. For men shall be lovers of their own selves, covetous, boasters, proud, blasphemers, disobedient to parents, unthankful, unholy; Without natural affection, trucebreakers, false accusers, incontinent, fierce, despisers of those that are good; Traitors, heady, high-minded, lovers of pleasures more than lovers of God; Having a form of godliness, but denying the power thereof: from such turn away. For of this sort are they which creep into houses, and lead captive silly women laden with sins, led away with divers lusts; Ever learning, and never able to come to the knowledge of the truth. Now as Jannes and Jambres withstood Moses, so do these also resist the truth: men of corrupt minds, reprobate concerning the faith. But they shall proceed no further: for their folly shall be manifest unto all men, as theirs also was. But thou hast fully known my doctrine, manner of life, purpose, faith, longsuffering, charity, patience; Persecutions, afflictions, which came unto me at Antioch, at Iconium, at Lystra; what persecutions I endured: but out of them all the Lord delivered me. Yea, and all that will live godly in Christ Jesus shall suffer persecution. But evil men and seducers shall wax worse and worse, deceiving, and being deceived. But continue thou in the things which thou hast learned and hast been assured of, knowing of whom thou hast learned them; And that from a child thou hast known the holy scriptures, which are able to make thee wise unto salvation through faith which is in Christ Jesus. All scripture is given by inspiration of God, and is profitable for doctrine, for reproof, for correction, for instruction in righteousness: That the man of God may be perfect, thoroughly furnished unto all good works."*

Whenever I read over these lines of Scripture, a bright light comes on up above my head. I can't help but think about the words that actually refer to the state of the world today, the current condition of the United States, the terroristic threats that have been aired on the television, the horrible acts that had already been performed by people in New Orleans, Louisiana and Mississippi after *Hurricane Katrina* had made her way up the coasts, taking lives, destroying homes, buildings, and ultimately—families! I am reminded of the devastation that occurred in Sodom and Gomorrah when God had probably gotten tired of the horrendous behavior of the residents in those cities! I can't say for certain, but I believe that He most likely had had enough of His children's behavior, those that He Himself had brought into existence!

God's children should pay some serious attention to the world and its *"goings on"* around them! It is *"time out"* for horse-play and just doing things *"our"* way! I don't know whether or not others are really taking notice of the things going on around them, but I have to admit that, finally, I sure am! I realize that although I was the product of my parents', Tony and Almarine Clayton's, coming together in 1956, God had a purpose for my being brought into His world when I arrived in 1958—*His* purpose! Satan knew that I would be willing to do what God brought me into His world to do, so he got very busy trying to keep me from the task! Although my having been sexual molested as a youngster was a horrendous mountain set before me, God had already given me the strength necessary to climb it! The terrible experience with my first husband took me across the country, to Los Angeles, California, in an attempt to get away from it, but six years later, God brought me right back home to Georgia. I had planned to reside in Atlanta, Georgia, having acquired a job with a major business company, but that was *not* where He wanted me to be! Days later, He brought me back to Columbus so that I could take care of the same man who had sexually molested me in my youth! And now, I have had to undergo my divorce from Derrick, the man that I had truly believed to be the husband that God intended for me to spend the rest of my life with!

Some time ago, I realized that I *had* to go *"there"* to get *"here!"* The good and the bad, the ups and the downs, the joys and pains, are all a part of helping us to become the persons that God brought us into the world to be! One thing is certain, He prepared us all *"ahead of time"* to deal with many things that awaited us in our futures, didn't He? Oh yes, I can attest to that! I returned to Georgia in 1990, and went back to Columbus College to become a high school teacher. I had *never* imagined that I would ever become a school teacher, but I set my mind on doing so. After graduation, I was hired to teach in a school located in a nearby county. In my second year of teaching in that school district, I was attacked by a student in my classroom. About a week and a half later, the local newspaper contained the story about the attack and as a result of that story being shared with the city of Columbus and surrounding areas, I was introduced to my sister, **Debra,** the sister that I had never even known existed! Somehow, I believe that God had allowed me to go into that classroom and undergo the attack so that she and I could finally meet each other! The classroom experience should have been enough to take me out of teaching high school aged kids, but it didn't. I was still bent on doing what I *thought* God wanted me to do, *my way,* of course!

Two years ago, my sister, *Debra,* and her sixteen-year old son, *Antonio,* were murdered in their home, by the husband that she had been married to for about two years. The news about the murder was brought to me in an early morning telephone call from Aunt Tisa.

I was on my way to the bathroom so that I could brush my teeth when I heard the telephone ring. I turned around, went back into the bedroom and picked up the receiver. *"Hello?"* I said.

"What are you doing?" Aunt Tisa asked.

"I just got up," I said. *"I was just about to brush my teeth and then iron the clothes I plan to wear to church today."* I had been Minister of Music at a Baptist church that was located in Columbus, and I had been playing there for about a year.

"Well," Aunt Tisa said, *"sit down. I need to tell you something."*

"What?" I asked.

"Just sit down," she replied.

So I did.

Then, Aunt Tisa told me something that caused my heart to skip a beat. *"Debra is dead,"* she said, *"Frankie killed her and Antonio this morning."*

I could hardly believe what she was saying! The words went around and around in my head! Debra's dead? Her husband, Frankie, had killed her? And Antonio, too? I was speechless!

"Did you hear me?" Aunt Tisa asked, her voice sounding hollow.

"Yes," I said. *"But how? When? Why?"* I uttered, hearing my own voice quiver.

As calmly as she could, Aunt Tisa told me the whole story. About two weeks ago, Debra's husband, Frankie, had had Antonio arrested, after having accused the teenager and a neighborhood youth of attacking him and taking some money from him. The boys had been put in jail, awaiting a court hearing. The day of the hearing, Debra had gotten up early, got dressed and gone to the courthouse, but Frankie had not shown up in court because he said that he had a headache, a cold or something. Because he never appeared in court, the judge released Antonio and his friend, and both of the boys went home.

A few days later, before dawn, on Sunday morning, in an act that nobody will ever be able to explain, Frankie stabbed Debra and her son, Antonio, to death! After he had committed the horrendous crime, he tried to run away, driving Debra's *VT Cruiser!* By the end of the day, he had been arrested and charged with two counts of murder and two counts of possession of a knife during commission of a crime. Frankie had stabbed both Debra and Antonio several times with an eight to ten inch kitchen knife. The police found young Antonio, dead, in the street, in front of their house, and Debra's lifeless body laying inside. My sister! The only sister I had ever had! The sister that it had taken me thirty-eight years to meet and get to know anything at all about! And just like that—she was gone!

Later, after the tragedy had occurred, I realized that God had indeed brought us together nine years ago, and He had given us enough time to get to know each other, talk to one another, laugh together and share our families with one another! Debra came and became a member of the church where I was the Minister of Music. Shortly after joining the church, she became a member of the choir. Her two younger children participated in the youth activities around the church. I believe that coming to the church and surrendering her life to Christ was something that she had not done before, but truly needed to do! It gave her a place to reside when her earthly existence came to an end! Since *no one* knows the day, nor the hour, when their life will end, they *must* have their lives in order! They *must* use the gifts that He has given to them for as long as they are able to! If it is singing in the choir, helping senior citizens who have been cast aside, teaching young people in Sunday school or leading the lost to Christ, we *must* do it before *our* time is up! And no one knows just *when* that is! I truly thank God for allowing Debra, my sister and her son, Antonio, and I to meet and get to know each other before their lives came to abrupt ends!

> *"Watch therefore, for ye know neither the day nor*
> *the hour wherein the Son of man cometh."*
>
> *Matthew 25:13*

Another season has come upon us. We have enjoyed the warm, sunny days of Summer. We have watched the leaves change from a bright green to glorious, colorful cinnamon reds, oranges and golds—but the chill of our mornings assure us that fall will soon enter the picture! Before we know it, winter will definitely be on its way! The seasons remind me a lot about life. Childhood is a lot like the season known as Spring. We learn a lot of things about the lives we have not yet begun to live. Things are not so serious when you're a child. If you fall, scrape your knee, or get a blister, you soon get over the little pain you've experienced. Many people have even savored the scrapes and bruises acquired during their childhood. Today, my sons proudly display some of the scars that resulted from many of the football games they have participated in. It seems that they didn't really hurt when they were received during the games. Some people even forget how, when or where the scars came from by the time they enter the later phases of their lives! But nevertheless, they feel that they simply *"came with the territory!"*

Youth is a detrimental phase. Young people are blindly searching around, trying to find out *who* they are, *where* they came from and even *why* and *how* they got there! It may be hard to believe, but although a couple of gray hairs have found their way into my scalp, I can still remember those feelings myself! I try to keep them in mind when my sons demonstrate their own *"blind"* behavior! Christopher, my fifteen year old, is still experiencing the joys of the Spring! Almost *everything* is **new** to him! He has been studying the Georgia Driver's Manual, although he doesn't know that I'm aware of it! His older brothers, Little Derrick and Tjai often laugh about that! They themselves have been experiencing the Summers of their lives. To them, Summer is fun! It is exciting! New things to do! New places to go! New people to meet! Of course, the climate is hot, but they can take off their shirts and wear short pants! They simply adapt! They don't even think about the fact that the upcoming seasons, *Fall,* and *Winter,* will eventually arrive. They will have to be ready though, prepared for those seasons and eventually, their ends.

So, what's next? Romans 10:4-9 says *"For Christ is the end of the law for righteousness to everyone that believeth. For Moses describeth the righteousness which is of the law, that the man which doeth those things shall live by them. But the righteousness which is of faith speaketh on this wise, Say not in thine heart, Who shall ascend into heaven? (that is, to bring Christ down from above:) Or, Who shall descend into the deep? (that is, to bring up Christ again from the dead.) But what saith it? The word is nigh thee, even in thy mouth, and in thy heart: that is, the word of faith, which we preach; That if thou shalt confess with thy mouth the Lord Jesus, and shalt believe in thine heart that God hath raised him from the dead, thou shalt be saved."* Whether you reach the Fall or Winter of your life or not, those words *must* be significant in the days that you live!

I have to reiterate that Satan has been after me ever since I came into existence! After undergoing the many years of disability as a result of the Grand Mal seizures that completely changed my life, my mind became clear enough for me to think with some clarity. I realized that Satan had gone to great lengths to stop me—a woman of God who had given her entire life to fulfilling His will each and every day of her life! Long ago, I had decided to do what God had brought me into His world to do! After the night of horror in East Wynnton, He had kept me in His arms! As a teenage girl, I had undergone many nights of sexual abuse, and later endured my aunt's anger and hatred as a result, but God sheltered my mind and enabled me to kept it stayed on Him!

I had married my first husband, and endured bitterness, hatred and physical abuse which I was not ready for nor deserving of. Perhaps the devil thought that would do it—but God had obviously said *"No!"* I had gone into teaching and endured some similar bitterness, hatred and physical abuse for which I had not expected. In my second year of teaching, I was physically attacked by a Black male student who was angry with someone other than me. Several years later, I was attacked by a White female student, but I was arrested and put in jail, accused of me attacking her instead! Surely, I believe that Satan thought that would have to do it! It didn't! In 2001, I had begun to suffer Grand Mal seizures that would afterwards bring about my label of *"disability."* And just when I thought that I had suffered *"enough"* in my forty-six years of living, I discovered that my husband, the man whom I had earnestly believed that God had brought into my life for His purpose, had been cheating on me—his *"disabled"* wife!

After I left him, I returned to my writing. I guess I needed something to keep my mind staid somewhere other than on my mental sadness and physical disability! In 2008, I realized that God had been watching, listening, and keeping me, in spite of Satan's numerous attacks to destroy me! In the midst of my state of being, I had kept Him at the forefront of my existence! He had enabled me to stay above board when initially, that old wicked one had intended to use my failing health to force me to throw my hands up and surrender to him. When I became earnest about sharing God's goodness with people all over the country, God had allowed the devil to attack me physically! When suffering Grand Mal seizures did not stop me from reaching out to people all over the country, in an attempt to help them get up and dust off the things that had been holding them down for many years, his attacks became closer, more preeminent in my life. Satan had used my position as a high school Language Arts teacher in his attempts to make me give up on the God who had kept me in His care for forty-nine years! When that wasn't enough, he brought things even *closer* to my home by destroying my marriage!

Well, once again, I am a divorced, single mother—this time, with three sons, I don't know just when I will be able to move beyond the pain and agony that I have suffered because of the break-up of my marriage, but . . . I believe that God can and He will see me through it! I'm not even sure when the sun is going to shine in my life again, but—I know that it can and eventually, it will, as well! I trust in God and I know that He will see me through it all! The only thing I have to do is continue to *TRUST* Him! I previously shared my testimony with people all over the country! My story has become even larger now, and for God's love, grace, mercy and kindness in the midst of it all, I thank Him for He has enabled me to endure it and share it with others! No matter how strong the winds may blow or how terrible the tempest may rise, God wants His children to trust Him and remain confident that no matter how trying, frustrating or demanding the trial may be, there **is *peace in the midst of the storm!*"**

Brethren, I count not myself to have apprehended: but this one thing I do, forgetting those things which are behind, and reaching forth unto those things which are before, I press toward the mark for the prize of the high calling of God in Christ Jesus."

Philippians 3:13-14